THE
QUIET GUNNER
AT WAR

Written for R, P and H

Sweet Chance, that led my steps abroad,
Beyond the town, where wild flowers grow –
A rainbow and a cuckoo, Lord!
How rich and great the times are now!

W H Davies

THE
QUIET GUNNER
AT WAR

El Alamein to the Rhine with the
Scottish Divisions

Richmond Gorle MC, RA

Pen & Sword
MILITARY

First published in Great Britain in 2011 by
Pen & Sword Military
an imprint of
Pen & Sword Books Ltd
47 Church Street
Barnsley
South Yorkshire
S70 2AS

Copyright © Richmond Gorle, 2011

ISBN 978 1 84884 540 4

Typeset in Ehrhardt by Chic Media Ltd

Printed and bound in England
by CPI

Pen & Sword Books Ltd incorporates the imprints of
Pen & Sword Aviation, Pen & Sword Maritime,
Pen & Sword Military, Pen & Sword Family History,
Wharncliffe Local History, Wharncliffe True Crime,
Wharncliffe Transport, Pen & Sword Discovery, Pen & Sword Select,
Pen & Sword Military Classics, Leo Cooper, Remember When,
The Praetorian Press, Seaforth Publishing and Frontline Publishing

For a complete list of Pen & Sword titles please contact
PEN & SWORD BOOKS LIMITED
47 Church Street, Barnsley, South Yorkshire, S70 2AS, England
E-mail: enquiries@pen-and-sword.co.uk
Website: www.pen-and-sword.co.uk

Contents

PART 3 – EUROPE

Introduction

This is the story of one man's adventures in the Second World War. No attempt has been made to write a war history, or even a history of a regiment: it is merely a personal story. Its only possible merit is that it may give some idea of what life was like under arms; it will help to fill in the gap that wartime separation left in the picture of family life.

Most stories need a background, and this one should be read against the background of the worldwide struggle to stop Hitler from making the world a German empire. It is a background that unrolls in phases, or changes like the backdrops of a theatre. The first of these is the pre-war phase, with Great Britain and the Commonwealth and Empire dominant in the world. The strength of the Commonwealth – scattered all over the world – depended on control of the Mediterranean and particularly on the control of Egypt and the Suez Canal. On to the stage comes Hitler, building up the German armed forces while we disarmed, rattling the sabre until we cringed, and then taking half of Europe with hardly a shot.

The scene changes to 1939: Britain and France call a halt to the German advance, making the occupation of Poland the dividing line between peace and war. Hitler crosses the line, so war is declared. Then follows the phase of disaster. Neither France nor Britain was ready for war. The fall of France and the loss of the British Expeditionary Force (BEF)[1] leaves us wide open to invasion, and the German Air Force tries to bomb the heart out of the country. We are alone in the war, facing the combined strength of Germany, Italy and Japan. In the Far East, Japan lops off the limbs of Empire, seizing Hong Kong, Malaya and Burma. India, Australia and New Zealand are all in danger, but Britain still holds Egypt and the Suez Canal. True, she cannot use the Mediterranean much – but neither can the enemy, as long as we have a naval and military base in Egypt, supported by Malta and Gibraltar. Always, that base is a threat to the enemy; through it, via the Cape of Good Hope, we can reinforce the countries round the Indian Ocean and beyond. Eventually we will use it to re-open the Empire route to the Far East.

The obvious German strategy was to seize Egypt and the Middle East, isolating the Commonwealth countries from Britain, their chief source of manpower and weapons. Mussolini was given this job, but the Italians failed dismally and the Germans had to take it on. However, they could only make it a ding-dong show until the middle of 1942, when for a time it looked as if they might succeed.

But the backdrop has changed again. In 1941 the Japanese make the mistake of bombing the American fleet in Pearl Harbour, bringing America into the war, and Hitler is foolish enough to attack Russia. No longer is Britain alone. The RAF has won the Battle of Britain: the invasion threat has vanished, and the waters are surging for the turn of the tide.

In October 1942 the tide turns at El Alamein, a little wayside railway halt in Egypt. There the German and Italian strength in North Africa is broken. The British and New Zealand forces push steadily on to Tripoli and link with the British and American First Army in Tunisia to drive the Bosch into the sea at Cap Bon. By the spring of 1943 the Mediterranean is open again. The Germans and Japanese can never meet in the Middle East and the Empire Route is re-established.

There remains but to knock a tottering Italy out of the war and start the long hard drive from Normandy to Berlin, crushing the remains of the German army between the Russians in the east and the huge American and powerful British forces. Meanwhile the reinforced XIVth British Army re-conquers Burma, and the Americans and Australians fight their way to Tokyo, finishing the war with the blast of the first two atom bombs.

And now, if you will descend from the sublime, you may read how the writer was carried on the crest of the wave, from El Alamein to Tunisia, and on into Sicily. Thence, omitting the fighting in Normandy (except for one hectic fortnight), follow his fortunes through Belgium and Holland, cross over the Rhine, take part in the drive to the Elbe and then experience the peace keeping.

I returned to Britain from India on 26 August 1939, and five days later, three days before war was declared, I received a telegram [see plate] telling me to report immediately for duty.[2]

Richard Gorle

Notes

[1] The BEF was sent to France at the start of the war. It was based from Bailleul to Maulde, north east of Douai. On 9 May, one day before the German attack, it comprised of nine infantry divisions with one other division (the 51st Highland) having been sent to the Maginot Line to bolster the defences in the Saar. It was well thought of, but too extended, and proved no match for the German onslaught.

[2] See plate 1.

Editor's Note

This book was completed in 1958. It was given to the family at the time. We read it and said nice things about it, but my father, being a modest man, did nothing more about it. The manuscript was bound in a single volume and has lain unread these many years. When I re-read it I found so much to admire, and so much skill and love had been put into its writing that I was sure it would be of interest to a wider audience. Editing has been minimum, tidying up a few references, expanding some of the military terms to make them more generally understood, and preparing an index of place names, units and people mentioned. Why *The Quiet Gunner*? One of his men said to him when he left the unit, 'We did not think you'd be much use when you came, you was so quiet.' In reality, they found him effective and valiant. He had already been mentioned in despatches in North Africa and was awarded the Military Cross at the Battle of Blerick.

My father was a career soldier. He had planned to join the Navy, but this was ruled out by colour blindness. You will note several loving references to ships in his writing.

He was plucked from the secure and certain British India of the time [see plates], where routine and detail were paramount, to join the scramble to train the part timers and new recruits who were to form the backbone of the Army at war. The regulars were often sneered at by these incomers for their constant attention to training and discipline. The result of their efforts, however, proved invaluable in the many crises that are faced in war.

After the war he served in Palestine, spent three years as a Liaison Officer in Fort Bragg, USA, home of the 82nd Airborne Division, and became an honorary member of the US Airborne. Other postings included UK and Hong Kong. After a period of ill health, which started with a serious car accident when he was about to command the Royal Artillery Regiment in Hong Kong, he died in 1971 at the young age of 61. He had retired as a Lieutenant Colonel and had taken a job in charge of administration at the Junior Leaders Regiment Royal Artillery in Bramcote near Nuneaton. He was there for thirteen years and it was there that he died. He was given a fine military funeral, including transportation of his coffin on a gun carriage, a red beret (the Airborne beret) proudly placed on it. A memorial plaque was affixed on the wall of the chapel there.

He, like many others who return from fighting, was often told not to bother people with what happened in the war. I do not remember him ever speaking of it, except for once during a walk on Dartmoor. We crossed the bed of a dry stream and I recall him saying that he had seen many like that in the desert, where they had been called '*wadis*'. That's all. But he did write his experiences down for posterity.

I am grateful for the help of my two sisters, Rosemary Fleming and Heather Ramell, and my wife Wendy for their help with reading and clarification of parts of the text, and also to Hilma Strudwick (my secretary for many years) for typing the manuscript into modern computer-readable format.

My thanks also go to others who provided material and access to resources, notably: Don Neale, who has carried out years of research and contact with members and descendants of 6th Battalion KSLI, which became 181st Regiment RA, resulting in *Guns and Bugles*; Anthony Sheil, son of Jerry Sheil, who has many mentions in this book; The Royal Artillery Museum; The Imperial War Museum; Michael Pegum's records of Irish war memorials; and Geoffrey Mason RN, Naval History Homepage (www.naval-history.net).

Peter Gorle, son, October 2010

Part 1

PREPARATION

Chapter 1

The Outbreak of War

Dark was the sky, and not one friendly star
Shone from the zenith or horizon, clear,
Mist sate upon the woods, and the darkness rode
In her black chariot with a wild career.

Philip Freneau

Plymouth, 70th Coast Defence Training Regiment
A switch clicked, and silence fell. We fixed our eyes on the wireless as if we
would wring from it what the future held.

It was 3 September 1939. Three days earlier the Germans had invaded
Poland, whose frontiers we had guaranteed, and now the Prime Minister,
Mr Neville Chamberlain, was to tell us what action Great Britain would
take. He wasted no time. In a few short sentences we heard that the country
was at war with Germany from that hour.

Faces were grave and thoughtful as we went back to our work: it is no
light matter to find oneself at the gateway of a major war. We found it hard
to realise that the whole course of our lives would be altered – that nothing
would ever be the same again – and harder still to accept that for some of
us there might be no future to worry about. A few may have been thrilled
at the excitement, but most of us soon gave up thinking about it and lived
only in the present. We had to: pressure of work left us no time to dream.

We were a hotchpotch that had been assembled at the Royal Citadel,
Plymouth, just three days earlier, and from all over the world. On the
fourth day men came in to us from the streets and the farms and the
villages to be turned into the gunners who would man the harbour
defences throughout the Empire.

It was most rewarding work. The keenness of those first volunteers can
seldom have been equalled, and it says something for the efficiency of the
pre-war Army that the Regiment – the 70th Coast Defence Training
Regiment – worked with hardly a creak a bare three days after its raising.

Hitler continued to 'extinguish the lights of Europe' as he overran the countries one by one. The BEF (British Expeditionary Force) was thrown into Europe to fight beside the French and the Belgians. At home we began the work of building a Navy, Army and Air Force that could drive the German back to his boundaries.

The time of the next six months became known as the 'Phoney War' because nothing happened. We were sure we would win; we were even impatient with the BEF for not advancing. We sang songs like 'We're gonna hang out the washing on the Siegfried Line' and goaded Hitler with 'Run, rabbit, run!' Little did we realise how close we were to defeat; how unarmed and defenceless we were. We wondered a little, perhaps, when our grass-green recruits were chosen to stand face to face with the enemy – albeit an enemy in chains. Yet I don't think we realised that no others were available!

The Regiment's first act of war was to provide an escort for some German sailors from a torpedoed ship. We had just skimmed off one trained batch, and their successors were really in no state of training to cope with such an assignment, having been soldiers for less than a fortnight. 'Right-turn,' said the officer-in-charge, and two of the party promptly and smartly turned to their left. Said a voice from the huddle of prisoners, 'What a mucking army!'

Then in the spring of 1940 the fighting began. In a bewilderingly short time, all was confusion. The Belgians capitulated; the wonderful French Army disintegrated; the BEF was left fighting for survival. Not even the BBC could disguise the blackness of the news, but even then I don't think we really understood how serious things were. We had infinite faith in Churchill, now Prime Minister, and seemed to imagine that there could be no disaster while he was at the helm.

Then came the evacuation of the survivors from Dunkirk, which brought Plymouth's Royal Citadel into a ray of the limelight. Thousands of our defeated army were landed at Plymouth and were fed, clothed and housed by us until they could be distributed inland. At the same time French and Belgian soldiers were landing at Dover and came to us to be shipped back to France. In a hectic week we coped with over 20,000 British, French and Belgian soldiers, some 6,000 of whom were housed overnight.

We also coped with one woman. She came with a French regiment, dressed as a soldier, and we only found she was there because someone discovered her stripped to the waist, washing at a basin with a crowd of soldiers. The Colonel's wife was brought along and offered to take the girl home with her, but the offer was declined. 'I've been through so much with them,' she said, 'and they have been so kind to me, that I will see this thing through to the end with them.'

One batch of French became quite mutinous because they were confined to barracks one night to ensure that they would be there when their ship came in early in the morning. Finding the main gate shut, they surged round the square until they found a sally port unguarded. The Orderly Officer was alive to what was going on and got there first. Immaculate in service-dress, wearing the Croix de Guerre among his ribbons, he confronted them with his polished swagger stick, and said, '*On ne passe pas!*'

At this, a huge *Poilu*,[1] head and shoulders taller than him, towered over him and said, 'So-oh! You have a little stick, have you! Well, I have a pistol – open the gate and get out of my way!'

But Stevenson-Payne still held the ace. He stood there and quietly fingered his Croix de Guerre. 'Are you going to make me ashamed of this?' he asked. 'Shall I tear it off?'

That was enough! Their sense of the dramatic was touched, they cheered him like mad, and then they went quietly to bed and gave no more trouble.

The stark grimness of war started to come home to me when I saw the survivors of SS *Lancastria*. By an amazing stroke of misfortune a bomb fell straight down her funnel and blew her bottom out. She sank like a stone, with over a thousand men. I talked with an officer saved from her who still had the horror of it on his face, and I began to understand a little of what one would feel if suddenly faced by mass death. Before that, my picture of the war had been unreal – it was something that one read about, but which could not happen to oneself. After seeing these shaken men, dirty and unshaven and in all kinds of clothes, it dawned on me that the survivors from Dunkirk were not dirty and unkempt from choice or from slackness, but because of the gruelling time that they had had. The few cases of bad discipline were not just 'bad soldiers': they were a warning of the shattering and disintegrating forces that war can bring to bear on a military unit.

I began to understand the officer's responsibility for combating these forces – by training his men to resist them; by setting an example of courage and endurance – and I wondered if I should be equal to it.

After Dunkirk, Great Britain was wide open to the German invasion forces, and every nerve was strained to counter them. Beaches were mined, hundreds of miles of barbed wire were strung into entanglements, and pillbox gun positions were erected in the most unlikely places. Roadblocks were constructed and every signpost and milestone was removed to make movement by road difficult. At night not a glimmer of light was allowed to be shown; travel by rail in the dark was stuffy and unpleasant, with every blind drawn and windows tight shut. Finding one's station was a matter of guesswork, as the only clue was the porter's 'musical' interpretation of the name.

Even with all these preparations, I think few people realised our extremity. Our Colonel gave the Regiment a pep talk, telling us that we were part of Britain's first line of defence.

'We have ten rounds of ammunition per man,' he said. 'You will take five of these to the ranges today, and learn how to fire a rifle. The other five you will use to drive the invaders into the sea.' I thought he was merely being dramatic, but it was the grim truth. There was no more rifle ammunition available. When Churchill made his famous speech of defiance ('We will fight them on the beaches … in the fields … in the streets …') it is said that he delivered himself of an aside to the effect that 'It will be with sticks and stones and broken bottles, as there are no rifles to be had!'

The BEF was shattered and all its equipment lost. In the whole of the British Isles there was, I believe, just one fighting Division. It was kept in reserve, and the beaches were defended by units scraped up from the BEF survivors, backed by a new force called the 'Local Defence Volunteers' – afterwards called the Home Guard – armed with pikes, pitchforks and a few shotguns.

Invasion really was on the cards, but we still felt that 'it couldn't happen to us'.

One day when I was Field Officer on duty I was called to the phone during lunch. 'JULIUS!' bawled the voice at the end of the wire, '… and if you don't know what that means, find someone who does, quickly!'

I whispered it to the Colonel, and he replied: 'Yes, it is something important, but I forget what it is – I think you had better go and ask the Adjutant straight away.'

The Adjutant was living with his family on the other side of Plymouth Hoe, and I felt quite annoyed at missing my lunch! He was almost scornful in his calmness. 'Oh, yes,' he said, 'that's the first half of the invasion warning, but there is nothing to worry about until "CAESAR" is sent.'

What a funny way to feel about an invasion – the Colonel doesn't know the code word, the Field Officer doesn't like missing his lunch and the Adjutant isn't worried.

Then came the Battle of Britain, when the Germans tried to annihilate our Air Force and got such a hiding that they gave up the idea of an immediate invasion and started to try and cower us by bombing the life out of our principal cities. London and the Midlands were the first targets, but Plymouth also had a taste of what was to come. At first there were a few daylight raids, just a bomb or two each, which were a source of interest and excitement rather than fear. The AA (anti-aircraft) guns made a grand row and the cotton-wool puffs of their shell bursts traced the course of the plane they were aiming at for us.

Night raids, when they started, were not so amusing. My family was living at Elburton and I used to bicycle into work. I disliked it intensely when the sirens went just as I got to Laira Bridge in the dusk, on my way to a tour of night duty. One felt very small indeed, pedalling through the deserted streets with hostile planes droning overhead. There were usually two or three small raids each night. In one of these, one of our master gunners and his wife and child were killed just outside the Citadel. That brought the war far too close. They were our friends – it could happen to us after all.

One night the Turnchapel oil tanks were hit and burnt with a flaring red glow, continuing to throw off clouds of thick black smoke for three days. Again, I felt very small when higher HQ wanted to know what was burning and I had to go up on the ramparts to see. It was depressing enough to see the eastern sky a glowering red like a doomsday scene without having to go out and – as it felt – become the principal target!

The worst place of all to be during a raid is in hospital. There you really do feel that every bomb is aimed at your personally, while you lie unable to move, as in a nightmare. I realised this to the full when I had an operation for haemorrhoids. Usually the part affected in this operation is so docile and unobtrusive that you never guess how sensitive it is to all you do. But let the Surgeon get busy on it, and you very soon learn that it is vitally concerned when you laugh, cough or sneeze, hiccup or merely move. When healing is still in progress, its reaction to a bomb burst is quite devastating: the muscles contract for dear life, sending a wave of pain right through you. Since that episode I have been a staunch supporter of the sanctity of the Red Cross.

Stevenson-Payne and I went for a stroll one evening on the ramparts during a small raid. The colours and flashes of the AA bursts were something to admire. Streams of red fireballs from the light AA seemed to be drifting gently upwards like ropes of flaming onions and there were continual flashes in the upper heavens where the heavies were bursting. Searchlights fingered the sky with their cool silvery beams, and now and then one of these would light on a plane. Instantly, two or three others would join it and form a beautiful criss-cross of brightness, moving in unison with the plane as it desperately twisted and turned to try and escape. At this, the fury of the guns would redouble as they hounded the struggling pilot, and, occasionally, there was a falling comet of fire as a shell hit home and the aircraft plummeted to earth.

Suddenly, a bomb came screeching towards us and crashed into the road below us as we crouched behind the parapet. Its hot blast swept past, though we were a hundred feet above it and protected by the unshakeable ramparts. It was my first experience of a close one, and I was quite shaken: in fact, I wondered if I could take it. I asked S-P about this, he being a much older soldier. How would one behave under real shelling? What was the secret of steeling oneself against running away, or becoming paralysed and useless from sheer fright?

He was most reassuring. 'You just get used to it,' he said. 'You won't run away, because you will be too frightened of being a coward. And anyway – there's nowhere to run to!'

There is a wealth of wisdom in those remarks. People do need to get acclimatised to the bumps and bangs of war, and that doesn't take the ordinary man very long. All the same, I do not think I should ever get used to being bombed in a town. The street I am in seems to be the only possible target, and my house right in the centre of the bombsite!

*

The Officers' Mess (living quarters) was a most attractive building of grey stone, arranged in a topsy-turvy fashion with the living rooms upstairs. From the ante-room you have a delightful view of Plymouth Sound, with Drake's Island set like a jewel in the blue waters and the green headlands embracing it on either side.

On a fine day, we used to enjoy watching the ships of the Royal Navy stealing quietly in and out of the Hamoaze as they went about their business, keeping the sea. The cruiser HMS *Newcastle* [see plate] had her berth just below us, almost in the Cattewater. The precision of her bugle calls was a delight to hear, and it used to irk me a little that we could never run up our Union Jack with quite the adroitness with which her Ensign was hoisted.

Another old friend and landmark was the aircraft carrier HMS *Courageous* [see plate], which used to anchor off the breakwater, until one day she steamed away into the mist and never came back.

When all was gloom, with heavy air raids, terrible shipping losses and not a glimmer of a military success, the Royal Navy suddenly handed the nation a glass of champagne ... the sinking of the German heavy cruiser *Graf Spee* by HMS *Exeter*, *Achilles* and *Ajax* in the Battle of the River Plate. It was a tremendous uplift, and one of the most moving moments of my life was when we stood and watched HMS *Exeter* pass between us and Drake's Island on her way home. Her funnels were riddled and scars showed on her upper works [see plate]. No salutes were fired from the Citadel in wartime, or she would have had of our best, but she was identified in time for the officers to rush and line the walls and salute her as she passed. I do not expect we were seen, but we had at least done our best to thank her ship's company.

Thus far, our war had been a very comfortable one; our consciences had been stilled by the knowledge that it was a sound policy to post regular officers who knew the ropes to run training regiments. We had been told that we would be transferred to the Field Army when we were needed there, and that in the meantime we were not to make extra work by asking for more active service jobs.

As time went on and there was not the least sign of a move, I realised that it was time I left this pleasant backwater. For over a year I had been responsible for paying, feeding and administering over a thousand men. I held every account in the Citadel and I was nominally second-in-command, though that was a sinecure. Then I managed to get command of a training battery, having picked up sufficient knowledge of Coast Artillery work to compete with the job. It was hard and exacting work, but work without a sniff of danger or hardship, so I asked the Colonel to release me. At that time we had just started to expand the Regiment into three, so I was asked to be patient until that was finished, and stayed a little longer.

One of my jobs during the expansion was to supervise the introduction of women (Auxiliary Territorial Services, or ATS) into the Regiment that we formed at Raglan Barracks. I was inwardly very ill at ease when I sat down to interview some forty or so young women with the Platoon Commander standing behind me in approved army fashion. Dealing with women en masse was a new and uncertain experience for me. Luckily, the ATS skirt length was one inch above the knee, and I happened to notice that the first poor girl's patellas were positively rattling with fright as she stood at attention before a male officer for the first time! Such a convincing demonstration that she was human helped a lot in making the interviews pass off successfully.

As soon as the expansion was finished I again applied to be posted, and was almost immediately sent to the 127th (H) Field Regiment RA, Aberdeen. That worried me, because I thought the 'H' in brackets must stand for 'Heavy'. I had no desire to go to the heavies and had been longing to get back to the Field Branch, in which I had served continuously for all my nine years of pre-war service. Nor was I re-assured when I arrived in Scotland, because I found everyone wearing (HD) on their sleeves. Almost my first words to the Adjutant were: 'They seem to have made a mess of my posting; I specially applied to get away from Home Defence, and here am I, posted to a HD Regiment!'

The Adjutant had been a sergeant in my peacetime regiment. He looked at me with a slow smile. 'I see I had better let you into a secret, Sir,' he remarked quietly. 'In these parts HD does not stand for Home Defence – you are now in the 51st *Highland Division*.'

The very night that I was on the train going to Aberdeen, the whole centre of Plymouth was laid flat in one of the worst raids suffered in this country. Nine bombs fell inside the Citadel: eight did only moderate damage; the ninth killed all twelve men of the Fire Piquet at a blow. The town was a shambles. Sixteen years later as I write this, it is still rising out of the rubble. The outskirts and most of the ancient parts of the city escaped the holocaust. But the fine shopping centre that you see today is quite different from the one that we knew.

Notes

1 Rough, bearded French soldier.

Chapter 2

North of the Border

Who are these coming to the sacrifice?
To what green altar, O mysterious priest

John Keats

127, 128 [H] Field Regiment RA, April 1940

Spring had already come to Devon, the primroses were out and the daffodils were bursting their buds, but as the train laboured past Montrose there was a biting nip in the air and a snowy landscape appeared in the cold grey dawn. In Scotland, April is a winter month – there may even be snow in May.

At Aberdeen I was met by a scruffy soldier speaking a strong uncouth dialect who took me to a dirty, badly painted car. Coming straight from the pre-war smartness and efficiency of the Citadel, I was quite appalled that such a turnout should have been allowed on the road, and wondered what on earth sort of Regiment I was coming to. It was the first of many shocks. When I had been there a week, the Colonel remarked: 'You think this Regiment is a "shower", don't you?' When I agreed, he said, 'Well, you should have seen them when I first came!' They were a second-line Territorial Army Regiment, one of those formed when the TA was doubled in frantic haste in the spring of 1939. The original Highland Division was overwhelmed at St Valery, and the new one was entirely second line, except for two regular Infantry Battalions.

Their discipline at that time was – putting it kindly – still in the formative stage. In other words, it seemed impossible to get the simplest order carried out. The Colonel, the Adjutant and I were the only regular officers, and we were all English. The others were various types of businessmen from Arbroath and such like places. They were all staunch Territorials, bitterly resentful of Regular Army interferences and, for the most part, hostile to Sassenachs.[1] On top of this, they were all related to each other, or at least had known each other for years, the result being that no one would give anyone else a direct order let alone administer a reprimand.

Doubtless the show would have worked if they had been good at their jobs, but to quote the Colonel, 'They know absolutely nothing about anything – and they don't even know that! They think they are absolutely marvellous!'

The men? They were the usual excellent raw material of the British Isles, waiting to be trained and led. There are no bad men – only bad officers! That's an old and trite saying, but it is very true. The Colonel, a capable man of sound methods, applied the only possible policy short of wholesale sackings – that of 'make haste slowly'. By concentrating on a few essentials at a time, discipline was gradually inculcated. The three Regulars had to follow each order through to completion, raising Cain at each delay and procrastination, checking at every stage, urging and encouraging, until at last the result was achieved. Hand in hand with this licking into shape went the technical and tactical training and the relentless struggle for existence. This last was the natural outcome of the Army's tremendous expansion.

There was no proper accommodation for us. We lived in huts, tents, vacant houses or ruined camps. Always we had to compete with cramped quarters, lack of stores and utensils, and the ever-present snow, slush or mud. Such hard standings as we had for our guns and vehicles were laboriously made by ourselves, from stone and rubble, pinched from 'don't ask where' or grudgingly given by people who had little of it to spare.

One story of rubble sticks in my mind as the only example of meanness we ever met in that most generous county of Aberdeen. During the invasion scare the Regiment had to dig gun pits covering the beaches from Cuden Bay to miles south of Stonehaven. These had to be floored with stone, or they would have been useless, so the Regiment got permission to draw rubble from a quarry belonging to the County Council. A year later a bill was sent in for £129 on the grounds that they had taken 'hard-core' instead of 'rubble'! Was the Regiment trying to defend Scotland or was it digging holes for fun?

Out of this mess of unruly humanity there eventually emerged a very good fighting Regiment, but, like Moses and the Promised Land, the Colonel and I were to see it from a distance only. He was not allowed to take it overseas because of his age and I was suddenly posted away after I had been with it for six months.

There was something fishy about my position, but I have never managed to find out the ins and outs of it. A reliable source told me that 'S' (the Colonel) eased me quietly out because I was not tactful enough in my handling of the Battery Commanders. If that was so, then I was stronger than I knew! It may have been that 'S' took a dislike to me. He was always friendly enough, but I believe he thought I did not treat the local Laird and his wife with enough respect. He was a self-admitted snob and enjoyed being billeted on them, where he probably heard of my shortcomings. These mostly centred on the mending of the soldiers' socks, for which 'Mrs Laird' organised the wives of the village into work parties. Do what I would, I could not prevent some feckless NCO from being late in getting the socks to these parties, for which she used to row me. The climax came when I was called away from dinner to deal with a fatuous note from her. I answered it politely on the only available paper, which happened to be very poor quality office memo paper, yellowish coloured. To make matters worse the despatch rider delivered it crumpled. She arrived next day, banged it down in front of me and asked – almost in as many words – what the devil I meant by writing to her on crumpled lavatory paper! She went away still convinced I had been intentionally rude. On top of that, her mean old husband sent us a bill for £2.10 for sand someone took from his sandpit to fill defence sandbags. I had already refused a similar and larger bill, so I refused that one too. Next morning the Colonel plonked my letter down, asked what I thought I was doing and told me to get it paid at once! So, putting two and two together, it looks as if feminine influence helped to decide that I would be better employed elsewhere.

My posting turned out to be the best thing that could have happened to me, because it gave me the good fortune of serving as second-in-command to Jerry Sheil [see plate]. I was to command an anti-tank battery in the Division, but was first sent on loan to the sister field regiment, 128 (Highland) Field Regiment. There I met Jerry.

Before I had been there a day I said to myself: 'I like that man. There is a nice atmosphere in this regiment ... I'm going to stay here.' And stay I did. Unashamedly, I set to work to demonstrate such efficiency as was in me in every possible way. Walking up to lunch, Jerry remarked, 'We ought to have a fence there to stop people cutting across the grass.' By tea time the fence was there. I knew what I wanted and I worked for it, and after the first month he asked if I would like to stay. My hope is that I did not slacken my efforts afterwards. I tried not to.

Jerry Sheil was an Irishman with a most attractive personality and great charm of manner, and as a soldier he was outstanding. His military knowledge and ability were in the highest class, but it was his power of leadership that made him so remarkable. His mere appearance when things were tough was enough to raise everyone's spirits sky high and make them treat the affair almost as a picnic. People felt safe with him there, no matter how bad the shelling or how great the number of bullets in the air. The ability to radiate such confidence is possessed by only a few: very few indeed.

He was a regular soldier before the war, but had retired as a Captain to breed horses. Recalled in 1939, he commanded a troop as Captain and made his reputation in the retreat to Dunkirk, so that he was promoted to Lieutenant Colonel at once and sent to 'pull 128 Regiment out of the mud'. From all accounts there was plenty of mud to pull it out of 'S''s policy of *festina lente* would not have worked there: the only remedy was the axe, ruthlessly used.

By the time I arrived things were in good shape. There were three new Battery Commanders and a new Quartermaster, and a leavening of young officers who had been through the mill of an Officer Training Unit, at which Jerry had been an instructor for a time after Dunkirk. In fact, he had pruned the tree and re-grafted it [see plate].

As we are going to war with this Regiment, I will set down what it consisted of. To begin at the top, it had a Regimental Headquarters (RHQ) to provide the Colonel with the means of controlling and commanding it. Then there were three batteries: 307, 308 and 492. These were the units that provided the firepower. Each was commanded by a major, with a senior captain as second-in-command (known as the 'Battery Captain' or BC), and was divided into two troops of four guns each, commanded by junior captains (called Troop Commanders). Thus there were twenty-four guns in the Regiment. Guns are big and hard to defend and are positioned well behind the front-line infantry.

The Troop Commander's place in action was at an observation post (OP). These OPs are in the area held by a Forward Company of an Infantry unit. From there he could see what to shoot, and he could keep close touch with the Infantry Company Commander to discuss likely targets with him.

The Battery Commander lived with the Infantry Battalion Commander, so as to be constantly in touch with what the Battalion was doing, and to be ready to plan gunfire support for each new situation as it arose.

The Troop and Battery Commanders were in constant communication with the Troops and Batteries and RHQ by wireless, with telephone lines too when it was possible to lay them. This close liaison with the Infantry was continued at every level, the Colonel living at Brigade HQ with the Infantry Brigadier and the Gunner Brigadier (always called the CRA – i.e. Commander, Royal Artillery) living with the General commanding the

Division. When working with tanks instead of infantry the system was exactly the same. Thus there was no danger of gunners or infantry fighting 'different wars' because they were closely linked at all levels from the bottom upwards.

Batteries provided their own Gunner Signaller, but there was a Royal Signals Troop attached to RHQ to provide communications between RHQ and batteries, and back to HQRA (the CRA's HQ).

Also at RHQ were the Survey Section, the Light Aid Detachment Royal Electrical and Mechanical Engineers (the LAD), the Medical Officer (MO) and his Regimental Aid Post (the RAP) and the Padre.

The LAD repaired trucks and guns, the doctor and padre mended our bodies and souls and the surveyors were the sorcerers. They made it possible – by what the Infantry always called 'Gunner Ju-ju' (magic) – for all three batteries to fire on to a target ranged by any one of them, and for the whole Regiment to fire on to a target found by any other Regiment within range. For accuracy's sake I must mention that the Survey Section only did the work inside their own Regiment: the outside work was done by their big brothers, the Survey Regiment RA.

Thanks to this branch of 'Gunner Ju-ju', this is what one Gunner Officer could do, crouching in a hole in the ground with a signaller and a wireless set: he could hit a target with one or more of his own four guns, or he could ask for the whole Battery, bringing in the other Troop. If that was not enough, he could call for a 'Mike' target, when the Regiment's 24 guns would answer.

If the target was important enough he could call in the other two Regiments as well – 72 guns. That was called an 'Uncle'. And if it was a really super target, he could say 'Victor Target', whereupon every gun within range would come in – mediums, heavies, super-heavies and all. To put down a Victor was everyone's ambition. It could mean a crash of up to 250 guns.[2]

General Sir Brian Horrocks has said in many a lecture of these concentrations of fire:

> although I am an Infantryman I would say that the Royal Regiment of Artillery did more to win the last war than did any other arm. The technical skill by which these huge concentrations of fire could be switched from one part of the front to another was never equalled in any other army. The Germans never succeeded in achieving anything like it.

*

We were billeted in Inverurie, except for 492 Battery, which lived on its own in Kintore, ten miles away. Our training took us through exquisite Deeside and into almost equally beautiful Donside, and as far afield as Elgin, Nairn and Inverness. Some of our exercises were as good as a summer tour through the Highlands. The Cabrach was one of our shooting areas, and we penetrated as far as Tomintoul, the highest village in the British Isles.

The grand finale of our Scottish training was a trip along the shore of Loch Ness to Fort William, whence we 'fought' our way back by a long and devious route, attacking every grouse-moor on the way with live rounds. It took us six days, during which I doubt if we got six hours' sleep in all. It was wonderful training, harder going than anything we met in war. At the end, when we reached Turriff and were waiting for a few minutes before going home, I was on the verge of hallucinations from lack of sleep. Sitting at the wheel of the stationary car, I felt as if it were moving, and the harder I put on the brake the more it seemed to move. However, I woke myself up, regained control and drove the forty miles without any bother.

Wherever we went the Scots were charming to us. One old man, pretty far north, was disappointed when I couldn't speak Gaelic, and a trifle surprised when I told him I was English, but even that did not dampen his pleasure at meeting troops of the Highland Division, raised in his very own Highlands.

At last the time came for us to go south for a final polish to our training at Aldershot. There we met an up-and-coming general whose name was soon to be famous all over the world: Bernard Montgomery. I went to a lecture of his at which he spoke as follows: 'I don't approve of smoking, so there will be no smoking. I don't approve of coughing either. You have two minutes now in which you may cough to your hearts' content – after that, NO coughing, please.' There was none!

His training programme was rigorous and any officer, particularly a CO, who couldn't take it found himself out. Fitness was his god. After a month or so of this training we began to wonder if war could hold any worse hardships. But we were now welded into a fine fighting machine, and we had not much longer to wait. Very soon we found ourselves at Liverpool, embarking in the Canadian Pacific Liner the *Duchess of Richmond* [see plate]. We arrived at breakfast time and had our first unrationed breakfast since 1939: iced grapefruit to start with, then as much of whatever you fancied as you liked to ask for. After three years of rationing we could hardly believe that such a thing was possible. The secret was that the ship victualled at Cape Town, where there was no dearth of anything.

And so, on 19 June 1942, the seventh anniversary of my wedding day, we set out on a great adventure, Many stirring events were to happen before we again saw our wives and children – events that would remove the nation from jeopardy and change the course of our lives.

Notes

[1] A word used chiefly by the Scots to designate an Englishman.
[2] See also the organisation table in the Appendix.

Chapter 3

Voyage to War

But why drives on that ship so fast,
Without or wave or wind?

Samuel Taylor Coleridge

128 [H] Field Regiment RA, June 1942

The routine bustle of the start of the voyage killed any tendency to homesickness as the ship inched her way out of the dreary Mersey into the open sea, and there most of us were absorbed watching the various islands and headlands of the coast slip by us and fade into the haze astern.

Next morning we found we were part of a huge convoy of beautiful liners, covering mile upon mile of ocean. From our place, second from the left of the front row, we could see the *Stratheden*, *Empresses of Australia* and *Asia*, the *Orion* – a particularly lovely vessel – the *Durban Castle*, the *Belgian Abosso*, the *Bamfora* and scores of others dwindling in size until they became lost in the distance. Completing the picture, on our flank was the squat, powerful-looking battleship *Malays*: out of date perhaps, but giving a comforting feeling of security. She had three or four destroyers, which she used to send round the convoy like sheep dogs rounding up a straggling flock. She also had a queer-looking survivor of the air world, a Walrus seaplane with a 'pusher' airscrew at the rear, which she used to look for submarines and to report on the progress of the convoy. Such was our escort: its capabilities were never tested, as the enemy left us in peace for the whole passage to North Africa.

The ship was terribly crowded.[1] Boat drill aimed merely at getting everyone up on deck where they would have a chance to swim for life; it would have been quite impossible to carry enough boats and rafts for all of us. Every morning we practised clearing the lower decks until it could be done in under four minutes. On the sounding of the alarm we pounded up the stairs to reach an open deck; there we stayed, packed like sardines in a tin, until the all clear went. If the alarm had been a reality, heaven knows what would have happened. It would have been very difficult to stage a 'Birkenhead'[2] with so much massed humanity.[2]

Fortunately, the *Duchess* steamed serenely on. Day after day the sun streamed on us and the bow wave made the only ripple on the glassy waters. The breeze thrummed a tune in the rigging and there was a rhythmic hum from below that could waft one to Dreamland long before one knew that one's eyelids had closed. Never a sign of a sub did we see. Our days were just pleasantly occupied: we tried to keep fit with PT, but shortage of deck space rationed our efforts to half an hour a day, so that all could have a turn. Lectures to the troops whiled away another hour or two, and then the officers met for discussions and lectures from those who had been to war. There was never a dull moment, but even so, there was time to read or just laze and look at the sea.

Our companions on board were the 2nd Seaforth Highlanders, the 5th Cameron Highlanders and the HQ of their brigade, the 152nd. It was a pity that the third battalion of the brigade, the 5th Seaforth, could not be on board as well, because of the friendship and mutual understanding that arose between us and the units we shared the ship with on this trip. They were the brigade to which we were affiliated, the one with which we normally worked throughout the whole coming campaign. 5th Seaforth were very much our friends in the campaign, but it seemed to me that the ties between us and the other two were just that little bit closer as a result of our time together on board.

51st Highland Division, order of battle at formation

152nd Infantry Brigade
2nd Battalion, Seaforth-Highlanders Seaforth Highlanders
5th Battalion, Seaforth-Highlanders Seaforth Highlanders
5th Battalion, Queen's Own Cameron Highlanders

153rd Infantry Brigade
5th Battalion, Black Watch
1st Battalion, Gordon Highlanders
5/7th Battalion, Gordon Highlanders

154th Infantry Brigade
1st Battalion, Black Watch
7th Battalion, Black Watch
7th Battalion, Argyll and Sutherland Highlanders

Support Units
1/7th Battalion, The Middlesex Regiment
2nd Derbyshire Yeomanry, Royal Armoured Corps
126th Field Regiment, Royal Artillery
127th Field Regiment, Royal Artillery
128th Field Regiment, Royal Artillery
61st Anti-Tank Regiment, Royal Artillery
274 Field Company, Royal Engineers
275 Field Company, Royal Engineers
276 Field Company, Royal Engineers

To start with, we won the triangular boxing tournament, which earned us considerable respect. Then we used to dine at each other's tables, so that the officers really were on Christian name terms by the time we landed. Thus we became 'their gunners' and they were 'our infantry', and both sides were much put out if the exigencies of battle caused a temporary change in the liaison.

We also had our Field Ambulance Unit with us, and affected a similar liaison with them. Several small units filled the nooks and crannies, including a bevy of eight nursing sisters, the only women on board. Only one of these was really attractive, but scarcity gave the others a greatly inflated value, of which some of them made full use.

One night as I stepped into the dark of the sun deck for a last stroll, my hand was seized in a gentle but firm grasp, which started to draw me into the shadows. 'What's going on?' said I, and there was a stifled shriek in the gloom. My hand was dropped as if it were red hot! It was Blondie, the only attractive one, anticipating the arrival of her friend the dental officer. The funny thing was that next day it was obvious that she knew it was me she had grabbed, but she was not sure if I knew it was her! I never let on.

Just where our good ship took us I shall never know as we cruised all around the ocean to avoid the submarine wolfpacks waiting for us. At last her wanderings brought us to Sierra Leone, off Freetown, the port where the slaves from the ships captured by the old-time frigates were liberated. We could not go ashore, but enjoyed feasting our eyes on the green of the palms, letting a tropical shower souse us as we stood in our bathing trunks and revelled in the unexpected coolness.

When the ship had re-fuelled, we resumed our lotus-isle existence: sunny days on the sun deck, hunting for patches of shade; cool nights also on the deck because the cabin was like an oven. As we crossed the 'line', we were treated to a royal visit. Over the side came Neptune with Amphitrite, his queen, and his physician, barber and court of bears. The Chief Officer met him with ceremony and presented the roll of those who had not entered his realm before, that they might be dealt with for their rashness, before being admitted to the select company of sea dogs.

First to be dragged before the court was our Infantry Brigadier, George Murray. His defence was to deny the court's jurisdiction. At this, his face was lathered with a whitewash brush and the barber shaved him with a huge wooden razor; the 'doctor' ladled a foul looking concoction down his throat, and he was tipped over backwards and ducked in a tarpaulin bath by the 'bears'. After all this, he ambled off, protesting and vowing vengeance if ever Neptune should dare to show his face in Murray's Highlands.

Last to be dealt with was a shrieking 'nurse', but it was soon seen that she was not one of the eight who had embarked with us. Here Amphitrite took a hand. 'What a costume!' she minced. 'Strip her!' Off came layer after layer of garments and corsets and whatnots, until 'she' was left cringing in a bra of stuffed pillowcases and heavy woollen drawers. 'Up-end her and spank her,' said the Queen of the Sea, and up came the end to reveal that the seat of her pants was one enormous Highland Division shoulder flash!

A few days later we put into Cape Town with its attractive harbour and friendly people. Table Mountain stood out sharp and clear among its attendant hills as we steamed in, with no sign of its usual misty Tablecloth [see plate]. At its feet, the town curved round the bay in a pleasing semi-circle, and a few small boats gave life to the scene. We had been promised a run on shore and we crowded the rails for a foretaste of the pleasure.

The morning was wasted by a very badly arranged route march, but the afternoon came at last, and we were free. 'Copper' Finlayson (Battery Commander of 308 Battery) and I set off to explore the town and found it good, improving more and more with acquaintance. In the evening we joined a queue that led to a promising-looking restaurant, only to be told 'House full!' when we reached the door. As we turned regretfully away, our arms were seized by an Afrikaans policeman. 'This is nonsense,' he said, almost dragging us back to the door. 'Make way for two British Officers, they are our guests – the guests of the Union! Find them a table, or I will call the manager!' Before you could say 'Knife', we were sitting down to an excellent dinner. Our benefactor just disappeared into the crowd before we could even thank him. As we had been led to expect coolness at least, if not open hostility, from the Dutch section, this act of friendliness was all the more pleasing.

Next day we went for a drive in the country and saw, among other things, the house of Field Marshal Smuts and the Rhodes Memorial. The latter is most impressive. High above the plain a huge statue on horseback gazes thoughtfully down on the town. The background is a magnificent temple front, apparently carved out of the rock. Crouching lions guard the figure of Rhodes, and the whole shrine is so beautifully proportioned that it is striking in its grandeur.

The visit was rounded off by a dance at a nice country club some seven miles out. This was most beautifully organised. Nothing had been left undone that could possibly add to our enjoyment: pleasant hostesses saw that all who wanted to dance had partners; food and drink were there in plenty, but nothing was forced on us. We were just encouraged to enjoy ourselves, each in his own way. The crowning act of hospitality: they knew we had to be on board by 2.00 am so the party finished sharp at 1.30, and we found buses lined up ready to take us back! The whole thing was a demonstration of how to entertain people from another country.

*

We put into Durban to join up with the ships that had spent their shore leave there and then turned northwards. Each night the Southern Cross appeared lower in the sky until one evening it was no longer there, and turning to the north we were able to see the Great Bear just above the horizon – we were north of the Equator once more.

Steamer Point, Aden, soon loomed ahead, as it used to when we were halfway home from India [see plate]. How strange it seemed to be approaching it from the south, while still outward-bound – we felt cheated!

In the Red Sea we broke convoy and each ship made her best speed. We were lucky to have a head wind, but even so the heat down below was 'stinking'. If you went near the galley it hit you like a blow and oppressed you until the sweat ran in streams, leaving you craving for water.

The evening before we came to our destination – Port Tewfik – I watched the setting sun for the green flash that one sometimes sees just before it dips below the horizon, and as I watched, it came – in the form of a 'V'. It seemed an omen of victory: in those days one badly needed such an omen. Victory seemed terribly remote at that time, with the Germans at the very gateway to Egypt.

Next day, 6 August, we landed. Packed in a lighter, we had our last view of the *Duchess*, our pleasant home for nearly two months. Handsome and friendly she lay there, raising steam for the homeward passage, but already she was part of our past. In war one seldom looked back. Forward, ever forward, one cast one's hopes, and the past faded as inevitably and completely as the wake of a ship.

Poor old lady! After the war they re-named her the *Empress of Canada*, and under that name she was gutted by fire in Liverpool Docks. Sailors have always held it unlucky to change the name of a ship.

Notes

[1] Orion, for example, was designed to carry 1,408 passengers and at the peak of her role as a troop ship carried 7,000 troops.

[2] The *Birkenhead* tragedy of 1852 is an example of the heroism displayed by the Black Watch Regiment, which gave rise to the tradition known as 'The Birkenhead Drill'. This requires a ship's crew to disregard their own safety, to remain calm, to give priority to the rescue of any women, children and civilians aboard, and to display endurance and courage beyond the call of duty. Worried that his men might swamp the lifeboat carrying women and children, the *Birkenhead*'s Commanding Officer ordered them to 'stand fast'. To a man, they all stood in quiet dignity as the ship broke up and sank.

Part 2

NORTH AFRICA

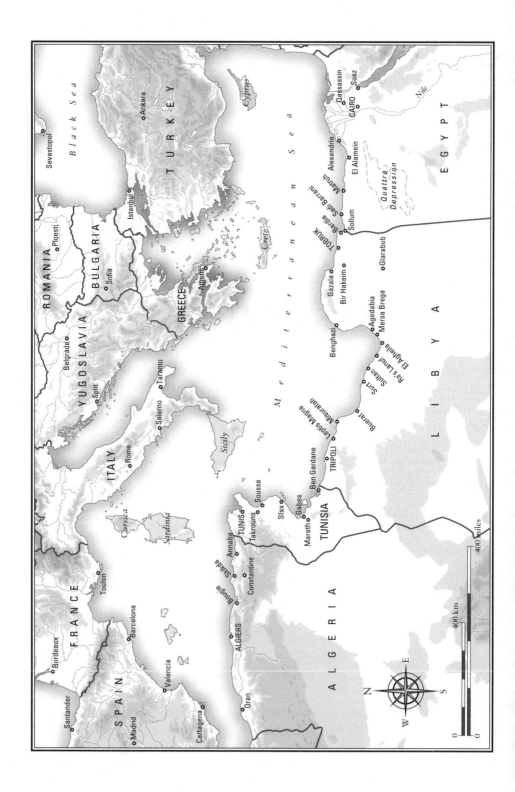

Chapter 4

The Land of Egypt

Hard by the lilied Nile I saw
A duskish river-dragon stretched along.
The brown habergeon of his limbs enamelled
With sanguine almandines and rainy pearl:

TL Beddoes

128 [H] Field Regiment RA

Port Tewfik at the southern end of the Suez Canal [now the passenger liner part of Port Suez] is full of smells and flies. We hung about there for most of the day, so I don't mean to dwell on it for a minute longer. A train came at last and carried us slowly along the Canal bank, past Ismailia, dumping us in the dark at a station without a name. From there we were taken in Royal Army Service Corps (RASC) lorries for several miles and then unloaded in the desert. 'Here is your camp,' said the RASC Officer, though all we could see was just sand and more sand, stretching to the horizon of the moonlit night. 'Good luck, and good night,' said he, and left us to begin our sojourn in the desert.

We were at a place called Qassassin, about ninety miles east of Cairo, which we did not realise at the time was pretty luxurious as living in the desert went. There were a couple of water taps, a shed for a NAAFI and another for a cinema. When the sun rose on the sand it seemed a pretty grim place: there seemed to be no escape from the heat, or from the ever-present dust, grit and flies. But when we looked round, we found a pile of tents had been left for us, and soon we made a sizeable village of canvas. Things began to look better. It is remarkable how soon one can get used to new surroundings, no matter how uncomfortable they may seem at first.

There was no time for moping. Guns had to be collected and put in working order, vehicles started rolling in, and soon we were a regiment 'in being' again, just itching to get out of kindergarten and get down to the business of war.

Kindergarten is quite a suitable name for this period, for it was at Qassassin that we learnt the rudiments of desert life. A team of experienced desert soldiers came and taught us most of what we ought to know: how to get a truck across soft sand (better still, how to recognise it before you got stuck!); how to make a half-gallon of water last the day for drinking, washing and shaving, filling the truck's radiator and – occasionally – washing one's socks. Above all, they taught us to treat the compass as our greatest friend. With a compass one need never be lost in the desert, even in the most barren and featureless parts of it. Without one you can get into a pretty pickle, particularly at night, when the whole country presents one vast miasmic sameness, stretching from you to a misty eternity on all sides with not a single clue to help you find where you are. I once got benighted without my compass in a strange part of the camp. I knew my bivvy tent was about three hundred yards away, and I set out quite confidently to go to bed. I got there two hours later, and then only because I happened to trip over a signal wire. I followed that to one of its ends, a Battalion HQ, and from there I followed another wire to our own RHQ, from which I knew the exact bearing to my bivvy. You may be sure I never forgot my compass again!

Our teachers showed us how to judge our direction from the sun by day and from the Pole star by night, and they made us experts in the use of the sun-compass. That is a most accurate instrument for desert navigation. In its simplest form it consists of a bit of string from the top of the windscreen to the radiator, which throws a shadow on to a chalk mark on the car's bonnet. More complicated instruments are made of steel and have lots of graphs and figures on them, but I don't think they give much better results. If you use them properly, either will get you to within half a mile of your point at the end of a twenty-mile trip. That is accurate enough if you are just 'swanning' – travelling about the place. If you have to meet someone, you will see his car at least a mile away, and can drive up to it when you have identified it as a friendly vehicle.

The magnetic compass is equally good, in spite of the metal in the car. To use it, you line up the car in the direction in which you want to go, and then place yourself and the compass where you intend to stay during the trip and rev up the engine. You get a reading that bears no resemblance to the direction in which the car is pointing, which is in fact the compensated compass reading allowing for the metal of the vehicle. You just steer on that.

You start by marking the route on the map as a series of straight lines making a number of 'legs' to avoid any known obstacles. Then you memorise it as 'so many miles on bearing X, then change to bearing Y for so many miles', just like laying off the course of a ship. Then there will certainly be a number of involuntary deviations, to avoid rough ground or soft sand. At the end, you average these out in your mind, and if necessary lay off a final short course to get to the point you are aiming at.

My most successful journey of this kind occurred when the regiment was caught in a real sand storm with visibility down to fifty yards. I laid off a bearing from where I thought we might be to where I thought the entrance to the camp was. The distance was ten miles. I had no real hope of getting there; in fact I was almost resigned to being kicked out of the regiment for losing them irretrievably! Imagine my joy when not only did the camp loom out of the brown dust, but my car was heading for the very centre of the gap in the minefield that was the camp gate! A fluke, of course, but it does demonstrate how reliable the compass is as a navigating instrument.

The distances were measured by the speedometer, tested over a measured mile at a certain tyre pressure, and allowing five-per-cent loss of distance for wheel-spin in the sand when on a journey. Tracks were no good as directional aids because everybody made a new one when they felt like it, so you couldn't tell if you were following one marked on the map or one made by the ration track of 'Z' Battery the night it lost its way and drove into the enemy lines! The exceptions were the divisional and corps axes. These were marked with the sign or the formation on iron stakes every hundred yards or so, and were lighted at night. They were a real boon – like buoys marking a shipping lane. But you could be caught by these too, on occasion. I remember doing a most careful reconnaissance for a move, memorising each divisional axis I would use: thus, 'Hit the "Red Square" track and keep on for two miles until you find the "Round O"; after five miles ...' etc. Unfortunately, these divisions moved just before we did, and pulled up all their signs as they went. I was left to my own devices and my good compass. I never again put my trust in someone else's markings!

*

We had arrived in Egypt at a very critical time. The first part of the campaign in the desert had been a series of ups and downs. First there was Field Marshal Wavell's masterly victory over a vastly superior Italian army, which took him up beyond Benghazi. He was then forced to deplete his forces to give support to Greece and at the same time the Germans reinforced the Italians. As a result he was forced back. His successor, Field

Marshal Auchinleck ('The Auk'), advanced to Agheila, but after much hard fighting he too was driven back, leaving a strong garrison in Tobruk, and occupied the last defensible position in front of Cairo and Alexandria, later called the Alamein Line. Here, the right flank rested on the sea, and the left on the almost impossible Qattara Depression – a 'sea' of soft sand [see plate].

While we were still on the way, Tobruk fell, which was a bad blow. It was considered a very strong position, which would be a thorn in the enemy's side, and Auchinleck intended to make full use of it in staging a comeback. There was then a tremendous upheaval in the ranks of command. 'The Auk' was replaced as Commander in Chief by General Sir Harold Alexander, and General Bernard Montgomery replaced General Neil Ritchie as Army Commander in the Field. These two found a spirit almost of defeatism. There had been talk of abandoning Egypt and at GHQ (General Headquarters) they had even burnt most of the secret files in anticipation of the capture of the HQ.

The new command soon changed all that. Montgomery found some soldiers digging trenches. 'What are you doing'? asked the General.

'Digging defensive positions, Sir', was the reply.

'Well, you can stop digging,' said Monty. 'You are going forward – you won't want defensive positions here!'

Alexander had decided to hold the Alamein Line come what may while he speeded the build-up of a force strong enough to break through the enemy's formidable position and, in the words of Montgomery, 'hit him for six, right out of Africa'. No longer was there a dearth of equipment. Tanks and other materials were pouring in from America and ammunition was becoming plentiful. It was a race as to which side could be ready to attack first, and we looked like winning it because the enemy's material had to come all the way by land from Tripoli, except for a little landed at Tobruk.

The enemy commander, Field Marshal Erwin Rommel, did put in one attack, which was thrown back with heavy losses. That was really his swan song, and after it our steady amassing of men and material continued unhindered. Of course, the Highland Division was an important part of the build-up.

Meanwhile, Egypt was still in considerable danger, and we were part of the last line of defence. As such we were moved into a defensive position at a place called Delta Barrage. The only incident there was the accidental killing of an Egyptian by a shot from a carelessly handled Bren gun. The Egyptian Liaison Officer with us thought this a great joke. 'But', said he, 'please do not kill more than one a day.' The very next day, two were shot and wounded, probably by a trigger-happy sentry. That put the Liaison Officer in a great paddy. 'I say only shoot one, and you shoot TWO! How this can I to my superiors explain – they with me will be very angry!'

From Delta Barrage we moved in a great hurry to the Mena House Hotel, near the Pyramids. So great was the hurry, and the secrecy, that no one knew we were coming and no one thought of telling us that there were already troops in the area to whom we should make our presence known before cruising about in their domains. That very nearly had unfortunate results as people were terribly nervous of spies in those days and treated all newcomers with suspicion until they had proved their bonafides. To make matters worse, we had no identify cards at a time when they had to be produced on every possible occasion.

The upshot was that I arrived with the advance party and started to reconnoitre gun positions. Out steps a sentry. 'Excuse me, Sir, may I see your identity card?'

'Sorry, I haven't got one, but I have orders to put guns in this area.'

He told me I must come to Company HQ and be identified, but I was racing against the setting sun to get finished in daylight, so I said I would go there 'after I've finished'. If he had been a seasoned soldier, he would have arrested me then and there, but I was too green to realise that and pushed on with my work, brushing aside sentries whenever I met them – a very dangerous thing to do in war.

After I had finished, I went to Battalion HQ to explain my conduct. There I met an absolute stumour! I regret to say he was a gunner. He was commanding a collection of goodness knows what scraped from goodness knows where, formed into a unit to make a last-ditch stand. As soon as I explained that we were from the Highland Division and had not yet got our cards, he started to lecture me pompously on security. 'It may seem strange to you,' he said, 'but the German is quite capable of producing a party like yours, all correctly signed and in British trucks, and speaking idiomatic English, and sending them to spy out the land.'

As I had about twelve trucks all full of men speaking idiomatic Scots, this was palpably absurd, and, being hot and tired, the moment came when I could stand it no longer. I drew my unloaded pistol and said, 'If I was a German I would have shot you long ago!' It was a very stupid thing to do, and I was nearly chucked into the guard tent, but it did at least relieve my feelings. Luckily for me, I suddenly remembered that we had met in India before the war, and the situation was saved.

While we were at Mena, we had an OP actually up one of the pyramids, and are probably unique as a regiment in having done so. Which leads to a story about our much-liked Padre. He was far too kindly and unworldly for the knockabout of war, but he did his duty manfully, and was an excellent influence in the Regiment.

One day he set out to visit 308 Battery, following the signal wire to guide himself. The wire led him to the pyramid where the OP was, so he climbed up and passed the time of day with the Troop Commander. When he came down again, up jumped the last surviving dragoman with: 'Me keeper of the pyramid; you see pyramid, you pay me fifty piastres!'

Well, this was supposed to be war! Any normal person would have told the man exactly what he could do with himself. Not so the Padre: he felt in his pocket and produced twenty. 'That's all I've got,' he said. 'I'll give you the rest next time.' I am afraid we pulled his leg unmercifully when he told us about it, but I believe he really felt he had defrauded that miserable dragoman.

Mena is only a few miles out of Cairo and is the centre of the part of Egypt that tourists used to know. Many of the scenes that we saw might have been taken straight from a gaily coloured postcard proudly displayed by the returned traveller: the sun setting behind palm trees on the banks of the Nile, for example, and of course the pyramids and the 'inscrutable' Sphinx. There were gardens and orchards, and if you cared to look for it just enough sand to show you what the desert might look like.

We found Cairo to be a dirty city with a handsome French town placed in the centre of it. Just turn into a side street and you leave civilisation behind you. In your hotel it would not be strange if you were kept awake until 2.00 am by the blaring of car horns and woken again at 4.00 am by the braying of a donkey. It was not advisable to venture alone into the back streets, as the 'street Arabs' were some of the nastiest people in the world – murderous cut-throats and purveyors of every known vice and perversion. Even in the main thoroughfares you would be pestered by touts from the brothels and had to be on the lookout for pickpockets. A favourite trick of the latter was to thrust a tray of cheap watches and fountain pens into your chest for you to choose. Meanwhile, nimble fingers pinched your wallet underneath the tray. The riposte was to bring your knee smartly up into the vendor's belly, doubling him up before he had a chance to rob you, but it was advisable to do that only if you were in a very main street and preferably near a policeman. A hostile crowd could surround you in a matter of seconds and could be very unpleasant, even dangerous. The same was true of Alexandria and Port Said.

The best time to see the native quarter is at night. I well remember driving through in the dusk and feeling the romance of it. Each little curio and sweet shop opened on to the narrow street with its wares spread in the light of a single unshielded flame of a primitive oil lamp. Carpets hung beside the rug shops and the tinsmiths and coppersmiths worked at their crafts, with the finished products scattered on the pavement. The effect was one of rows and rows of fairy lights glinting on brass and copper, accentuating the swarthiness of the owners' faces against the whiteness of their cotton robes. To bargain for a rug, or for any trifle, was fun, but you really needed a reliable guide to keep the curious crowd at bay or your enjoyment would be quite spoilt as soon as the touts joined in. The shopkeeper would look after you while you were in his shop: after you left, it was your wits against theirs.

Barely had we sampled the comfort of the famous Mena House Hotel when we got the order to move. This time it looked like business, as we were not told our destination. Our orders were to report to 'Movement Control' at Amarea, on the Cairo–Alexandria road. That meant that we were passing from the command of 'British Troops – Egypt' (BTE) to that of 'Eighth Army'. The latter was the fighting army, while BTE controlled the base troops, sometimes called the 'Shepherds Hussars' because they were so often in the luxury hotel called Shepherds. Another name was 'Gaberdine Swine'. People have always been unfair to base troops. Some of them may have been scrimshankers, but I'm sure most of them worked as hard as any to help win the war.

However, passing from BTE to Eighth Army was like going from a fuggy room out into the cool of a moonlit night, so let us move on to close the chapter on Egypt. We were not leaving the country yet, though: there were still some stirring events to come before we were clear of the 'land of flies'.

Chapter 5

Life in the Desert

You arrive and arrive, and once more you arrive – and once more you see the same vast nothing you are arriving from. Believe it or not, that is the very charm of a desert – the unfenced emptiness, the space, the freedom, and the unbroken arch of the sky. It is forever fooling you, and yet you forever pursue it. And then it is only to the eye that cannot do without green that the Karoo is unbeautiful. Every other colour meets others in harmony – tawny sand, silver-grey scrub, crimson-tufted flowers like heather, black ribs of rock, puce shoots of screes, violet mountains in the middle distance, blue fairy battlements guarding the horizon. Above all broods the intense purity of the South African azure – not a coloured thing like the plants and the hills, but sheet colour existing by itself and for itself.

It is sheer witching desert for five hundred miles, and for aught I know five hundred miles after that.

GW Stevens, *From Cape Town to Ladysmith*

128 [H] Field Regiment RA

The move from Amarea was the first of many races with the declining sun. As second-in-command it was my duty to go ahead with the regimental reconnaissance or advance parties to prepare the position for the regiment. The regiment, as often as not, was moved under cover of darkness, which was quite easy if the advance parties had enough daylight to choose and prepare the site. But doing this in the dark was altogether a different matter. Time and again we would not get our orders for the move until late in the afternoon. Then the sun would seem nice and high in the heavens when we started, but it would soon be hurrying down to the horizon. There it would turn into a ball of glowing red and suddenly plunge out of sight, with the curtain of eastern night falling almost immediately.

This time, I was in charge not only of our own reconnaissance parties, but also had those of the rest of the Brigade under me. I was just a little nervous of my responsibilities, as this was the first time that we had ventured into the real desert, right away from civilisation.

My orders were definitely scanty. I was merely told to meet a staff officer of XXX Corps at a spot ten miles away in the sand, and I did not get these orders until 5.00 pm, when the sun was already low. To crown everything, the leader of the infantry parties came up just as we were starting and told me that his trucks were nearly out of petrol. I left him to get his trucks filled and dashed on myself with my dispatch rider, giving the others a rendezvous at which to meet me. The dash soon became a crawl because no one had told us that motorbikes are simply an encumbrance in sand. I discovered this when poor old Milburn, the dispatch rider, came a purler for the third time. After that I reduced speed to ten mph and tried to will the sun not to set.

Actually, I wasn't too worried, because there was a railway line to guide me as far as El Hamman, from which I could set off on a compass source for a couple of miles to my rendezvous with the Staff Officer. But when I got to the station of Hamman, my troubles really began. Instead of a nice open plain with just one car on it – that of the man I was to meet – I found the place strewn with vehicles for miles. It was a unit in camp, with its trucks dispersed 100 yards from each other and their inhabitants peacefully sleeping or going about their business. A needle in the haystack would have been easier to find than the car of my would-be friend.

And then the sun went down. I never did find him.

After scouring the desert unsuccessfully in the forlorn hope of meeting with my advance parties, I set a course back to Hamman Station, hoping that they would have the sense to collect there when they could not find me at the rendezvous and cursing myself for not having thought of telling them to do so. The station was just two deserted huts and a water tank. There was not a sign of the others. I was now worried stiff, because none of us had the slightest idea of where we were supposed to be going! My only hope was to collect the advance parties and then try to find someone who could tell me in the morning. But for now, here was I – and where in the world were they?

Then, when things seemed at their worst, someone suddenly materialised out of one of the huts. Of all people, it was a military policeman! Still stranger, he had a message for me. It turned out that the advance parties had come to the station, as I had hoped, just before I got there, and the Brigadier, George Murray, had found them and taken them on. The message said that they had gone to 'J' Box. That meant precisely nothing to me, so I said to Taylor, my driver, 'Here is where we sleep,' and, relieved of our responsibilities, we slept very well.

Up at first light, we started questing along a track in the hopes of meeting somebody. Very soon we came upon an armoured car, its occupants lying round it, stretching the sleep out of their systems. It was a Gunner OP party, and by good fortune they belonged to the Regiment we were to relieve in this mysterious place, 'J' Box. They had broken down and had been benighted before they could carry out their repairs. 'No one moves at night unless he has to,' said the captain in charge of the party. 'It's so much simpler to doss down where you happen to be when the sun goes down, and then you won't go barging into a minefield in the dark!' 'Don't move at night unless you have to' might be one of the rules of the desert, but the trouble was that one nearly always did have to. After a shave and breakfast the captain led us to 'J' Box where we found the rest of the advance parties, and a little later we were joined by the Brigade and our own Regiment.

The 'Boxes' were simply large areas of sand enclosed by barbed wire and minefields, which served as 'fortresses'. A brigade-group would spread itself out in one of these, secure from being overrun by tanks because of the minefields, and protected from an infantry assault by the barbed wire. The guns were put in the middle so that they could strike out at anything approaching from any direction, and the infantry and Anti-Tank Artillery manned the perimeter. They were part of a method of defence that had been evolved to deal with the situation when the German tanks outgunned both our anti-tank guns and our tanks.

We were still nowhere near the enemy, but in a day or two we moved on to 'H' and then to 'E' Box on the Alam Halfa ridge. At the latter, things were getting warmer. Only a week before the troops there had beaten back the last attempt of the enemy, under Marshal Rommel, to break through to Cairo and Alexandria. There were burnt-out tanks in front with German markings, and we were shown a captured 88-mm gun – a splendid weapon, built for anti-aircraft defence, found to be a fine anti-tank gun and also used with excellent results as a field gun. There was also a burnt-out truck of our own side, hit by a dive-bombing Stuka aircraft, which the second-in-command of the regiment retrieved and presented to me. That came in very handy, providing the bits and pieces to make a roof rack for my car. After the attack the Germans had withdrawn, and we were now some nine miles from the front line.

'E' Box was about sixty miles west of Alexandria. You reached it by series of tracks made in the desert by bulldozers. These had been lovely level roadways when first made, but by the time we arrived they had been worn into a million potholes that jarred one's bones at every turn of the wheels. The passing of countless trucks and tanks had ground the surface into a fine powdery grit that billowed behind your truck like a smokescreen and settled on everything like a rain of dirty-white volcanic ash. Provided you went fast enough to leave the cloud behind you, you were all right; but when you met another truck, you were completely engulfed in a swirling, almost-liquid gritty fog. As you were sure to be sweaty, your face, neck and eventually your whole body became encrusted with this harsh powder. After a drive on these tracks people were comical sights, their hats and clothing white as a miller's, with luminous eyes peering out of paste-white faces with dust-encrusted eyebrows and moustaches.

Away from the tracks the country was sandy, with brown stony patches, flat and bare, except for minor folds and undulations. There were clumps of dead-looking plants like heather, which actually was very much alive and would blossom as soon as a drop of rain fell. Tucked into its branches were numbers of snails that also looked dead, but they came to life and foraged for food in the lightest downfall. There were birds in the larger clumps, and also butterflies. In fact, this seemingly barren waste was teeming with life, including scorpions and other insects, and – where man had been – myriad flies.

The nights were almost chilly and any clothing left outside one's bivvy-tent would be soaked with dew in the morning. At 7.00 am the sun began to be felt and by 10.00 am the heat was sweltering. In the heat there was a continuous shimmer and haze, which destroyed visibility. Mirages were common. These were generally familiar objects distorted: a tented camp became elongated into white streaks dancing in the air, and men and camels could be stretched into very queer-looking objects. Pools of water would appear where there were none, and everywhere the distance seemed vague and unreal.

At about 5.00 pm the haze disappeared and one could again see into the distance. The desert then became most fascinating and attractive, its surface was continually changing colour, passing through all the shades of purple and blue as the sun sank lower and the shadows lengthened. I never failed to enjoy this constant change of colour. Even when the sun was at its height, it only needed a passing cloud to change its shades and hues, and if there was no cloud, a sandstorm would suffice.

Almost exactly at noon every day the wind would blow steadily from the north west and raise a horrid dust storm. The sand from this penetrated everything. It permeated the bread or biscuit, and it sanded the sugar. Your teeth gritted on it whenever you ate. You were spared drinking it, because it sank to the bottom of the cup, but it always spoiled the porridge, and your pillow was harsh and gritty when you turned in at night. We called these nuisances 'duststorms' because they were not proper sandstorms. They were entirely due to the churning up of the surface by our trucks. Only occasionally was the wind strong enough to raise the sand where man had not broken the surface. When it was that strong, it gave you something to remember!

*

> The stinging lash of sand whipped up by storm
> Has scarified your face, and bleared your eyes
> As desert djins brought night to mid–day skies
> And hurled their wrath at every living form.

In this desolate place we learnt to live in the wilderness, and almost to like it. Our day started half an hour before first light, when we 'stood-to', or manned our defences. Often it was very cold and we would eagerly watch the sky grow pale and then turn orange as a sign that the sun was on its way. The light would grow, and then, at last, a huge red ball would float up from the horizon. That was the time when the Stukas were most likely to attack and a single twinkling fire could attract them to one's locality. Not a fire was allowed and not a man could stir from his post until the sun was right up and had changed from red to blazing brightness. Then when the signal to stand-down was given and a hundred little fires would spring to life: the first mug of tea and shaving water were on their way.

Days in camp were hot and sweaty, and one got very tired of trudging about in the yielding sand, but more often than not we were off on our own, training. When out of camp there was no cookhouse or mess. Each truck was a self-sufficient unit, carrying its own rations and water, its occupants cooking and eating when and how they could. The rations were mostly tinned, so it was easier than it sounds, and most people much preferred the picnic life, though it was nice to go back to communal feeding for a change after a long spell of vehicle cooking.

We were now training for the battle that was to start the turn of the tide. We moved into the line with the Australian Division to gain a little war experience in a quiet part of the line, and they were fine teachers. After that we did several divisional exercises in a locality chosen because of its similarity to that of the ground where the battle was to be fought. Seldom has such thorough training for a battle been given in the history of war.

On 12 October 1942, I went to Alexandria for ten days' leave.

My stay in Alexandria was quiet but luxurious. I had a room with private bath at the Hotel Cecil and sampled the Union Bar, Beau Rivage and many other places of interest. But I was to be recalled three days early because it was time to start the final preparations. It was a shock to find my car waiting outside the hotel when I came back from one of these expeditions, with orders for my immediate return.

We got back to 'E' Box after nightfall and a second shock awaited us. Everyone had moved, lock, stock and barrel. The place looked just like any other part of the desert and there was not a clue as to which way they had gone. Then my car got stuck in the sand – the first and last occurrence. I can only suppose she had a perverted sense of humour. Certainly she couldn't have chosen a worse time. When we got her out, I chose a track going north and hoped for the best. It turned out to be the right choice and my ego got a great fillip when we caught up with one of the batteries ploughing through the dust.

We settled down a few miles east of Alamein railway station. The area was full of dummy lorries made of wood and painted canvas, and each of our guns and trucks had to be put under one of these. The battle was brewing and a gigantic deception plan was afoot: the enemy was not to know that tanks or guns had moved into this area, while every effort was being made to convince him that a huge concentration of guns was being built up in the south. Every day columns of trucks were sent southwards, raising clouds of dust, and every day the German spotter planes reported more tanks and guns in that locality. At the same time his signal experts reported a tremendous amount of wireless activity from a new station there that appeared to be an Army or Corps GHQ. Everything pointed to it as the concentration area for the attack that they well knew was coming.

But the trucks were coming back each night to make the same weary journey next day; the tanks and guns were made of canvas and wood or rubber, inflated with air [see plate]; and the wireless net was sending dummy messages. Seldom or never has a deception plan been so complete or so successful. Even when our attack started in the north, von Thoma – commanding in Rommel's absence, as he was on sick leave at the time – was convinced it was a feint and kept his main counter-attack forces watching the south for at least a day, if not longer.[1]

Every night we took working parties forward to prepare our battle positions. Gun pits were dug and camouflaged and dugouts for command posts, slit trenches and weapon pits had to be made. Telephone cable was laid and buried a foot underground so that it would not be damaged by tanks or shell fire. We managed to borrow a couple of pneumatic drills, but by far the greater part had to be done by the back-breaking pick-and-shovel methods, and the ground was like iron under the first thin layer of sand. By dawn every trace of the night's work had to be hidden lest the enemy planes should smell a rat and come and look more closely.

Side by side with this went the ammunition dumping programme. In addition to our own twenty-four guns we were to have another three troops (twelve guns) attached for the first night of the coming battle. For each gun there was to be 500 rounds of ammunition. That means about a hundred lorry loads and some three hundred tons to be unloaded, carried by hand to the guns and dug in for concealment's sake. It was quite a task.

The dumping task was made harder because the RASC trucks that brought the shells had only rear-wheel drive (four-wheel drive is essential in soft sand). There was an incline near our position and every one of those trucks got stuck on it every night! We had trucks with winches there to wind them out, but even so the work was slowed and was made much harder, more of a race against time.

As the day of battle approached we were told to move in one gun a troop each night and conceal it in its pit under camouflage nets. There were to be no fresh trucks in or near the troop positions, no trucks there, and not a man or a mouse was to stir in daylight. Not a rock or a bush was to be disturbed. The place was to look as it had looked since the Australians left it six months ago. Secrecy was absolute. We did not know the date of the attack until the day before, and we were not told the time of 'zero' hour until the day itself.

This careful attention to the details of deception was very irksome at the time – particularly when our supply lorries were taken for the dust-raising trips – but it paid a wonderful dividend. The enemy reconnaissance planes were completely deceived: the date, direction and time of the attack came as a complete surprise.

Notes

[1] von Thoma briefly took command of the combined Axis army when its commander, General Stumme, had a fatal heart attack during heavy bombardment at the start of the battle.

Chapter 6

The Battle of El Alamein

The Zenith opened to a gulf of flame,
The dreadful thunderbolts jarred earth's fixed frame,
The ground all heaved in waves of fire and surged
And weltered round me sole there unsubmerged.
Yet I strode on austere;
No hope could have no fear.

James Thomson

128 [H] Field Regiment RA

23 October 1942 dawned just like any other day. We ate our usual breakfast of tinned bacon, hard biscuits and marmalade, and, of course, there was the same old mug of strong, sweet tea. There was no sign that the long period of waiting was over and that the turning point of the war was at hand. But as the morning wore on there were many more comings and goings than usual at RHQ. Signallers were busy testing telephone lines and finishing burying the cables, there were last-minute queries about targets, and final orders were given. Last of all, dressed for battle, the battery commanders and observing officers came for their final briefing by the Colonel. As he wished them good luck and they saluted before going to join the Infantry, the thought came to me: 'This is *it*!' One might not see those good fellows again. Casual though the occasion was, just like the start of one of our many exercises, it was a moment to be remembered.

After that, the day dragged on interminably, but at long last the desert sparkled with a thousand little cooking fires as the evening brew got underway. We had a fine meal of steak followed by tinned peaches, served by Livingstone and Fowler in an improvised mess in a quarry-like hole in the ground. We all ate well, I think – there seemed to be no battle nerves, even though this was to be our war baptism.

The men were in fine spirits. A simple and direct personal message from Montgomery had made a deep impression on them, and each was determined to do his best and a bit more besides. Witness Livingstone's contribution. As we left the table, he said quietly: 'There will be hot coffee ready all night, in case you have time for it.'

The sun went down as we finished our meal and walked across to the command post. Having no immediate duties, I stood for a while and watched the night descend on us. As the last glow of the sun faded, the sky paled and then quickly darkened to midnight blue, silver-pointed with stars. It seemed too calm and beautiful for death to be abroad. As I watched, the eastern sky glowed gold and suddenly, with startling haste, the full moon floated over the horizon and glided into the canopy of blue. And what a moon! ... brilliant, gilded copper, flowing with frozen fire. Her light streamed over the desert and transformed it to a place of magic beauty. It was truly magic, for no magician could have shown a more deceptive scene: the smallest detail of the landscape seemed to be revealed before one. But the deep shadows contrasting with the brilliance played tricks, hiding many things while showing others that were not there at all.

A sudden burst of gunfire shattered the peace as I turned to go into the command post, and for a moment or two we wondered if the enemy was going to get his attack in first, but it proved to be only a short 'hate', which soon died down and left the peace of the night undisturbed.

The Command Post – the nerve centre of the Regiment – was a six-foot-deep trench roofed with poles and corrugated iron and covered with a thick layer of sand. A recessed shelf served as a table for the maps and telephones and other implements of war. Dan Ridley, the Adjutant, was quietly checking that our fire plan data was right and occasionally talking to someone by phone. Next to him was 'Gubby' Allen, bespectacled, solemn and tough. He was the Survey Officer, whose work could make or mar the Regiment's accuracy. In a corner a wireless set was chuckling away to its signaller, filling the dugout with speech now and then, when one of the OP Officers called up to give us news. At the far end sat the Colonel, watching and waiting.

One could imagine the final preparations being made at the batteries – a drop of oil on a breech-block, one more box of ammunition opened and the shells stacked ready, a peep through the sights to confirm that the crosswire was dead on the aiming lamp, and then there remained but to wait. Slowly, the minutes ticked by, though the watch hands seemed never to move. This was the apex of all that we had trained for and tensely we wondered how good we should prove to be. Outwardly calm, we were inwardly keyed to a pitch of excitement that tightened the chest and quickened our pulses to racing speed. Away in the west the Germans and Italians were settling down for another peaceful night.

Dan stared hard at his watch – it was nearly time. 'Stand-by!' said he to the phone, and the men on the guns stiffened. It was 9.39 pm. Just one more minute to wait. 'One-oh seconds to go ... Five ... four ... three ... two ... one ... FIRE!' The flame of the hurricane lamp popped up the chimney, a cascade of sand fell on the plotting board and the world seemed to fill with concussion and noise. A thousand guns had fired as one.

Outside, the night was filled with flickering lightning; the air throbbed with a majestic rhythm as from gigantic drums that rolled and crashed unendingly. To the north, to the east and to the south, wherever one looked there were flickering flashes. When guns near us fired, the moon paled and the desert was bright as day, with every detail momentarily picked out in brilliancy [see plate].

There were flashes in the west also, but they were insignificant compared with ours. Our guns had smothered the enemy artillery and gagged them by smashing their cables. It was a full forty minutes before they could make an effective reply. Through the din, intensifying it, we could hear the shells from guns behind us passing overhead in droves, moaning and screaming and whistling as they hurtled to their destruction and the enemy's. The Division's historian wrote:

> A soldier might have described that mighty barrage passing over his head as the noise of many wings, and the couplet of the old poem might have come back to his memory:
>
> The angel of Death spread his wings on the blast,
> And breathed in the face of the foe as he passed. [Lord Byron]

For twenty minutes this avalanche was directed at the enemy guns. Then, at 10.00 pm, the range was shortened and the bursts tore into the forward positions. That was the cue the Infantry had been waiting for.

The sappers had already been making gaps in the deep belt of mines, and through these the infantry advanced. The distance to the final objectives was over three miles, though it was not expected that we could penetrate as far as that in one night. The aim was to break the back of the defence by dawn and then to dig in and hold fast until another attack could be launched.

The 5th Camerons were given the job of forming a firm base on the far side of the minefield. News that this had been done reached the Division from Jim Inglis, our OP Officer with them. Then his wireless became silent – he had been killed. Our first casualty, and a great loss in every way. Jim sadly died because when he reached his OP he found that his microphone had been left behind. He was returning to fetch it when he was killed by a mine. His brother John was also with the Camerons and kept us informed of their doings for the rest of the night.

The rest of the Infantry pushed steadily on. Bofors guns of the Light Anti-Aircraft Regiment helped them keep direction by firing streams of tracer shells on either flank, but even so it must have been terribly hard to keep straight in the smoke and confusion. Many were killed or wounded, chiefly by machine-gun fire, but the others pressed on. Resistance was slight where they were able to capture a post just after the guns had lifted from it on the heels of the shelling, but there was plenty of grenade and bayonet work when the defence had had time to recover or had been missed from the fire-plan.

We had two other officers forward – John Connel and Ian Beaton. They were both with the 1st Black Watch, as our two Seaforth Battalions of 152 Brigade were in reserve. They were there to deal with the unexpected, to give flexibility to the fire-plan by calling in reserve guns to deal with emergencies. They were there too to tell us what was happening, and where the Infantry had reached. Information of this kind is vital in war. The plans of the General depend on its accuracy and freshness. Much depended on these officers, both under fire for the first time, and well indeed they rose to the occasion. At first their reports were frequent and full. The picture they gave was one of steady progress under heavy fire. But the battle grew more and more mixed and confused as they penetrated more deeply and their messages grew more and more vague. At last they told us that the Infantry were digging in. The final objectives had not been reached, but they were consolidating where they were. Where that was, no one knew.

So ended the first night of the Battle of Alamein. For our part, we fired for five hours and twenty minutes, and each gun fired four tons of shells. Not one shell came near us, so for the men on the guns it was just a sort of endurance test. At the end they were deaf from the noise and half-dead from weariness, but they had smoothed the path of the Infantry and were largely responsible for the victory, for Alamein was a gunner triumph.

At 3.00 am the last round was fired and there was silence in the batteries – a silence that rang in our ears.

When dawn broke the Colonel went forward to size up the situation and place the OPs to his liking. Our attack had bitten deep, but we were still a long way from the final objectives. In fact we were to have another ten days of fighting before the crowbar was through the wall and a breach made for the tanks to pour through and round up the enemy.

In the course of the morning I was ordered to move the Regiment to an area beyond the enemy minefield near the gap that the Camerons had used, which they had christened 'Inverness'. When I got there I found a New Zealand Battery getting a good dose of shelling and the whole place was decidedly unpleasant and noisy. During my reconnaissance Gubby Allen (the Survey Officer) saved me from mishap by warning me that a line of tins looked suspiciously like the markers of a minefield. He was dead right too. A few minutes later there was a bang and a pillar of black smoke indicated where he had entered it from the rear and run over a mine. Happily, he was only a bit shaken and given a blackened face. Later on, when we knew more about mines, we realised how lucky he was. The truck had its front axle broken and the engine damaged, leaving us with less transport than ever.

I selected a Battery position as far as possible from the New Zealand one and sent for the Regiment. Just then, the Colonel arrived. 'This place is too unhealthy,' he said, and told me to put 492 Battery right forward, behind a ridge where it was only 1,700 yards from the enemy, and to put the other two behind 'Inverness'. That was a much more comfortable arrangement, and 492 were reasonably safe there because the height of the ridge protected them from all but the plunging fire of the mortars. Also, they were able to reach far into the enemy position.

That evening Sergeant Gray, a West Country man who ran the domestic side of RHQ, arrived late with the water and rations. He explained shamefacedly that he had lost his way 'and gone all through the 'Kantara Depression'. As Kantara is a town in the Delta and the 'Qattara Depression' was thirty miles to the south, and impassable to vehicles, I couldn't help pulling his leg. I told him his story would not hold water, so perhaps that was why he was late bringing it. Everybody liked old Gray. A story was told of him that he heard someone say: 'Let's get cracking on this.'

'Never you mind about Bombadier Crackin',' Gray is reported to have said. 'Ee's in the wagon lines – you can get on an' finish the job yerselves!'

We stayed put for several days while other Divisions enlarged the gap in preparation for the final breakthrough. During that period we fired for one Division or another every night, also shooting by day as well. The Colonel was continually on the go, getting the OPs into better places, pushing them forward, and scanning the country for new targets. Illey of

492 was smuggled by night to a position in no man's land, only a mere 150 yards from the enemy. He had some good shooting there, and gathered some useful information. He was close enough to hear them speaking in Italian.

Other OPs had their share of excitement. Norman Owen (307 Battery Commander) took his Captain to a viewpoint by a burnt-out carrier, where the enemy saw them and gave them a good pasting. Mercifully, they both came back smiling, though the machine guns were turned on to them as well when they moved.

Copper Finlayson came over a ridge in his carrier and was engaged by a nest of machine guns. The engine then stalled and refused to start until it had been primed with petrol. Then, when they got it going, they found the steering had been hit and damaged, and it would only steer to the right, which forced them to make a wide sweep under fire before they could get under cover again.

Ian Beaton saved the Argylls from a nasty mess by knowing where he was on the map. He had re-sectored his position by compass bearings to three groups of shell bursts from our guns – which of course were surveyed. When the Battalion Commander gave a bearing for the attack, Ian saw that it was wrong by miles, so he spoke up and corrected him. It says a lot for the CO, Lorne Campbell – who afterwards got the VC at Wadi Akarit – that he accepted the Junior Officer's correction without question, merely remarking that he would always trust a Gunner's map reading. In passing, it was just impossible to read a map accurately in that country: there were no features to 'read' and the map was little more than a blank sheet.

No words can be too good for our Colonel, Jerry Sheil. He was just everywhere and he could size up a situation before the ordinary person had realised that one had arisen. His clear orders and cheerfulness gave the OP Officers great confidence, and his wide knowledge and experience made their job a lot easier. As well as this, he taught the Infantry how Artillery should be used, and that it should be used to the full the whole time if they were to get the best out of their own efforts.

The next few days were uneventful, except that the batteries had a man killed and two wounded by shell fire, and RHQ also got shelled a little. Then the tanks tried to break through and failed, losing nearly a whole Regiment in the attempt. The rest came and parked in and around our troop positions until there was a tank or trucks every twenty-five yards. Never have I seen so much armour in so small a place. There were Crusaders, Shermans, Grants, Valentines and a hotchpotch of armoured cars. Stukas came and bombed the mass of vehicles, which was very unpleasant, but they didn't do much damage. The Light Anti-Aircraft (LAA) had great fun defending us all.

The Colonel and Norman Owen became involved in a tank battle one afternoon. It must have been a bit nerve racking, as they were only in a light armoured car, which would have torn like paper if a tank shell had hit it. Apart from that, the fact they were differently mounted from the rest drew attention to them and marked them as Gunner OPs. Tanks were churning all round them, banging at each other and going up in flames, but the little armoured car – known as 'Ben Nevis' – came out of the action unscathed.

They got to a place from which they could observe and scattered an enemy tank regiment by bringing down twenty-seven rounds of gunfire from all twenty-four guns. Several tanks were hit and badly shaken, and the rest closed their tops, thereby lessening their efficiency. The Colonel then helped some of our tanks, which were getting the worst of it, in laying down a smoke screen, which enabled them to withdraw and re-engage in more favourable circumstances. An exciting afternoon's work.

After that engagement our tanks placed themselves hull-down behind a ridge from which they could snipe at the enemy tanks. I went with the Colonel when he visited this area next day. I stayed in Ben Nevis while he went off to see the CO of the Argylls. The tanks were lined up behind the ridge at what I thought was far too close an interval, but space seemed to be limited, so I squeezed Ben Nevis into a gap and watched with interest.

It was most amusing to see the Cavalry Officers lounging about outside their tanks, as if they were on manoeuvres at home. By raising my head I could see the enemy position, about 1,000 yards away, shimmering in the haze, yet these people were wandering about as if no enemy existed, brewing tea and so on.

Every so often, the tank on my right would bang off a round at something I couldn't see, and an answer from the opposition would hit the crest in front of us. Bombardier Beales, driver of Ben Nevis, would say: 'Here's another of them! – but you should have seen the stuff there was flying about in the tank battle, rattling on the sides of the car, it was!'

When the shells began to get closer, I began to look round for a more comfortable place. Just then a shell burst right under the 'bows' of the tank on my left and its wireless aerial toppled over like the mast of a ship when the stays break. A Medical Officer's car was whistled up and someone was pulled out of the tank with a nasty arm wound. At that, General Post started: everyone, including me, moved to a different position. A shell chased us as we left, the splinters tinkling against Ben Nevis's sides. Shortly after this the Colonel came back and we left the tanks to sort themselves out.

The tanks sharing our gun positions left us a little later and I found where they had gone when I had to go to 154 Brigade HQ about something. There they were, huddled together just as they had been with us. One of their Royal Horse Artillery Batteries was there with all its trucks bunched behind the guns. The area was – to say the least – 'unhealthy', and every time the shelling happened, the Battery lost a truck or two. Heaven knows why they did not send the unwanted trucks to a safe place in the rear.

Meanwhile, the Infantry had been steadily gaining ground, and we were getting close to the limit of the range of our guns, so the expected order to move was received. The Colonel and I drove through the area the CRA had allotted to us with mounting despair. There were tanks and trucks all over it, with no room to slip a gun in edgeways. It was a good thing that the RAF had driven the Luftwaffe out of the air or there would have been a massacre.

At last we found an area clear of the tanks and trucks – a desolate, windswept bit of rocky ground where the digging was terribly hard. From there we were to have fired a barrage in aid of an attack by the 1st Gordons and a Tank Squadron, but the Tank Commander had it stopped because he thought his tanks had reached the objective. They hadn't, and the Gordons suffered heavily as a result: proof, if proof were needed, that the Infantry cannot advance in daylight without Artillery cover.

During this attack, John Connel suddenly saw a whole host of enemy tanks in the haze and reported it post haste. This caused a major 'flap' at all levels, because our Intelligence branch had accounted for all his tanks and said there were none in that sector. John pounded them with 'Mike' targets from the Regiment until the haze cleared a bit. He then saw that he had been engaging the burnt-out skeletons of a former battle.

On the night of 2 November we fired our last fire programme in this battle, in support of 4th Indian Division. They advanced magnificently and secured the final objective. Next morning the hole was punched right through and the wall fell down. It was now the turn of the Armour, and it was unleashed to complete the victory. Score upon score of tanks and lorries full of Infantry went roaring past us in a pall of dust. The X Armoured Corps and the New Zealand Division were taking up the chase. We sat on our haunches in the turmoil and hoped our turn to advance would soon come.

I wrote a small Christmas mail remarking that I thought we had won a big victory, not realising just how big it was. Later on I went to 152 Brigade HQ, and there a Military Policeman told me he had heard that the church bells at home had been rung to celebrate the victory. It seemed a nice idea, but I did not really believe him. One was too close to events to appreciate their full effect.

So ended ten days of hard fighting, with little rest, plenty of uncertainty and quite a lot of excitement. As an introduction to battle it was a great success. We were veterans from then on.

*

EL ALAMEIN
A Ballad of Battle

The Harvest Moon is round and full tonight,
Come, roam the fields and watch her steep
The sheaves of golden corn in silver light,
Contrast with shadows dark and deep.

Such beauty holds me, makes me catch my breath,
And wafts me back to desert sand,
To Alamein, that fateful night of death
The night a thousand guns were manned.

That night we saw a sudden curtain rise
To show Selene[1] girt in light
Cross swiftly o'er the threshold of the skies,
To take her place as Queen of Night.

The moon, her throne of glowing frozen flame,
Encanopy'd in deepest blue,
Arose and o'er the sun-dried desert came
To lend enchantment to the view.
And there on high she stayed, while deeds of fame
Were wrought that saved the world anew.

The day had slipped away like other ones,
And evening saw our twinkling fires
Snuffed out – like lives – as night embraced the guns

So soon to light such ghastly pyres.
It's true the day had passed like other days;
But with the sunset – came a thrill!
We knew we'd left behind the waiting phase –
T'was time to act! For good or ill.

Around the guns men talked in lowered tones,
Sometimes one heard a breach-block clink;
They set their sights, and linesmen tested phones;
And cooks brought cans of tea to drink.

The shells were stacked in heaps around each pit,
Five hundred there for every gun;
To front and rear the aiming lights were lit,
And all that could be had been done.

At RHQ the barrage plan, though right,
Was checked and counter-checked again,
In case through slip or careless oversight
The guns should shoot that night in vain.

Away in front the Jocks were forming up,
With Lochiel's pipes to lead the van.
Alas! a' mony there w'd drain tha cup
That robs a lassie o' her man

And forward too, were those who wear, the 'Gun',
Hawk-eyed and nerved with tempered steel;
Their task to lead the barrage to the Hun,
To crush him 'neath its flaming heel.

Then slowly, slowly, crept the minutes by,
While History paused just off the stage,
Suspense consumed us, mounting fever-high,
Those minutes ere we loosed War's rage.

And then – at last! This message thrilled the wire –
'Eighth Army's thousand guns will open fire
To-night! One hundred minutes after eight!'
Which gave us just ten seconds more to war

'FIRE' a FLASH – intense, quiv'ring, silver-bright:
It poised a silent instant there –
Then, CRASH, a rending thunder split the night,
And ripp'd and tore the peaceful air.

The guns, like drums of Death, hurled forth their wrath
In steady rhythmic symphony;
And lightning from their up-raised muzzles' blast
Outshone the moon in brilliancy.

And droves of shells screeched past the waiting Jocks
With screams and howls, and whistling moans,
That drowned the skirl of 'Aden's Barren Rocks',
And thrilled the marrow in one's bones.

Soon crashing burst brought panic to the foe,
Whose men lay sleeping unawares;
But that soon passed, for each had work to do,
And manned his post despite his fears.

T'was forty minutes ere defensive fire
Brought comfort to the enemy;
Our guns' onslaught had ripped their signal wire,
And gagged the Bosch Artillery.

And now the Jocks set out to take a hill
Of sand they'd christened 'Aberdeen'
The air was thick with smoke, and things that kill,
And flares enhanced the horrid scene.

With them went Inglis, new to battle, yet
Defying bullet, shell and mine.
He paused upon a battered ridge to get
The guns to shoot a different line.

Kismet! They'd left the microphone behind!
So back across the shell-torn zone
He went, right through the belt the Bosch had mined
He came not back. He died alone.

And such is fate! Someone had dropped the thing
Unnoticed when the party moved.
For penalty, a Soldier of the King
Was snatched away from those he loved.

The moon watched through the night, then in the west
Sank down in weariness of soul,
And left the Jocks to fight on without rest,
Through smoke and carnage to their goal.

The morning sun looked on a land gone wild,
With bodies sprawled like dolls left fall
Uncared for, by a spoilt and careless child
Who heeded not their loss at all.

The guns were moving up to close the range,
And wounded men were limping back.
To everyone the ground was new and strange,
And strewn all o'er with wreck and wrack.

Exhausted men, in lulls slept where they lay,
And roused to meet the battle's tide,
Which ebbed and flowed in doubt throughout the day,
But quietened down at eventide.

The snake was scotched – but not yet killed, men saw,
But action had been justified:
They'd smashed the front of Rommel's elite Corps,
And now were on the winning side.

For nine days more the battle rose and fell,
And we slipped the Armour through –
His stricken legions broke, and fled pell-mell!
Then – for a while – we'd naught to do!

Notes

[1] Selene, ancient Greek moon goddess.

Chapter 7

Left Behind

Thousands at his bidding speed
And post o'er land and ocean without rest;
They also serve who only stand and wait

John Milton

128 [H] Field Regiment RA, November 1942

Montgomery's plan was to surround then destroy the retreating enemy with his Armour, supported by the New Zealand Division. The rest of the Eighth Army was left behind for the time being, as it would not have been possible to supply a bigger force in an advance that was so rapid, and over so great a distance. He came within a hair's breath of success but was foiled by an unseasonable fall of rain, which held up our tanks and allowed Rommel to withdraw a large part of his army in reasonable order.

Meanwhile, we had to stay where we were for a couple of days to give the pursuit force elbow room. The most abiding memory of those days is the stream of prisoners that seemed as if it would never cease [see plate]. Most of them were Italians, and their tameness and docility was amazing. One carload of officers actually drove up and asked the way to the prison cage, apologising for troubling us because they had lost their guide. The word 'guide' summed up the situation – there were no guards, just an occasional British soldier plodding along to one side of the dusty column, disinterestedly shepherding it in the general direction of the back areas.

We then moved on a few miles to a railway station called El Daba. There, a heap of scrap metal that had once been several Messerschmidts and Heinkel bombers showed that the RAF had been busy as well as us, but the great attraction of the place was a well full of water. Never had water been so welcome. My first action was to get old Pike, my batman, to dig a hole, line it with a tarpaulin and pour in several gallons of boiling water. The bathtub may not have been Ritzy, but I don't think I have ever enjoyed a bath more – it was over a month since I had had one!

Soon we were thrilled to see a train come wheezing along the railway, and fresh bread and meat appeared on the table. This was luxurious living and for a time we revelled in it. Impatience soon intervened, though: we did not like being back numbers. We laughed at the rumour that a platoon of ATS[1] was coming to join us, but we really began to feel in our hearts that the show would be finished without us, and that was not an ending that appealed.

After about three weeks at El Daba we moved a few miles into a more fertile neighbourhood where there were patches of wild flowers and some flowering scrub. Butterflies rather like tortoiseshells helped to make the scene quite pretty. The desert here was what is called 'poached egg' country, because of a kind of shrub that collects wind-blown sand. As fast as the sand rises, the bush grows over it. The result is a cross-country motorist's nightmare, hummocks eighteen inches to two feet high, so closely spaced that you cannot avoid them and must bump and grind over them until your bones ache. They may be a godsend to those who want to reclaim the desert, but to us they were anathema.

Then we really began to move. In one day we passed through Mersa Matruh, Buq-buq and Sidi Barrani, names that had become household words from the number of battles that had been fought round them. They were not much to look at. Matruh was a small village by the sea; Buq-buq was a notice board and some debris; Sidi Barrani was a collection of ruined houses. At sunset we came to Sollum, frontier 'town' of Egypt, in time to enjoy the beauty of its bay as the sun's last rays glinted on the waves. And as we climbed the twisty road up the escarpment, the biggest traffic jam of all time [see plate] gave us the chance to watch the moonlight shimmering like shot silk where the sun had been.

We would have enjoyed that more if we had not been looking forward to the journey's end and supper. Our wait was enlivened by a New Zealand lorry nearly plunging over a precipice as it took a hairpin bend too fast.

Early to bed and early to rise. Sunrise found us ploughing along the 'Trigh Capuzzo', a famous camel route crossing Libya from end to end, straight as a die and monotonously level, through bare and featureless immensity. As is usual in the desert, each traveller had picked his own path and each column of trucks had made a track of its own to avoid its predecessor's dust and ruts and potholes, so the camel 'track' was in fact a belt of ruts and potholes and criss-crossing tracks some two miles wide.

That sort of route is one of the hardest to find your way on – the ruts make navigation by compass impracticable, while the infinite variety of paths is like a maze and can completely bewilder you when you are trying to decide where to turn off to get to your destination. That was my lot as darkness began to fall. I knew we had come about the right distance, but I could not have placed myself on the map to within a mile or two! Peering into the purple gloom, and making up my mind to strike off right in another mile, I suddenly spotted a faint light, the only tangible thing in the vast hazy nothingness. I hardly dared hope that it could have anything to do with us, but I swanned up to it in case. Imagine my relief when I found it was a Military Police Traffic Control post, and one of our own Division's. We had reached the turning-off point and the 'Red Cap' gave us excellent directions to our bivouac area. In peace the saying is that the soldier's worst enemies are his rifle – because the smallest speck of dirt on it gets him 'Jankers' (military prison) – and the Red Cap. In war it is quite the reverse. The Military Police (MP) were invaluable: they marked the routes, they lighted the paths through the minefields, and they were helpful in every way.

For all that, I cannot help telling one story about them. In Scotland there was a standing order that everyone – no matter who or where – must wear his gas-mask from 11.00 am until 12.00 pm every Thursday. Also in Scotland, the General used to have all the Officers together for a lecture at frequent intervals. The security measures for these lectures were very strict. Two policemen stood at the doorway and identified each officer from the photo on his identify card before letting him in. One of these lectures happened to be on a Thursday at 11.30 am. With my own eyes I saw these two MPs solemnly look at each identify card photo, compare it with the gas-masked owner and allow him to pass!

But never have I been so glad to see a Red Cap as I was that evening.

We turned off the Trigh Capuzzo near El Adom, near Tobruk, which is now a big airport. In those days I think it was a fighter aircraft landing strip, though I never saw any sign of human activities on the ground there. Our camp was said to be at a place called Acrema, but I never saw any sign of life there either.

Our stay there was notable for one of the worst gales and sandstorms that we experienced in the desert. It lasted for three days, and those days were among the coldest and most miserable that I have ever known. Of course, the coldness was only by comparison, and because we were in tropical dress. Nevertheless, we felt quite blue with it, and were thankful when the wind dropped at last. Then, when the air cleared after the sandstorm, we could see Tobruk, ten miles away, unreal and mirage-like in the distance. The sight – vague and distant though it was – seemed to give the desert a boundary: it reminded us that there was a civilised world and that the desert was not as boundless and infinite as it had seemed when we were on the Trigh Capuzzo.

All this time very little news of the war had filtered through to us. We simply went where we were told when we were told. No one had the time, or the communications, to keep us *au fait* with the situation. All we knew was that the people on ahead were chasing the enemy, having been unable to surround him as had been hoped, and that in due course we should take their place when they had shot their bolt.

At last we heard that our advance had been halted near Agheila – the furthest point reached by Auchinleck's Army – and that we were to close on the leaders and take over from them. It was good to know that we had not been forgotten after all.

Notes

[1] The Auxiliary Territorial Service (ATS) was the forerunner of the British Women's Royal Army Corps.

Chapter 8

Ships of the Desert

So on I went. I think I never saw.
Such starved ignoble nature; nothing throve.
For flowers – as well expect a cedar grove!

Robert Browning

128 [H] Field Regiment RA, December 1942

For the next 200 miles we travelled like a fleet at sea: a flotilla of trucks on an ocean of sand. Our Regiment and various other troops were placed temporarily under the command of 142 Infantry Brigade, forming a Brigade Group, and this was ordered to cut straight across the Libyan Desert from Bir Hacheim to Agedabia, so as to leave the Coast Road free as a supply route for the troops already forward.

Between us and our destination was ... just nothing but thousands of square miles of emptiness. Provided a lookout was kept for holes and rocky outcrops, a truck could go anywhere and 'swan' about as its driver pleased. Thus the obvious way to travel was spread out, like a big fleet, and that is how we went.

We formed 16 columns abreast, each truck keeping 200 yards from the one on its left, and 100 yards from the one in front. Away ahead was the leader, called the navigator, flying two pennants on his wireless mast so that we could identify him, exchanging the flags for blue lamps at night. The column leaders had to keep the navigator in sight while they picked the easiest route for their columns. The whole fleet was controlled by flags. The navigator raised two when we were to get ready to start. At once every truck repeated the signal as it saw the truck in front raise its flags. When he crossed his flags, everyone else did the same, and the signal rippled through the fleet like the flame of a powder fuse. Simultaneously, each driver let in his clutch, and so the whole formation of over 1,000 vehicles started almost as one.

The advantage of moving in this open order will be apparent when I tell you that 1,000 vehicles at 100-yard intervals occupies 50 miles. And travelling at our daytime speed of fifteen miles per hour, the head of a column fifty miles long gets home nearly four hours before the tail. There was, of course, in our case no question of the rear getting into camp after the front: when the front halted, the rear did so too. We were grouped in a straggling rectangle roughly a mile wide and three miles from front to rear. Where a truck halted, there its occupants stayed, fed, slept and had their being, so no time was wasted in getting in or out of camp.

Carrying the fleet analogy a little further, each vehicle was, like a ship, a self-sufficient community. Each carried food and water for four days. There was no filing up to the cookhouse for your meal – there was no cookhouse. You just opened a tin of stew, added what you fancied and heated it as best you could. The lucky ones had petrol cookers. The others made little scrub fires. These crackled merrily in the evening and gave quite a pleasant tang to the tea. In the morning, the fires of the wise crackled merrily as before, but the fires of the foolish – who had not covered their scrub from the dew – burnt with a sulky coldness and gave forth columns of smoke.

All cooking was done in a 'brew can' made from an old petrol tin. We nearly lost the war because these tins leaked so much that up to thirty per cent of the petrol was lost, but we should have been lost without them because they could so easily be made into wash basins, baking tins, field ovens and many other things. The 'four gallon expendable petrol tin' was a wonderful invention – for everything except carrying petrol! Eventually we gave up on them and used captured 'jerry cans', which were excellent and never wasted a drop.

The journey lasted three days, which was just the right length for the novelty to be retained. We travelled until it was too dark to see and rested until the moon rose, when we moved on again. This meant starting at 1.00 am the first day, to catch the moon, with a later start each subsequent day as the moon rose later. Each morning we halted at 7.00 am for breakfast and a wash and shave. The moon went down, leaving us in the dim half-light before dawn. We would be cold and hungry, and we longed for the navigator's flags to go up as we stood in our trucks with greatcoats wrapped round us. Then the smell of sizzling tinned bacon was delicious as we hurried through the routine, and one felt so much better after a shave. That hour and a half, which was all we were allowed, passed like lightning. If one was well organised and pressed on without dawdling there was just ten minutes free at the end to have a peaceful pipe and feel that all was well with the world.

By the time we moved the sun had gathered most of its strength and the desert began to shimmer in the heat. Every two hours there was a short halt, and most welcome these halts were ... just time to stretch and limber the joints. Both driver and lookout – the latter standing up to pick the path – got quite cramped, grinding and bumping along, mostly in low gear. Do not get the idea that the desert was flat and smooth. Most of the time we were clattering over rocks and stones, dropping a wheel into a hidden hole, or clambering over 'poached egg' hummocks. There were stretches of hard gravel where we could have travelled at thirty or forty mph, but even there the potholes were waiting to break your springs, and the rocks lay in wait to tear the bottom off your crank-case.

At midday we halted for half an hour: time to brew a mug of tea, swallow some bully-beef sandwiched between two hard biscuits, top up the radiator and get on the move again. Then, after ploughing through a rather tiring and monotonous afternoon, we stopped for an hour to have the evening meal – the big meal of the day. This was tinned 'M&V' (meat and vegetable stew), some sort of a pudding, and a mug of tea, of course. The food was good, but there was no variety for the whole of the campaign, and we were to get sick and tired of it by the end. Can you wonder that I wrinkled my nose when I was on leave and my wife produced some bully that she had been saving as a special treat!

We started the journey in a terrible flap because the Regimental Quartermaster Sargeant had lost himself with our water supply for the trip. It is not a good thing to barge into Libya with nothing to drink! We also had a shower of rain, which made us feel cold and wet, like a lot of bedraggled chicken in a fowl run. Luckily for him – and for us – he caught us up by Bir Hacheim with the water, so we were able to continue in a more relaxed frame of mind.

On the first day we passed the 'Knightsbridge' battlefield, littered with burnt-out tanks. We were shocked to see many Shermans amongst the wrecks. Worst of all, many of their turrets – weighing perhaps three tons – had been blown about thirty yards away, making us wonder if they were as good as they were said to be. They were then America's latest. The charred remains of the crews were still left in some of them. When a tank is hit and penetrated, you must dismount smartly if you intend going home by troop ship. It becomes a blazing volcano in no time, and then the ammunition explodes, which is what blows the turret off. You may feel safe in a tank, but it is a false security.

When dark came we put in a few hours' sleep and got up when the moon rose. Within five minutes, all was chaos! The 2nd Seaforth had left unfilled the trenches, which they had dug when in the Advanced Guard position, and we drove slap into them. Judging by Brigadier Murray's remarks as the confusion was unravelled, they would know better next time.

Driving by the light of a rather dim moon was quite hair raising. Great shapes loomed up in front and dissolved into nothing as we slowed down; others appeared and did not dissolve. That made the driver very careful for a bit, but then the navigator's blue lights seemed to race ahead, and we would work up the speed again, until another jarring crash reminded us that eggs can be horribly hard-poached.

By day, the desert was alive with a mass of crawling, growling vehicles, each raising its own dust cloud. But if you stopped and let the last line of trucks pass out of sight, the solitude closed on you as if man had never existed, rather as Walter de la Mare describes it in 'The Listeners':

> Ay, they heard his foot upon the stirrup,
>   And the sound of iron on stone,
> And how the silence surged softly backward,
>   When the plunging hoofs were gone.

It was surprising how much wildlife there was in that seemingly barren waste. One day, on a plain of hard sand with hardly a patch of scrub for miles, I saw a covey of partridges. They seemed a bit annoyed at being disturbed, but did not bother to take to the wing. Further on, someone shot a pair of bustards. I also heard that some small deer were seen, probably a relative of the Indian Chinkara deer.

One evening when Pike was cutting some scrub for the fire he found a viper ready to strike and quickly lopped its head off. As we gathered round to try to identify it, someone put his hand down to pick up the head. Before he had touched it, that head raised itself on the inch or so of neck that was left to it, and tried to strike. It was all done in slow motion, as it was a very sick snake, and gave a perfect demonstration of the mechanism of its fangs. First the mouth opened wide, then the two fangs dropped on hinges from the roof of the mouth, then head moved forward to bite. This was not a reflex action, because the head had not been touched: it was still able to see the hand approaching and to take action accordingly. It had been about fifteen inches long with a head shaped like that of an English adder, and was probably very poisonous. At any rate, it made us probe the scrub pretty thoroughly for a bit before pulling it up by hand.

On the third day we made an especially early start before it was light to try and finish the journey, but it did not do us much good. It happened to be a rather misty morning, added to which the reconnaissance of the route by the Advanced Guard was rather ignorantly performed. The upshot was that the Camerons and our 492 Battery plunged into a lake in the gloom. It was just a shallow depression filled by the shower that snatched Montgomery's victory from him, so little harm was done, but we were held up for an hour while they got out of the mess.

Our scouting wasn't too good either. Hardly were we on the move again when we came upon a 'wet wadi'. The leaders had to stop in a hurry and all those behind came piling on top of us. For a while there was complete confusion: trucks were stuck in the wadi, others were milling about in each others' way, people were trying to stop those behind them ... in fact, it was no ordinary shemozzle! The Brigadier wisely cut the Gordian knot by ordering the breakfast halt, during which we unravelled ourselves. A 'wet wadi', by the way, is what one would call a stream in an ordinary country, but in these parts the 'streams' are nearly always dry, so when there is water in one it is called 'wet' because it is unusual.

Next morning the journey really did finish. I was sent ahead with our Regimental Advance Parties to find a 'harbour' near the oasis of Agedabia. As we drew near, the oasis looked enchanting. First there was a dancing white mirage that flickered and flowed like a flame; then the flame crystallised into gleaming white towers and minarets set in a park of green palms. Then the enchantment was destroyed as we came to a dirty and deserted Arab village, tumbledown and dusty, the plaster peeling from the walls. Our three-day desert march was over. We had come back to reality and were in the war zone again.

Chapter 9

A Land of Green Valleys

Far in the western brookland
That bred me long ago
The poplars stand and tremble
By pools I used to know.

A E Housman

128 [H] Field Regiment RA, December 1942

The valleys were not really green. They were for the most part bare and stony, but there were some patches of grass, which made the place seem verdant and pleasant to our sand-blown eyes. The mere fact that we had come to a land of valleys was a novelty. We seemed to be tucking each troop into a little box of its own when we deployed instead of spreading the Regiment out on the floor as we had done in the desert proper.

We found the Rifle Brigade – which was a Motor Battalion – holding a wide front with M Battery RHA. The Germans held a strong position in a little village of Mersa Brega, on a hill, which dominated all the approaches from our side and prevented us closing with their main defences at Agheila, a few miles further on. It was intended that the Highland Division should take up a position in the low foothills that the Rifle Brigade had been holding and drive the enemy back to Agheila.

The CRA warned us that we had outstripped the fighter cover of the RAF and we were told to disperse ourselves widely to avoid casualties from the unopposed attacks of the Luftwaffe. So we really did spread out, RHQ over twice the area that it normally occupied on a flat plain clear of the valleys. Tactically, it was an excellent position, but there was no moon. It was a nightmare finding one's bivvy in the dark. Some people spent half the first night trying to find their beds and the air was full of disembodied voices cursing despondently as they wandered round in circles. The next night was almost as bad. The Padre set out from the Command Post at 10.00 pm, and came back at 3.00 am, still not having found his place. I too suffered. My bivvy was 400 yards away, so I took a bearing and hitched my eye to a star and walked on confidently, counting my paces. Unfortunately for me, I had been out all day and did not know that the Adjutant had borrowed a bulldozer and had pits made for all the trucks to go into as a protection against bombs. One of these was plumb in line with my bearing and I just walked straight into it. I thought I must be falling down a disused well. Then I hit the bottom and felt as if my leg were broken. It was only a twisted knee, but it made me lame for six months: one of the hazards of war!

We fought no battle at Mersa Brega. The Bosch timed to a nicety the time we should need to gather the information necessary for the staging of an attack. He pulled out just before we were ready and he left the area so cleverly mined and booby trapped, with demolitions at key points on the route, that we could not gain contact until he had slipped right out of reach and was well on his way to his next main position at Buerat, 250 miles further on.

In spite of that, our stay was of interest because we ran into map trouble. When Gubby finished his survey and compared the results with the map, he found that, apparently, one battery was in the sea and the other two were north of the coast road when in fact they were both south of it. Knowing that 'the map is never wrong', he did it all again – and got exactly the same answer. Then he went to the Colonel and told him the map was wrong. Jerry Sheil laughed: many an indifferent map reader has tried to prove the map to be inaccurate. 'Go and do it again, Gubby,' he said, 'and take a drop of water with your whisky!'

Poor old Gubby put in another weary couple of hours of traverses and rounds of angles and came back with the same story. That convinced us all: Gubby was a first-class surveyor and had trained his team well. There could be no doubt at all. The map was hopelessly inaccurate and we had to do something about it, or else we and the Infantry would be fighting wars of our own in different parishes. We pored over it for hours and tried every form of trace and conversion table, but the errors were quite irreconcilable.

Something had to be done, and the Colonel rose to the occasion. 'We'll make our own map, by shooting,' he said. By this he meant that we would accurately range on to as many points as possible, using a single gun. The position of that gun was accurately 'fixed' by Gubby's surveyors. It follows that if it fired on to a target and its compass bearing was found to be, say, due west, and the range was 3,000 yards, then the gun could be plotted, a line drawn on a bearing of 270 degrees (due west) and a mark made at 3,000 on the correct scale. The result would be the same as if you had surveyed the target.

That is what the Colonel did. He studied the front from each of our

OPs and had all the prominent points ranged. In this way each visible house was surveyed as well as each bend in the enemy's wire perimeter and sufficient points on the road to permit its course to be drawn. The result was a remarkably accurate map on a scale of 1:25,000, the scale generally used for shooting and planning.

So far so good, but it still had to be 'sold' to the Infantry, who preferred their tidy enlargements of the printed 1:500,000 map. At first they said, 'Gunner Ju-ju! You use it if you like, but we'll stick to the proper one.' In the end Jerry got the General interested and a Subaltern of the Argylls was ordered to come to RHQ after a night patrol. I remember how tired and bewildered he looked as the General and Jerry fired questions at him – what bearing had he marched on, did he have a checker counting his paces, what did he see when he got there? and so on. As a consequence of the cross-examination, the fact emerged that he had not got to the place he meant to get to, which he had chosen and measured from the map: he had run into a wire entanglement long before he had expected to, with a small house just beyond it, which he did not expect to find there. Then a comparison with our shooting map showed that the bearing he had taken and the distance travelled would take him to the perimeter exactly where that small house was.

That convinced the General: he almost snatched the board from us and had it flown to Cairo for photographic reproduction. At the same time he gave Jerry some heart-warming compliments, saying among other things that no one else had been able to give him such a clear picture of the front. The pity of it was that the RAF then caught up and were able to produce a photographic map before ours was ready. However, it was satisfactory to find that theirs agreed with ours in almost every detail, proving the old saying 'The gun is an excellent surveyor.'

This steady firing of a single gun gave the enemy-locating devices great fun. A single gun is very easy to pinpoint, and pinpoint him they did, and fired off a lot of ammunition at him. They would have been well advised to save it because we were not foolish enough to fire from one of our troop positions. We moved the gun a long way to a flank, away from everyone else, and dug a deep pit for it. When the OP was ready to range, we hurried it into position, the ranging was finished in ten minutes or so, and off went the gun to a safe spot from which its detachment could watch the Bosch strafe the empty gun-pit. They thoroughly enjoyed this game of tag.

The expected air attack did not materialise, but there was one rude awakening. A Troop of the LAA Battery that defended our guns was caught moving in the half-light before dawn. They had moved closed up, as was usual at night, and were just too late in opening out to day distances. An early Stuka spotted them and came screaming down on them with a stick of bombs. These landed fair and square on a gun and lorry and nine men were killed outright.

Apart from that, our sister Regiment, 126, were the only ones to get hurt. They had a major killed and another wounded, both by the same mine. They also had some shell fire casualties. We lost quite a few from jaundice, including the doctors, John Grant and Dan Ridley the Adjutant. Dan's place was taken by 'HJ' Decker, a fat and jovial Captain from 307 Battery.

News that Jerry Sheil had been awarded the DSO for Alamein reached us at Brega, and fortunately we had a drop of whisky left to celebrate it. Seldom was a DSO better earned.

Just as we were ready to attack, we found that the bird had flown, so prepared to advance. We had first to wait while the mines were lifted. 275 Field Company RE did some pretty heroic things in cold blood, lifting those mines. Many were booby trapped against lifting, but still the Sappers pressed on, finding ways to circumvent the Germans' ingenuity. After a long wait a narrow way was cleared and we were able to move slowly on.

While we were hanging about a Gunner of the LAA Battery with the Camerons precipitated a horrible tragedy by flatly disobeying orders. Because the houses were known to be booby trapped, strict orders were given not to go inside. This poor fool found curiosity too strong and entered one. He touched a hidden trigger and was blown up. His Sergeant went in to help him and was badly wounded. The Cameron Company Commander tried to get him out and had an arm blown off. His Sergeant Major, in spite of the obvious danger, went in after his Officer and was killed.

That shows what these devices can do. The opening of a cupboard door can spring a mine; lavatory chains are connected to a charge in the tank; an attractive watch apparently left behind by mistake has killed many a soldier who did not know it would trigger a grenade if moved. Often a charge was put under the hearth and brought the house down when the fire grew hot. The only safe motto in country where the enemy has been is 'LEAVE IT ALONE!'

Outdoors there were 'Jumping Jimmies'. These were small canisters hidden in grass or scrub with black threads attached. When you hit the thread a small charge popped the bomb to about chest height, where it exploded and filled you with ball bearings. One day when I was idly watching two little tortoises playing something made me look down at my feet. My right foot was six inches away from a black thread! The temperature seemed to drop to zero. I traced the thread with my eye and saw the little black canisters about six feet away. As I looked round, frozen in my tracks, I found I had wandered into a clump of these jumpers. Not a nice position to be in.

Meanwhile, a force of tanks was sent along the sea shore, some of them towing 307 Battery's guns. The going was appallingly rough, but they managed to make a detour and get to the road beyond Brega. There they were faced with demolition after demolition, all sited to hold us up where there was no way round. We had to give up the chase. It was now known that the enemy was going right back to Buerat. This is the other side of the Gulf of Sidra, so there was nothing for it but to call a halt until sufficient petrol and ammunition had been collected to cover the 250 miles and the storming of the new position.

It was now 19 December 1942, so we were quite glad to have a rest for Christmas. There were also some training matters that needed attention, and although we were in a rest area for three weeks the only days on which we did not work were Christmas and New Year's Day.

Chapter 10

On! On! To Tripoli!

If ye gallop to Fort Bukloh
As fast as a bird can fly,
By the favour of God ye may cut him off
Ere he win to the tongue of Jagai!

Rudyard Kipling

128 [H] Regiment RA, December 1942/January 1943

The enemy had now taken up a rear-guard position in a nexus of wadis round Buerat at the western angle of the Gulf of Sidra. The Eighth Army kept touch with armoured cars while feverishly bringing forward petrol, rations and munitions to the area round Agheila, where we were, from 250 miles back.

Not only did Supply Services compete with the build-up of hundreds of tons of ammunition and convoy after convoy of petrol, and with ten days' rations for three Divisions, but they also brought up the normal Christmas dinner of turkey, pork, plum pudding and all the trimmings. How they did it, only they know. We did justice to it in a delightful cove by the sea and were thankful.

Montgomery's aim was to get to Tripoli with speed, before Rommel could build up a force to stage a comeback. He considered he had sufficient time to build up supplies for ten days, and his plan allowed exactly ten days to reach Tripoli and capture it from the time the build-up of supplies was complete. If we failed to get to Tripoli before supplies ran out the Army would have to withdraw and start again.

There was a strong position to capture on the way – the Buerat position – and the distance to be travelled was 500 miles: 500 miles with a by-no-means-beaten enemy disputing the way. The Highland Division was to attack and clear Buerat and then to advance astride the road. The New Zealanders and 7th Armoured Division with the rest of 10th Corps were to do a 'left hook' with the aim of surrounding the enemy. The key note was *speed*. We were to 'give battle by day and by night'. We did so, and we reached Tripoli in ten days exactly. When our Regiment reached its final position one Battery had petrol left to take it precisely three miles and the other two had enough for seven miles. The ration of sleep had long been exhausted.

But we in our Christmas camp were not yet aware of the frenzied planning that was afoot. We lived from day to day; our planning was all short term because we never knew when sudden orders for a move would come. Our job was to be ready for anything, and we continued training, tuning the Regiment to something like the pitch of perfection.

As time went on we were plagued with rumours and keyed up with orders to move that were cancelled until we became quite jittery. The real thing came at last and irritation vanished with the excitement of movement. The Colonel and the Battery Commanders were ordered to move ahead to start planning for the battle and I was left to bring on the Regiment. Jerry left everything cut and dried for me, but he might as well have saved himself the trouble: orders for the journey were changed. We were to do it in two-and-a-half instead of four days – the pressure had reached us! Speed was indeed the word.

The entire programme of stages had to be reorganised and new arrangements made, but things came right in the end and we struck our flag and ploughed off through the dust. Our feelings were mixed as we left our delightful camp by the sea. We were delighted to be on the move again, but three weeks there had made it seem like home, and it was quite a wrench to leave.

This part of the Eighth Army's route has been described as the most barren and inhospitable in the whole desert, but the recent rain brightened it for us. The wilderness was rich and lovely with wild flowers. Swathes of blue and red anemones stood out from a background of golden daisies; there were blue pimpernels, a kind of speedwell, purple violets and many another flower that might have come from an English hedge. We were some miles inland, with no coastline breaking the sweep of the land, so we seemed to be cruising through a fairylike prairie, a country of gaiety, far from the war.

We passed 'Marble Arch', the Army's name for a great archway, Arco Philaenorum [see plate], built by Mussolini on the boundary of Cyrenaica and Tripolitania. Isolated from everything, it seems quite out of place – civilisation gone haywire in the sandy immensity – but there is a legend that gives point to its being there.

It is said that in classical times the Carthaginians and the Cyrenians disputed the boundary between them. To settle the argument, they agreed to each send a pair of runners from their territories and to plan the boundary post where the pairs met. The Carthaginians chose the brothers Phileni, and they ran so well that they met their rivals well within Cyrenian country. At this the Cyrenians were so angry that they refused to accept the result unless the Phileni agreed to be buried alive at the spot. To their surprise, the Phileni sacrificed themselves for their country and submitted to being buried. So now 'Marble Arch' commemorates this rather unlikely story and the downfall of its builder.

Next day the track was abominable and progress was slow. We were told to stage at Sultan, and the distance was said to be 110 miles. What we were not told was that the staging camp called Sultan was nowhere near the little town of that name, which is on the coast. Nor were we told that the distance was only a guess. Small wonder, then, that no city loomed out of the dark and no welcoming advance parties appeared when my mileometer registered 110.

The moon rose and set again, and still we bumped and growled through the gloom. The night grew darker and more dreary, the miles clicked steadily on the instrument, and the track became worse and worse. In theory it was the 'HD' axis, marked with an occasional HD sign. In practice it was like the Trigh Capuzzo, a dry morass of tracks some two miles wide, and after the start we saw no more signs. When the mileage was nearly 130 and the time was after 1.00 am, I decided that we must have overshot Sultan and called a halt.

It was a trying situation because our advance parties had our petrol and food for the next day. We could manage without food, but we could not go much further without refuelling. On top of that, we had to send the advance parties on at the crack of dawn to prepare the next halt. All I could do was to appoint emergency parties, filling their tanks from the main body, and hope that we could find the others in the morning.

Having settled the Regiment, I went off to investigate a dim light in the distance. There was not much hope of its being any use to us, but it might give some clue, and so it did. I found a Military Policeman there, one of the Division's as well. He told me that the rest of 152 Brigade was just in front – if I had gone on another mile, I should have driven on to their bivvies! It all goes to show that worrying is never worthwhile. I went back to my car and slept like a log.

The first glimmer of light found me driving round a somnolent bivvy area. The first person I ran into was our own Quartermaster, Willoughby. 'Have a cup of tea!' said he, and very good it was. I heard from him that the advance parties also had trouble over the name Sultan. The leader got to hear that there was a town called Sultan on the coast and went straight there by road, thinking that he had been given wrong orders. He then had to go on a compass bearing for thirty miles through soft sand, hunting for the place where the camp was to be.

The next day's trip was quite pleasant and there was a nice surprise in store for the afternoon. Sitting on the roof of my car picking the route, I was in a world of my own – a slightly troubled world, because I had no idea how to find my journey's end. Behind me the Regiment had just crossed the chasm and broken ground of the big Wadi Tamet and was widely spread in little groups, each trying to avoid the other's dust clouds. In front was a shimmering immensity of scrub-patched sand with here and there a dust-devil spiralling upwards until it spread into a brown cloud and lost its shape again. Otherwise all was emptiness.

Suddenly, a small grey cloud caught my eye on the horizon. It approached steadily, a trail of dust streaming behind it, until I could pick out a truck with a tall, thin man standing up in it. Focusing my glasses, I was delighted and amazed to recognise Howard Graham – Jerry had sent a Battery Commander to meet us! So we had travelled nearly 300 miles, by track and by no track, and had linked up with the Colonel as planned, though I'd had no idea where this would be, within fifty miles, until Howard met us. It was a most satisfying reunion.

At dawn we found the Colonel and his party in the huge Wadi Ouesca, his camp by the only landmark for miles: two minute bushes we named the 'Twin Trees'. We went forward at once and prepared positions for the Buerat attack. The Regiment was to rendezvous at dusk at the Twin Trees, safe from observation in daylight, and from there I would lead them forward under cover of night. It was quite a tricky journey with several wet wadis that could only be crossed at certain places, so I reconnoitred the route with infinite care until I could almost have led the Regiment blindfold. Then I swanned off on a compass bearing to go straight to the Twin Trees, a simple journey of ten miles, with the comforting thought that I couldn't possibly miss the Wadi Ouesca – a huge chasm – and then could easily find the Trees.

Couldn't miss it? When I had gone twelve miles I began to wonder. At fourteen I stopped in a panic. What could have happened – was I bewitched? Was there a deposit of lodestone to upset my compass? And what would happen to the Regiment? No one else knew the route to the gun positions.

Then I pulled myself together and started to reason it out. I measured the bearing on the map, thirty degrees; I checked the set of my compass – and then I laughed. I had set it at fifty! A careless mistake, but at least I now knew what was wrong. I quickly laid off a rough course and started to race the setting sun over some vile rocky country that gave the car springs a terrible jolting. As we came to the Twin Trees, there was the Regiment eating their evening meal. The sun went out like a candle and one of the back tyres went flat with a hissing sound. What a relief! If that tyre had not lasted just so long what a predicament to have been in. The secret of missing the wadi was simply that there was no chasm about a mile above the Twins, just a slight fold in the ground. They do sometimes play tricks like that.

'Pop into my jeep,' said the Colonel – it was then the only one in the Regiment – 'and put Aitkinhead into an OP that Tony Thicknesse will show you: he's at point so-and-so.' So I gave up my idea of a quiet amble round the Batteries and went off to meet Tony, the Commanding Officer of 126 Field Regiment. He and I were old friends of pre-war days, when he was Adjutant of the 8th Field Regiment.

By good luck he, Aitky and I all converged on the point together and Tony showed us the enemy positions. It was a bare, featureless bit of country, and we had to stand on the bonnet of a jeep to see anything at all. When I had absorbed as much as I could, I asked him about the OP. That meant nothing to him: he had gathered from Jerry only that I was to be shown the enemy positions, so I was left to solve that problem myself.

A heartbreaking problem it was. There seemed to be just nowhere with a view. The enemy had scored a direct hit on one of Tony's OPs that very morning and was making quite a nuisance of himself with mortars, so we had to go carefully. At last we found a place where he could see a little and get a little cover from a knoll. There I left Aitky with orders to dig himself in well. That was my first experience of siting an OP in war, and the enemy rounded it off by dropping a mortar bomb almost on my tail as I drove off.

When dark came we fired a programme for 153 Brigade, who carried out the attack. It was an anti-climax, as the enemy had pulled out straight away, leaving the usual number of mines to contend with. One of 492's captains drove over one and was wounded in the foot. He was our only casualty.

Our troubles started after the battle. About 4.00 am when all was quiet and I was gently nodding in the Command Post, the Brigade Major of 152 Brigade rang up and started discussing our move. Soon it was clear that a message had failed to reach us: we knew nothing at all about a move; we had no petrol; our lorries were anything up to thirty miles away collecting some, and drawing ammunition. The Brigade Major insisted that they were expecting us to join them, about thirty miles away, in three hours. They were to lead the race to Tripoli with us.

We rang up the Batteries to find out how much petrol they had and got vague 'couldn't care less' replies – everyone was very tired, and it is no easy matter to round up the sleeping drivers of trucks scattered over acres of desert in pitch dark. At last we found that 492 had enough for thirty miles, so they were detailed to go with the Advance Guard. The others had only about ten miles' running time, so they were to move later.

The next few minutes found me on the way to 152 Brigade to arrange things, and Gubby dashing off with four trucks and orders not to come back until he had found petrol – and to be quick about it. Meanwhile the Quartermaster arrived, dead-beat from trying place after place, all empty, so the outlook was a bit gloomy. At Brigade I found the remains of a flap that must have equalled ours – when the Battalions were told to move, it had transpired that they had no petrol either.

Eventually, we moved at 11.00 am, still without petrol. We formed up with the Brigade in 'desert formation', as we had moved on the Cyrenaican march. Everything went peacefully at first. But as I was jogging along, without a care in the world, the Staff Captain swanned alongside and asked if I thought we were going in the right direction. I told him that he was the one to know that: we had merely been told to travel with them, and I knew of no destination other than Tripoli, the ultimate one. He rather shook me then by telling me that the Brigadier had dashed on ahead with the Brigade Major, that he (the Staff Captain) hadn't been told where we were going, and that I was the Senior Officer left. So no one knew! A nice situation. All I could do was to keep on as we were going and hope that we should eventually catch up. We were heading north, having rounded the western angle of the Gulf of Sidra, so I got the sun just behind my left shoulder and kept going, wondering when the guns would run out of petrol.

Moonrise saw us stumbling through country covered with low bushes and patches of a deliciously aromatic shrub that filled the air with sweetness as our wheels crushed it. In the midst of the scrub, we came upon an iron stake stuck in a bush. What a welcome sight. It carried an HD sign, meaning that the leaders had laid a trail and we were bang on it. We pushed on happily and soon ran into the back of the Advanced Guard. They had halted and were full of rumours that the enemy had been bumped by the vanguard, so I went on to find out the form. Before I had gone far, the Colonel appeared, as always seemed to happen when he was wanted. He said the Camerons had brushed the rear guard and 492 had some lovely shooting and 'flushed the birds'.

Just then, Gubby arrived with the petrol, and we almost fell on his neck for joy. Now we could carry out Monty's orders: 'We're going to Tripoli. Good luck and good hunting!'

Chapter 11

Nothing Shall Stop Us Now

The trumpets sound, the banners fly,
The glittering spears are ranked ready;
The shouts o' war are heard afar,
The battle closes thick and bloody.

Robbie Burns

128 [H] Regiment RA, January 1943

152 Brigade and our Regiment were now in the lead, and the pressure from behind was intense. With us was the Governor Designate of Misurata, who was to be installed post haste. This was the first military government to be set up by the British in this war – a big lift for the nation's prestige. This, by the way, but added to the force of the drive to get to Tripoli.

Montgomery twisted the General's tail – which needed no twisting – and the General breathed fire down Brigadier Murray's neck. That grand solid old soldier carried on unmoved by it all, making haste slowly, without relaxing a single military precaution.

Jerry Sheil was up with the advanced guard with 492 Battery in his pocket, and also a Battery of 5.5-inch guns from 64 Medium Regiment that had been lent to us to add force to our punch. Every time the enemy tried to make a stand, Jerry let fly with both, and German and Italian alike made off almost before the Infantry had got out of their trucks.

I was plodding along with the Brigade HQ group, but this time I was definitely in charge of it, having made a bit of a fuss about the last effort. In the afternoon we breasted the top of a ridge just as the advanced guard had quite a spirited little skirmish in the plain below us. The 5th Camerons 'motored into battle', that is, they stayed in their trucks too long and were ambushed. Their Colonel, Ronny Miers, was wounded, and several men were killed by shell fire before they had time to dismount. But in almost a matter of seconds the great black bursts of the medium shells and the smaller crumps of 492 Battery's shells turned the tables, and the enemy made off long before the Infantry could attack them.

This was a copy-book example of how to use Artillery to keep an enemy on the run, and it is a great pity that the Division history makes no mention of it. It merely says:

The 5th Camerons (the leading Battalion) were not too lucky. Colonel Miers was wounded. Many trucks were put out of action, and the men inside them killed and wounded by the enemy rear guard long-range artillery. But after a temporary stoppage the advance was continued ...

Strange it is, in such accounts, that again and again one hears how 'a few enemy guns' held up the advance or broke up the attack, but seldom is the credit given to our guns when a hostile attack is repulsed – are our shells less lethal?

As we were settling for the night after the evening brew we were suddenly told to push on to Misurata and to be there by dawn. So on we went. My group was to follow the 5th Seaforth, but they went off at such a gallop that I soon gave up trying to keep up with them, and went at our own pace with the moon to light us and the friendly Pole star as guide.

Suddenly, out of the gloom, the Intelligence Officer of the 5th Seaforth appeared. They had got off course and got stuck in soft sand. I was now ahead of them, so would I please incline to my left and come up behind them again? 'Perhaps you can lead us to them,' said I, not wishing to strike the same bad patch. He said he couldn't be sure of finding them, and dashed away into the night.

We wheeled left, hoping we were past the sand, but our luck was out. What grinding and digging, and cursing! We had a lot of ambulance cars and other two-wheel-drive vehicles, so it took some time to winch and dig and tow them clear. I sent an officer to try to find a way round. He found none, so I gave up trying to join the Battalion and took the group back to our former track.

When we were nicely on the move again, a strange apparition swanned up to me and yelled, 'EATER! Have you got a doctor?' When he saw I didn't much like his greeting, he explained that *he* was 'Eater' – not me – and explained that he was a member of the OETA, or Occupied Enemy Territory Administration. He said there had been an ambush a mile or two ahead, near a little village called Crispi. That made me sit up and take notice! We lent him a doctor and I tried unsuccessfully to get a coherent picture of the situation from him.

As he could not give me any information worth having, I decided to halt and wait for daylight, which was about an hour away. True, it would make us late into Misurata, but I had no patrol to send ahead and the HQ was not a fighting unit, so it did not seem sensible to push on regardless.

It was very cold hanging about waiting for the sky to lighten, alert for a possible raid on the column, but the Quartermaster created a lively diversion by arriving at 4.30 am and handing out the home mail. Among it was a letter from my mother, hoping that I was getting enough sleep and not feeling the heat ...

We moved on at first light, picking up a platoon of Seaforth that had got lost, and found that the ambush had been mopped up after causing a few casualties to some Sudanese troops. It was a pocket of determined enemy that the advanced guard had missed.

Misurata has been described as 'the first of a line of pleasant green oases stretching to Tripoli'. The abiding memory I keep of it is the sight of acres and acres of Asphodel or, as we called it – knowing no better – Crusader Lily. It stood about two feet high, with many branched stems. The dainty flowers were a waxy white with pink veins that gave a delicate tinge of colour to a delightful picture.

After a morning of meetings and conferences concerning our future moves, the Military Governor made a triumphal entry, driven by Bombardier Beales in 'Ben Nevis', but I saw nothing of that. Pike put my bed among the lilies and I was dead to the world for a wonderful two hours.

Another night march brought us to a bivouac area some two or three kilometres short of Homs, one of the green oases. It was a bad area, allotted to us in the dark, full of irrigation ditches and terraces, which forced us to bunch the guns and trucks into a small, cramped space. When daylight came, we saw a huge craggy hill in front of us, completely overlooking our position.[1] Having a rough castellation of rock on the top, it was at once dubbed 'Edinburgh Castle'.

'I'll put an OP there,' said the Colonel, and went off to do so. On the way he met the CRA and told him his plans.

'Good gracious – you can't do that!' said the Brigadier. 'The enemy are there!'

'Holy Mother!' said Jerry. 'My Regiment is in full view of it – they will be massacred!'

And as he got back to us, the shells began to fall. Not many, or there would indeed have been a massacre, but there were casualties at once. In a couple of minutes there were two killed and several wounded, including a Subaltern, Peter Carr, badly hit in the stomach. The prospect was not at all bright.

Said Jerry, 'We must get out of here *at once!*'

I could only think of pulling back and was wondering where we could find cover from that all-seeing hill without losing all our range, but the Colonel's brain was quicker than mine.

'We won't go back: we'll go forward, into action!' he said, pointing to a thin black line of the map. 'That looks like a wadi, about a mile down the road – see if you can get the guns in there.'

Leaving orders for the reconnaissance parties to assemble and await my return, I leapt into my car and Taylor drove off like a shot from a gun. For some reason the Bosch had stopped shelling the Regiment, all bunched and helpless as it was, and was concentrating on the road. He chose a point on it and dropped bursts of three there at unpleasantly frequent intervals.

The road was straight for about a mile and then entered a line of trees, which I hoped was the wadi. We went down it at sixty, just missing a burst. The wadi was practicable, and out of sight of the 'castle', so we hurried back for the recce parties. This time we had two bursts to starboard and one to port as we passed the danger spot and the old car shuddered. I was wondering how to get the guns through. Perhaps we could time it so that each avoided a burst – but perhaps he would bring more guns to bear. That did not bear thinking about.

Gubby and Taylor (the Signals Officer) and the battery parties were all teed up, so down the road we went. A burst nearly got Taylor – blackened his windscreen – but he waved OK, so on we went. The Colonel joined us and helped allot the gun positions, and in no time the guns were steaming down the 'mad mile', their tyres whining like a circular saw at work. They came 300 yards behind each other, each Number One (the sergeant in charge) standing up as usual, holding on to the windscreen. Some were smiling with excitement, others looked tense and anxious. Each one gave a smart 'eyes right' in salute as he passed me standing by the roadside, waving the speed down so that they could turn the corner into the wadi. A salute at such a time says a lot for their discipline, when you come to think of it.

Anxiously, I watched the vicious blasts that rose in dust and smoke as they passed the danger spot. It seemed too much to hope that not one shell should find its mark, but gun after gun appeared, bouncing like toys on their springless carriages at the unfamiliar speed, and soon all twenty-four were tucked away in the friendly wadi and answering calls for fire. It had been an exciting quarter of an hour.

That German OP Officer certainly missed his chance! I can only suppose that he was sited where he could not see us and that the shells that disturbed us so were fired at random.

We were in action, unknowingly, right next to the ruins of the old Roman city of Leptis Magna [see plate]. The Padre discovered this and advised me to take a look at it. The Italians had done some very good excavation work, and I believe the place is quite a showpiece now. I have always regretted that I did not take a walk round, as there was a lull in which I could have gone, but at the time I felt too keyed up and tense to take time off to look at ruins.

Various flanking movements took place, and by afternoon the Germans had withdrawn. This I discovered when I went to see Bill Field, BC of 492 Battery, in his OP. I approached very carefully on my belly, so as not to give the place away, only to find everybody sitting about in the open. Bill was just going to 'stroll to the next ridge', so I strolled with him. It was a delightfully peaceful walk through orchards and green meadows bright with flowers and growing barley. The only reminder of war was the sight of two or three of the Black Watch with their red hackles, resting in a copse. I left Bill still questing ahead. The tide of war had obviously receded.

That night the M&V stew was bad and made me quite ill for a bit. We also had petrol worries and the ammunition was late in coming up. The petrol arrived in the very nick of time – just ten minutes before we moved.

'Nothing shall stop us how,' Monty had said. He was right: nothing did stop the Army. But if he had known just how bad the enemy demolitions of the road would be, I wonder if he would have been so confident! As usual, the place was infested with mines and Jumping Jimmies, but it was the demolitions that slowed the advance. Where the road wound along the side of a hill the Germans had blasted it away, leaving a precipice, with all approaches to it mined. Up came Major Lloyd and his 275 Field Company RE and up came the mines. Then huge bulldozers appeared and tons of earth and rock were sent cascading down the slope until there was a way over and through the debris. On the heels of the bulldozers came the Military Police with red caps and HD signs, controlling the traffic with white gloves, and through the gap the column slowly wound its way. Except for one more battle, that was the story for the rest of the way to Tripoli.

*

This city now doth, like a garment wear
The beauty of the morning; silent, bare,
Ships, towers, domes, theatres, and temples lie
Open unto the fields, and to the sky;

W Wordsworth

We left Leptis Magna at 2.00 am on 21 January 1943, seemingly on a normal night move, but as we were humming gently past the 'castle' that had caused so much trouble there was a sudden commotion at the side of the road.

'I'll put the leading Battery in here,' said the Colonel. 'Find a place for the next behind them, and tell Gubby to get the other in somewhere – no fancy work; get 'em in quickly.'

The Battalion ahead had bumped the enemy and the crack and bang of battery firing soon confirmed that we had wasted no time in 'getting 'em in quickly'.

You will have gathered that we were out of the desert for the time being. Indeed, we were now entering some rough, hilly country that continued until we were nearly in Tripoli. The enemy, after leaving Edinburgh Castle, had left some posts in these hills, into which the 5th Seaforth had now bumped.

As a rule, full-scale attacks are not made until there has been an opportunity to reconnoitre the enemy position by daylight. But in the present urgency the General ordered an attack to be made at dawn, knowing that there could not be great resistance. This was a nightmare for all concerned. The Battalion Commander had to do the best he could by moonlight, and the Gunner OPs had to register the targets under the same difficulties.

Observed shooting by moonlight is, generally speaking, impracticable. Even if you can see your target, it is very difficult to judge where it is. The shell bursts show as momentary flashes and are gone, so it is almost impossible to see where they are falling in relation to the target. On this occasion even the moon failed us and hid behind a cloud most of the time. The gun-end has its difficulties too. Survey takes three times as long when there has been no daylight reconnaissance, and there are many extra causes of inaccuracies.

In spite of the difficulties, the attack started on time. Then the Seaforth found themselves in trouble. Great chasms appeared in what the moonlight had shown as flat plain; the ground was rocky and steep in places, and the enemy machine guns were well sited. On top of this the artillery fire was inaccurate – as had been expected – and, also as expected, our machine guns were not in the right places. Consequently, the enemy's fire was not neutralised, and the Seaforth had many casualties. In fact, things were in doubt until the Gunners could see to correct their fire and the machine gunners to get to the right places. At last, after some hard fighting, the Germans withdrew and the way to Tripoli was open.

Open? Far from it! The way was well and truly blocked with mines and demolitions, but there was no more active resistance. The Sappers were busy all that day and after. The advanced guard reached Castelverde the next day and then had to set to work with pick and shovel to help fill in the craters in the road. In the middle of the night there was a full-chested bellow of 'Jerry! Where are you?!' It was the General himself, calling for more pick and shovel parties, and soon nearly everyone in the Regiment was busy digging and filling.

Early next morning, 23 January – exactly ten days from the start of the advance – the road was clear for vehicles. At 5.30 am the 1st Gordons rode into the town on the tanks of 40th Royal Tank Regiment, closely followed by a company of the 2nd Seaforth in lorries. The Division's ambition had been achieved. The town that had been like a mirage for so long – ever beckoning, yet ever distant – had fallen at last.

Close behind the leading troops, in his jeep and unescorted, came General Wimberley. Seeing Howard and Bill Field by their armoured cars with a road-mending party, it evidently struck him that he was disobeying his own orders in so travelling. At any rate, he called out to them, 'Come and be my escort!' So 128 was also represented in the triumphal entry.

There is a story that the uppermost thought in his mind was to mark the town with the 'HD' sign as soon as possible. It is said that one of the first men he saw there was the Pioneer Sergeant of the Gordons (Pioneers being carpenters and handymen). 'Ah, Sergeant!!' said Wimberley. 'Where are you going to put the "HD" sign?

'Weel, Sir, we ha' na tha paint yet,' said the Pioneer.

'Oh, that's all right,' said the General. 'I've got it!'

Before they had been there half an hour, the most prominent building in the city was decorated with the biggest 'HD' ever painted [see plate].

During the night of the entry, the Regiment was ordered to Castelverde, and I found myself once more reconnoitring by moonlight. This time it was in sandy country, made beautiful by the glint of the light on the bright flowers and shiny leaves of an orange grove.

When all was ready I stretched out on my bed to wait for the Regiment and enjoyed the peace and beauty about me. When I woke up it was broad daylight and I was surrounded by the men of RHQ, dead to the world.

Notes

1 Not to be confused with the Takrouna outcrop mentioned later.

Chapter 12

The Mirage Clears

The worldly hope men set their hearts upon
Turns ashes – or it prospers; and anon
Like snow upon the Desert's dusty Face
Lighting a little hour or two – is gone

Edward Fitzgerald, from *The Rubáiyát of Omar Khayyám*, 16

128 [H] Regiment RA, January 1943

At Alamein the British Lion sprang; when Tripoli was reached, the quarry's death was certain, though it took another year to die.

The capture of Tripoli was a triumph because without it the Germans could not stage a comeback in North Africa. Its fall opened the Mediterranean, saved Malta and ensured that the European end of the Axis powers could never link up with the Japanese. As well as this, the prestige conferred by such a clear-cut victory was enormous.

We knew all that and were glad, but the town itself was something of a disappointment to us. For more than six months we had slept under the stars, water we had known only as a lukewarm fluid that trickled sparingly from a tin, women had vanished from our world and we were sick and tired of the unvarying monotony of M&V, bully and hard biscuit. In fact, we wanted a dose of civilisation.

The town in the mirage had promised us this. We thought we saw there lights and colour, appetising meals in pleasant surroundings, entertainment and the bustle and excitement of a visit to town. But we were to be disappointed. Such bath water as there was was unheated and the 'chain' would not pull. The food was army rations, faintly disguised by Italian cooking. The nearest we got to entertainment was the Divisional Concert Party, and the bustle of city life was provided by a few woebegone Italians and a lot of dirty-looking Arabs.

One day Jerry and I set out to give the place the once over. We drove past orchards of pretty pink almond blossoms, past red-roofed Italian bungalows and Arab mud huts, and along a fine avenue of eucalyptus trees that led through the suburbs. We looked at the almost-empty shops and had a sweet and sickly drink at an exorbitant price. Then we went to the best hotel and found it being converted to an officers' club. The windows were blacked out with dismal blue paint and the lights were dim. We asked for coffee, and it was weak and cold. They said we could have a bath, but there was no fuel to heat the water. The main dish for dinner was – bully-beef stew.

The Infantry were to 'beat retreat' in the main square so we went to watch, but the rain came down in buckets and washed out the show. So then we went home. Our comfortable little bivvy tents with a tin basin of boiling water and the cheerful company of our officers in our tattered little Mess tent had more to offer, we said, than the whole of Tripoli! As far as I remember, neither of us went there again, except on duty.

Our camp was at a dirty little village called Tagiura, half-Italian, half-Arab, fifteen miles east of Tripoli. The Italians lived mostly in outlying bungalows on their farms and were in terror of the Arabs. Their fear was understandable. Jack was now not only as good as his master – he was top dog. The more distant Italians were in danger of being beaten up, if not murdered, and the Arabs consistently stole their poultry and farm products.

They were a nasty lot. They used to unbury our dead and steal their clothes. One was found with the identity disc of a Seaforth Sergeant. He professed ignorance of where it came from until someone suggestively loaded a rifle. That made him think better of it, and he led the soldiers to a wounded man who had been left for dead, after being kicked and robbed and finally clubbed on the head. If they could do that to a member of the conquering army, no wonder the Italians were afraid.

Our efforts to vary the menu were not too successful. A fine sheep we bought was stolen in the night and there was not much else available except eggs. These were small – quite tiny – but plentiful if you had plenty of tea, which was the only currency that the Arabs would accept. Occasionally we laid hands on some good Chianti, but mostly it was poor stuff. I liked the local cigarettes, which had a strong Turkish flavour, but most of the others turned up their noses at them.

The tea currency was rather amusing. Every Arab carried at least two small eggs in his robes and every soldier had a handful of tea in his pockets, and bargaining took place whenever the twain met. One day I found the whole of RHQ sitting down to a breakfast of two fried eggs each, so I congratulated the cook and asked how he managed it, as tea was not all that plentiful.

'Well, Sir, it's like this,' said the cook. 'I dries the old tea leaves in the sun, what I've made tea with; then I puts them in the oven, and they all goes black and crisp, like. They think that's what tea should be like!' Trust the British soldier to extract the kernel from the nut.

Our stay was pleasant and restful, though we were kept busy refurbishing for the next lap of the campaign. We were also called upon to provide a ceremonial guard in Tripoli. Only one day was allotted to the Divisional Artillery, so, it being an honour, the fifteen Batteries of the five Artillery Regiments had a drill competition for it, which our 307 Battery won. They were a real credit to the Regiment. In fact the Garrison Sergeant Major told us in confidence that they were the best guard produced by anyone. He begged us not to quote him, as he was a Cameron. The Highland Infantry were not used to being outsmarted, but neither were the Gunners.

The big event of our stay here was the visit of Winston Churchill, the Prime Minister. In his honour the Division staged a nearly full-scale ceremonial parade. I say 'nearly' because the Divisional Artillery was only allowed to send a token party, a composite Regiment composed of a composite Battery from each Field Regiment. The excuse was that we should take up too much room if the whole show was on parade. Personally, I should have said that it would have added considerably to the impressiveness of the occasion! However, what we did send looked mightily fine as the guns rolled past the saluting base, in perfect line, with shining paint and burnished steel [see plate].

The Prime Minister drove along the line of troops and was cheered to the echo, the Arabs breaking the cordon to give him the 'V' sign. Churchill smiled and stuck up his two fingers, raising the cheering to a magnificent crescendo, and went on to the saluting dais with Alanbrooke, Chief of the Imperial General Staff – the greatest soldier of the war – Alexander and Montgomery.

The massed pipes and drums of the Division were formed up opposite him, a magnificent sight in their kilts and with bannerettes streaming. Leading the revue came the General, his carrier 'Beaumont Hamel' wearing the six tartans of the Infantry Regiments on his wireless mast. Then came the Artillery, a picture of precision and smartness, the guns rolling by to the Royal Horse Artillery March, 'Bonnie Dundee' – presumably because the pipes could not encompass 'Keel Row' on their scale. The Sappers and Signals came next in smartly painted trucks, followed by the Middlesex Machine Gun Battalion, also mounted.

Then, as one looked down the long, straight street, the marching Infantry came on in waves, the sun glinting on the bayonets and the kilts of the Camerons catching the eye with a welcome touch of colour [see plate].

It was a splendid parade and a wonderful closure to this part of the campaign. It is said that the sight brought tears to the Premier's eyes. We will close with his message to the Eighth Army:

> You have altered the face of war in a most remarkable way. The fame of the Desert Army has spread throughout the world. When a man is asked after the war what he did, it will be sufficient to say, 'I marched and fought with the Desert Army.'

Chapter 13

The One-Day Battle

The canon standing at stiff-arm salute
Discharge their duties in the innocent air

L Frankenberg

128 [H] Regiment RA, 1–6 March 1943

Soon after Alamein the First Army, part British, part American, landed in Algeria and was directed on Tunis. I felt rather irritated at the time – it seemed to be a violation of Eighth Army's preserves! At first the two armies were independent of each other, but when we reached Tripoli a Supreme Headquarters was set up at Algiers, with the American General Eisenhower at its head, to control all operations in North Africa. Our General Alexander was appointed Deputy Commander and the direction of the actual fighting was largely in his hands, Eisenhower confining himself to the political aspect and to integrating the American and British staffs so that friction was avoided.

Thus Rommel became a rat in a trap with the two allied armies steadily converging on him. Unfortunately, one side of the trap was not yet rat-proof. The Americans suffered a very considerable reverse at the Kasserine Pass,[1] which jeopardised the whole First Army. So considerable was the reverse that we found ourselves on the move westwards a whole week before we expected. Montgomery had been very reluctant to move because he was not ready to give battle. The port of Tripoli was well and truly blocked, so the build-up for the advance was necessarily slow. However, Alexander pointed out that if he did not act to ease the pressure quickly, there would be a major disaster.

We rolled along the via Balba – as the coast road was called – until we reached the Tunisian frontier. There we came to a ten-mile stretch of perfectly vile French road, purposely left unrepaired to discourage any attempt by Mussolini to add Tunis to his empire. The country was flat and rough, interspersed with salt marshes, mostly bare except for scattered clumps of heather of a kind with sage and a sort of lavender growing amongst it that pleasantly scented the air. There were many wadis, some of them wet and harbouring wild duck. The Colonel shot a brace of teal in one, and there was an occasional hare to be seen. Cultivation was restricted to the fairly frequent small oases, except for a few green patches of corn swathed with blue chicory or the like, where an enterprising Arab had found a patch of good soil.

To the north the plain was bounded by the sea, and to the south were the Matmata Hills, which swept in a large circle westwards and north, stopping some fifteen miles from the sea at the Mareth Gap. In this gap the French had built a miniature 'Maginot Line' against the Italians. Unfortunately for us, the French had sited and built these fortifications exceedingly well, for it was here that Rommel intended to bar the Eighth Army's way.

The Division was directed on the Mareth Line, but was not to close with it yet because of Rommel's reaction to our move. Knowing that Montgomery could not have finished his preparations, and having put the First Army temporarily out of action, he staked all on catching the Eighth off balance and hurried everything down to our front, including his 150 remaining tanks.

Things were tricky for a time because we were almost the only troops on the front. Montgomery calculated that 3 or 4 March was the earliest date that Rommel could attack us, and that 6 March was a more likely date. He himself could not be ready until then. So there was an overlap of two or possibly three days when we might have to bear the brunt alone. We were told, 'Backs to the wall; hold him until 6 March – that is all I ask of you!'

We didn't know all this yet as we motored through the little oasis town of Ben Gardane, bright with flowers and almond blossoms, and continued towards Medinine. That night we camped in a grove of trees that were new to us. They were olives.

The water was foul. We had already met brackish water, but this actually curdled the tinned milk, and we had to drink our tea with horrid particles of suspended solid in it. Most of the Tunisian water was like that. It contained quite a lot of magnesium sulphate (Epsom salts), so it was a laxative as well as nasty to the taste. In some areas it was a strong purge, quite undrinkable.

We were now approaching the Mareth Line and came into action near a little village called Makralouf. Here it was difficult to find gun positions that were not overlooked by the enemy in the distance. We found one of the few available places and were a little peeved when a Medium Regiment came and sat down on top of us. We told them to go away, but they said they had nowhere to go to: 'Anyway, we're fighting the same war, aren't we?' There was no answer to that, so we all became friends. I'm glad they did not fire while we were there, as they make a most disturbing noise!

In a few days we got the order to move and as I was choosing the new position the Colonel wirelessed 'meet me at the waterfall at once'. That had me beaten for a bit. I remembered passing a little cascade some days ago, but I could not recall where. Careful retracing of the paths of memory rediscovered it at last, and soon we were enjoying the pleasing sight of a waterfall in the wilderness.

After choosing a position there for the Regiment we had time on our hands, so we slipped along to see Brigadier Murray and his Brigade. He took us to see the Infantry position, on a long bare ridge with a wide flat plain between them and the enemy – so flat that I wondered how they would ever be able to cross it and get to grips with our foe. Murray was puzzling about the same thing. He wanted to know if it was as flat as it looked, or if there were any folds to hide in. At the same time he did not want to send a patrol out because he wanted to keep his position secret. Here Jerry stepped into the breach. He too wanted to know what the ground was like, so he said he would take a jeep across, arguing that one jeep would never be spotted if it went circumspectly, because of its low silhouette.

So off we went into no-man's-land, keeping to a rough bearing and exploring the small folds and hollows, noting the state and direction of the various tracks. We were right out in the blue, edging towards the enemy side, when Jerry stopped and pointed at two men crawling on a little hill. A careful look showed British tin hats, so we relaxed.

Jerry found a convenient hill and got out his telescope to study the enemy positions. He was a great person for the telescope. Most people preferred the handier binoculars, but the telescope has a much greater magnification and is first class as an observing instrument if there is enough cover to hide it while you take a long, steady look. I kept lookout while he became absorbed in penetrating the veil. In a quarter of an hour he had collected a sheaf of new facts about the position that no one had even suspected.

A little further on we caught a glimpse of an armoured car and shot into a fold, out of sight, creeping stealthily up to study its lines. 'One of ours,' said Jerry. It was one of 127 Field Regiment's OP trucks. We approached cautiously and exchanged news, then we set course back to 152 Brigade again, where the Colonel was able to give George Murray a route for his advance and a picture of the country in general with most valuable details of the position. He was always scouting about like this. One Infantry Battalion Commander described him as 'The man I meet coming back at dusk from the place I'm wondering if it's safe to go to in the dark!' To him it was part of the day's work – he wanted to know what was at the back of the hill, so he went there to see.

The Regiment now carried out its first and only withdrawal. The troops were most puzzled when they found they were going backwards and expended a lot of soldiers' wit on it. 'Monty must be 'ome on leave – 'e wont 'arf create about it. 'E said there wasn't goin' to be no more withdrawals!'

In fact, we were preparing for the three anxious days, and had been told to get our 'backs to the wall'. Having a very long front to hold, the General decided to occupy three separate 'keeps', each with a Brigade Group. George Murray said there wasn't room for us in his keep, and we were told to go back a couple of miles and form a keep of our own. We were warned that the expected tank battle was likely to happen all round us and told to kill as many tanks as possible. That meant siting the guns in a primary anti-tank role, which made our normal job more difficult. That had to be accepted – guns are not good if the tanks hit them first.

We had quite a nice setup and were full of confidence, but the General said we were too valuable to be left out on a limb and ordered us into 'Fort George', the 152 Brigade keep. This gave us quite a problem. We had come to the first of the days when Rommel might attack, and the Division could not afford to be caught with our fire power unavailable through the guns being 'on wheels'.

Eventually the Intelligence Branch told us that they estimated that the attack would come by 3.00 pm or not at all, so I was told to prepare the new position, wait until 4.00 pm, and then slip one Battery forward at a time. Bang on the hour 492 pulled out and rolled on its way. Then, just as the next was to move, John Inglis, from his OP, called for a big dollop of fire – the attack was coming in. Hastily I cancelled the rest of the move and got on the wireless to find out the form and tell the Colonel. At that moment communications with the OP broke down. The Colonel was out of touch! So there we were, 'caught with our trousers down', as the saying goes, the Regiment split in two: not the easiest situation to control.

It proved to be only a feint. The Colonel got a message through that the move was to proceed. Then the General took a hand again when the other Batteries were on the move. 'You are still too exposed,' he said. 'Get the guns right into the keep!' So with the guns almost on our heels, we had to do a lightning reconnaissance to find new positions, and direct the Batteries to them. Their training was evidently better than we ever admitted, as it all went smoothly with hardly a check.

My troubles were not over. In the hurry I sited RHQ badly, too near the perimeter, and had to move them again at first light. That made me very unpopular with the Signal Section as they had to reel in all the phone cables and re-lay in a hurry, the likelihood of attack becoming greater every minute.

Next morning, the fun started. At 7.00 am precisely the Bosch opened fire and started the advance. It was 6 March – the day that Montgomery had chosen for Rommel to shoot his bolt. Monty must have been rubbing his hands with glee. Everything was ready. The New Zealanders and 7th Armoured Division and the 11th (Independent) Guards Brigade were all in position and we had all the ammunition we could possibly use.

We used it, too! All day long we blazed at the attacking Infantry, and every attack was broken and sent reeling back before it could reach our Infantry. We fired as a Regiment, we fired Uncles – the three Regiments on one target – and we fired with the Mediums. Our fire was murder! Only on 154 Brigade's front did they penetrate, killing some of the 126 Regiment's men with rifle fire, until the 7th Argyles counterattacked and drove them out.

The tanks came in on the front of the Guards Brigade and 7th Armoured Division chiefly and were routed. Fifty out of one hundred and fifty were destroyed. 76 Anti-Tank Regiment RA and the Guards Anti-Tank Platoons accounted for most of them. At one place the Guards were short of mines, so they put up a wire strand marked with red triangles – a dummy minefield. That was gloriously successful. Seven tanks turned sharply to avoid it and followed it round to find a gap. This brought them into a little valley covered by four anti-tank guns (whether Gunners or Infantry I do not know).[2] The guns held their fire until the leader was only a hundred yards away, then they let fly and destroyed five with six shots. The Troop Commander said afterwards that he wanted to wait for all seven, but the Infantry were getting a bad time from them so he thought he had better put paid to them. A man of iron nerve.

By late afternoon the attack had failed in complete disorder and we were able to rest our nearly red-hot guns and weary gun detachments. That was 'the One-Day Battle', Rommel's last desperate thrust. From then on he was on the defensive and we could prepare for the assault on the Mareth Line without hindrance.

Notes

[1] Significant as the first large-scale meeting of American and German forces in the Second World War, the untested and allegedly poorly led American troops suffered heavy casualties and were pushed back over fifty miles from their positions west of Faid Pass in a rout. In the aftermath, the US Army instituted sweeping changes from unit-level organisation to the replacing of Commanders. When they next met, in some cases only weeks later, the US forces were considerably more effective.

[2] They were 76 Anti-Tank Regiment RA.

Chapter 14

The Mareth Line[1]

Then shook the hills with thunder riven,
Then rushed the steed, to battle driven,
And louder than the bolts of heaven
Far flashed the red artillery

T Campbell

128 [H] Regiment RA, March 1943

We stayed in 'Fort George' for several days after the battle and received quite a lot of attention from a battery of German 80-mm guns. 492 got the worst of it and had several casualties. One of their Subalterns, Kerry, was particularly unlucky. He left the Division to volunteer for war service when we were in Scotland and then moved heaven and earth to get back when he heard we were in the Desert. The very day he arrived, a shell splinter took his hand off.

I found myself in the centre of the target of one outburst and did not like it at all. The shelling seemed to go on forever as I tried to make my body sink through the ground, sweating with fright. Shell fire is most alarming. It shakes morale to the core, but it is a very wasteful way of killing people because so much of the burst goes either up in the air or into the ground. Its effect is quite unpredictable: one Officer saw a big shell burst beside a jeep a hundred yards away. To his surprise, the occupants got up and shook themselves, none the worse for it. A second later, his own driver fell dead at his feet, hit by a splinter from that same shell.

One day about a dozen of us were crowded into the Command Post, which we had burrowed into the hillside, when the shelling started. The first shot just missed a light anti-aircraft gun and the rest fell all round us. I was sitting in a kind of porch of sandbags, there being no room inside, when one fell just the other side of the sandbag wall and exactly six feet from where I was sitting. It made all our ears sing, and covered us with dust, but no one was hit. The bits all flew forward and straight through MacPhee's bivvy, tearing his belongings to smithereens. He was so angry when he came back and seemed to think it was our fault! But this was understandable, because one's few belongings in war are all necessities, so their loss means the loss of one's personal comforts, almost of one's home.

The jumping-off place for the attack on the Mareth Line was a conglomeration of wadis that afforded concealment on the far side of the wide plain that we were now overlooking. It was planned to move there the night before the attack because it was no place to hold for any length of time, all isolated as it was by day. But there were many preparations to be made there beforehand, so the advance parties were slipped across by night with orders to lie doggo by day and get on with the job under cover of darkness.

We got there and fitted our trucks into little niches in a deep wadi, covering them with moss and undergrowth until they were so well hidden that even the owners had difficulty in finding them again.

It was a nice peaceful existence, though we kept on the *qui vive*, there being only a thin screen of Infantry in front of us, and one of our OPs. In the dark, the ammunition lorries would sneak forward to us, to be led to the gun positions that we had chosen. We had a road to make, with an improvised bridge made out of oil drums and stones cemented with mud. There were dugouts and slit-trenches to be dug, gun pits to be built. Everything had to be tidy and hidden by dawn, so there was enough work to make the nights pass quickly. In the daytime I would walk round to see that the camouflage was right and pass on the plans for the next night.

On the last night we had everything finished and ship shape quite early, so I went to my bivvy, hidden in a cranny, got into my pyjamas and hit the hay. Just as it was getting light I woke with a start as a big voice boomed through the wadi. It was the General's. Normally I was pleased to see him, but this time the circumstances were wrong. The booming was to the effect that: 'If you go to sleep without taking elementary military precautions, you will end in the BAG! You'll be walking to ITALY!'

Here was I, in my pyjamas, within easy reach of a probing patrol. I was dressed in less than a minute.

He had gone by the time I had found Sergeant Gray, who was on duty with our defence posts. 'It's all right, Sir,' he said, 'the General didn't know we was 'ere until he 'ad my rifle in 'is stommick! Very pleased 'e was, too, that we see'd 'un before 'e 'seed us!' The object of his anger was a carrier crew of the Seaforth, whose vehicle had broken down. They found we were there, so went to sleep without posting a lookout.

It may have struck you that the modern General does not command his army from the rear, as is sometimes supposed. You never knew when or where to expect Douglas Wimberley. He would pop up in the most unexpected places, a huge, gaunt man folded into a jeep with his knees up to his chin, an enormous Tam o' Shanter pancaked on his head. He had boundless energy and drive and his voice could be heard above any din of battle. We all went in considerable awe of him, and there was not a man in the Division who did not know and admire 'Tartan Tam'.

His great love was the Highland Division, to him the embodiment of the Fighting Spirit of Scotland, entrusted with the honour of a hundred generations of the world's toughest fighters. It irked him that there should be a high proportion of English in the Gunner Regiments, and at one time he threatened to replace them with Scots. When we told him that we just could not give up so many trained men in return for untried recruits he gave in.

For all that, he was never anything but friendly to us 'mercenaries in the pay of the King of Scotland'. He tolerated us and in the end admitted that we had deserved our places in the Division.

The attack on Mareth took place on 20 March. Our Infantry had to do a small preparatory attack to gain a bit of ground that overlooked the route of the main attack. That was made by the 50th Tyne and Tees Division. We shot for both attacks and had a very busy time, but it was rather humdrum as we had no OPs to tell us how the affair was going.

What might have been a tragedy, when a gun burst, was saved by sheer good luck. A fragment of the breech weighing over 50 pounds landed harmlessly at RHQ 400 yards away and no one was hurt. A bursting gun can cause heavy casualties.

After very heavy fighting, the attack was called off. It is said that Montgomery had been woken up at 2.00 am and told the bad news. He told them to abandon the frontal attack and set in motion one by a flanking force that had been secretly advancing through the Matmata hills. Then he went to sleep again. Such calmness is one of the marks of a really great commander. His job was to plan the battle and to have alternatives ready, such as this flanking move. Having done that, his work lay two or more months ahead, planning for the next affair. He could do no good by lying awake worrying. Rest was essential to his health, so he rested.

The flanking force made fine progress through the country that the opposing side thought was passable only to men on foot and pack mules. In due course Rommel found himself out-flanked and pulled out in a hurry.

People who had time to examine the defences said it was a good thing that the flank move had succeeded as the front was pretty nearly impregnable, with massive concrete posts, well-sited wire entanglements and, above all, the colossal obstacle of the Zigzaou. Once more Montgomery's famous 'left hook' had come off.

Notes

[1] The Mareth Line broaadly followed the Wadi Zigzaou for 35 kilometres (22 miles) inland from the sea to the Matuâta Hills, crossing the coastal road. The wadi provided a natural defence line, with steep banks some 70 feet (21 metres) high in places. It was reputed to be the most difficult military defence line in North Africa.

Chapter 15

The Battle of the Wadi Akarit

The midnight brought the signal sound of strife,
The morn the marshalling in arms, – the day
Battle's magnificently stern array!

Lord Byron

128 [H] Regiment RA, March/April 1943

The day we moved from Mareth we were nearly rushed off our feet. I was given position after position to prepare, only to be told to leave it and push on to the next. The General was like a flea on a hot shovel. 'Get the Infantry off the road and let the Gunners through!' 'Clear the road for the tanks!' 'Where are those Camerons! How can they get past when those tanks are blocking the road?'

He met me laying out a gun position. 'What are you doing here? You should be at least ten miles on, push on!' So on we went. The Gunners had again been given priority on the road, so my party hummed along until we found we were ahead of everybody except some half dozen carriers leading the advanced guard.

'Generals should stick to commanding Divisions,' said George Murray, almost shaken out of his imperturbability. 'He's been commanding my Brigade all morning – and now he has taken over the Camerons. I might as well have a rest!'

As I was cruising about choosing a gun position, McLean my driver, suddenly exclaimed, 'There's enemy over there, sir!'

'Don't be stupid,' I retorted. Reconnaissance takes a lot of concentration when one is trying to fit the guns into the allotted area so that they are able to do their job properly. My drivers soon learnt not to be chatty on these occasions. My mind was so much occupied that I hardly heard McLean, and I certainly did not take in what he said.

This time he was not to be squashed. 'I tell you, there *is* enemy over there – lots of them. They look like Eyeties to me'.

That made the penny drop and we zipped into a small wadi out of sight and crawled up its side to have a careful look round. He was right – the place was lousy with them. Their one idea seemed to be to surrender, and I think they had thrown their arms away. But there is always the chance that the mood of such people will change if they find you are alone, so I was very relieved to spot one of our OP armoured cars in the distance. We swanned up to it in the jeep and got the officer, Stephenson of 492, to round them up and hand them over to the Battery when it arrived. The Italians had long lost their zest for war.

We caught up with the Germans holding a strong position in the 'Gabes Gap', a bottleneck north of the little town of that name. Here there was a dominant feature called Roumana, with an almost impassable wadi, the Wadi Akarit, running from it to the sea. A well-made anti-tank ditch added to the position's strength and a broad flat plain in the front made approach to it difficult.

Covered gun positions were few and far between, but the Colonel found some little hollows which just gave the troops cover from Roumana, and no more. It was a funny sort of position, rather topsy-turvy. RHQ was a mile in front of the guns because there was no cover for it in its more usual place behind them. The approaches to it were in full view of the distant Roumana so I had to take special precautions to get the trucks in. I took the Officer who was to lead them in to a safe spot and pointed out a tree some way off, telling him not to pass that spot until it was dark enough that he could no longer see the tree.

That proved quite a good definition of dusk, but it did not save them from being shelled. By some mischance the enemy opened fire just as they had passed the tree, making quite a lurid war-like picture as the little column of some twenty vehicles loomed out of the dusk with shells banging and crashing all round them. I was afraid there would be heavy casualties, but the only damage was a hole in the radiator of the doctor's car. The luridness was added to by a brilliant white flare dropped by a hostile aircraft. That was usually a prelude to a bombing attack, and we felt rather tense for a bit, but none came.

The men were quite elated at passing through a sharp bit of shelling with no one the worse for it. Bombardier Beales remarked to someone: 'It does you good to have one or two near you sometimes; give you a bit of excitement – keeps you up to the mark, like.' My old Fordson car was not so lucky. She was standing a bit apart, by herself, when a shell landed right under her stern and played old Harry with the back axle and chassis, damaging her beyond repair. So passed an old Veteran. She came all the way from Scotland to find a grave in Tunisia. She had been a grand car, only a two-wheel drive, but she only got stuck once and handled like a jeep. She carried a battle scar that we were very proud of, from the Leptis Magna affair, where a shell splinter hit her windscreen but failed to penetrate. 'Them's too damn close,' said Driver Taylor at the time. 'You nearly lost your batman.' He was quite right too: Pike was sitting in the front seat, and without the windscreen he would have had a hole in his skull. Her engine was undamaged and within twelve hours it was in the car of Hugh Perry, then commanding 127. That was its third car, as I got it out of the Padre's 15 hundredweight when he drove over a mine at Mersa Brega.

Pike and Taylor were near the car when her end came. There was a lot of shelling at the time, but Pike pulled my kit out of her in spite of it and was most annoyed with Taylor for hustling him away to safety before he had found my scarf. He went back for it later and got shelled again. One did not deserve such devotion to duty on one's own behalf. Pike was like that. On one occasion before Alamein he had just dug a hole and pitched my bivvy in it when a shell fell over 100 yards away. He stood gazing thoughtfully at the drifting smoke for a few seconds, then he remarked quietly, 'I see we must go down deeper than this,' pulled down the tent, and started digging towards Australia.

We started the attack at 4.00 am, an unusual time, which caught the forward defence napping. But not so the remainder. There were Germans on Roumana and they fought desperately all day. There was attack and counterattack and from RHQ the hill was completely enveloped in smoke and dust. We engaged target after target, for all three Brigades.

The 7/10 Argylls had a particularly tough job crossing the wadi and anti-tank ditch, and their CO, Lorne Campbell, was awarded the Victoria Cross for this battle. The citations for it ran into fourteen paragraphs. The last was as follows:

> This Officer's gallantry and magnificent leadership when his now tired men were charging the enemy with the bayonet and fighting them at a hand grenade range are worthy of the highest honour, and can seldom have been surpassed in the long history of the Highland Brigade.

All the Battalions fought magnificently and the *Times* described the battle as 'one of the greatest heroic achievements of the war'. The Divisional History says: 'There can be no doubt that the day marked the fiercest fighting that the Division had experienced in this campaign.'

Our OP Officers and men gave them fine support. John Connel steadily directed fire for the 2nd Seaforth all day. Jim Henderson, with the 5th Seaforth, found himself the only unwounded officer with utter chaos all round him. He rose to the occasion, rallied and reorganised the remnant of the Company, and led them to retake the position they had been driven from. I'm glad to say that he was awarded the Military Cross.

Taffy Wilcox of 307 Battery had a fine OP on Roumana and lashed the enemy with fire, at the same time wirelessing back excellent reports of the battle. His last message told of 'hundreds of enemy coming in to surrender with their hands up'. Unfortunately, the would-be prisoners found he was alone, so they took him prisoner instead.

Norman Owen, 307's Commander, saved the situation for 2nd Seaforth by a clever and daring bit of shooting. The enemy had regained a small knoll and placed there a nest of machine guns that defied any attempt to recapture it. The knoll was the key to further advance, so just had to be taken. Our troops were so close to it that there was a real danger of hitting them instead of the enemy, if artillery were brought to bear. Norman was equal to this. Very carefully, he ranged on to the target, starting well beyond it and gradually shortening the range. Then, when he was satisfied with the ranging, he brought down the fire of a troop on it so accurately that the defenders' nerve failed and they were easy meat when the Seaforth charged them again.

Late in the afternoon, when the battle was over, the Colonel and I went forward to find new gun positions. While I was reconnoitring these, seven large Heinkel bombers returning from a raid flew up the valley at a height of 300 feet. Obviously they did not know that their people had been driven back and were flying low to evade our fighters. Our LAA were on to these sitting ducks like lightning. Five were shot down and in almost as many seconds. Two of them toppled and crashed right in front of us. It was all over in an instant. As they hit the ground a gigantic column of flame shot 100 feet into the air, and then they burnt steadily with black smoke pouring out of them. The rest were caught by a Battery further forward.

Ill luck struck us the next morning. The Colonel's party inadvertently parked in a minefield. When they moved, their big Signals lorry disintegrated with a roar, the body flying apart from the chassis. A signaller was killed and the driver wounded, but the Officer in the back escaped with a shaking. He was saved because the floor was covered with their kitbags, which insulated him from the blast.

After that we pushed on with hardly a pause until we bumped the enemy rear guard in the afternoon. The Regiment then did a 'Crash' action – into action from the line of march as fast as ever possible. This is a horse artillery manoeuvre that one practices in peace for the verve and élan and instantaneous reaction that is engenders, but seldom has the chance to execute in war.

The cry – 'Action!' – with the map reference of a target came down on the wireless and the guns of the leading battery roared off the track and dropped their trails. I had just had time to wave the other two to each side of the track before the first gun fired. That first round was off in under three minutes, which was not bad at all. Coming into action in war is usually a slow and deliberate affair, generally at night, with a slow, cold-blooded efficiency. The rear guard left in a hurry.

Two days later Sfax fell. We pulled into a rest area, opened the Messes and settled down to a little comfort. After being continuously on the move for nearly three months, it was nice to give up picnicking and have a 'communal feeding' for a change. After a week of this, we had the CRA and Brigadier Murray to dinner one evening. They assured us that there was no possibility of a move for at least a month.

Next morning, at 9.00 am, we were told to be in action miles away at 11.00 am!

Chapter 16

Journey's End

O Captain! my Captain! our fearful trip is done;
The ship has weathered every rack, the prize we sought is won

Walt Whitman

128 [H] Regiment RA, April 1943

We had again arrived at one of those awkward places where the enemy had ensconced himself in hills overlooking a wide plain. A big volcanic feature called Takrouna [see plate] standing alone in the plain provided an outpost position that made the main position even stronger. Happily for us the New Zealanders, in a most heroic action, took Takrouna before we arrived so we were spared a most difficult and costly assault, and were able to use it as an OP.

For some reason we supported 154 Brigade for a time instead of our usual 152. I relieved the Colonel for some days as Liaison Officer there and quite enjoyed my stay. I created quite a stir at my first breakfast there by asking for sugar with my porridge. The dyed-in-the-wool Scots looked appalled at my request, but the English Commander of their Anti-Tank Battery spoke up and said, 'Thank heaven someone has at last dared to ask!' That broke the ice completely.

We were in cactus country, where the fields were divided by hedges of growing cacti – a most effective barrier, and most unpleasant to collide with in the dark. The tall hedges shielded the camp from the enemy in the distant hills, but there were plenty of 'windows' through which we could observe, although the distance was too great to spot movement. When time was a bit heavy on our hands we used to collect at one of the windows and I would put down some fire for their amusement. One target was a special favourite, numbered 'Monkey 34' (Monkey being then the phonetic word for 'M'). A patrol said there was an OP there, so we delighted in making life miserable for the unfortunate German observer.

In due course 152 Brigade came back into the picture and I was sent to liaise with them. On presenting myself to Brigadier Murray I asked him what sort of a day he had had. 'Day!' he said. 'Do you realise it's Easter Sunday, and the worst Easter Sunday I've ever spent? Why, he landed a shell just where you are standing. Come inside before he lands another there!' 152 were very excitable because an Arab had stuck a red flag in a tree, and almost immediately they had been heavily shelled. The Arab said the Germans told him to mark the place his house was with a flag so that they would know and not shell it. I think the Arab did it in good faith, not knowing anything about aiming and ranging marks. But 152 were convinced he was a spy, so he was probably shot.

I went up Takrouna one early morning to visit the OP and to call on the 5th Camerons. Said Jerry, when describing the route to me, 'When you get to the bend where the black rock juts out, stop and smoke a cigarette: that's about the time the Bosch starts his morning "hate" – it's better to sit quiet while that's on!' The view was magnificent, reminding me of looking down from an aeroplane.

I found the Camerons' HQ in a cave right next to the rubbish heap of the little village that crowned the hill. It had a pretty good pong of its own, but that was put in the shade by the stench from some long-dead enemy corpses that the New Zealanders had left there. The Camerons kept complaining about the atmosphere, but it did not seem to strike them that dead men are best buried.

After a few days we were told to hand over the position to the Free French Forces. Their Commanding Officer came round with me and criticised everything, apparently knowing little about anything, but he finally took over our exact positions without a single alteration. 'They are all like that,' said the British Liaison Officer with them. 'They will chatter interminably and argue about the very stones on the ground. Just let them chatter away and they will end by taking whatever you give them.'

I took him up a hill to point out the enemy position by shooting at some of them, firing at targets that we had recorded previously. When I called up RHQ I found that the Regiment was already doing business, so I was rather flummoxed. My opposite number in 126 Regiment saved the situation. 'What targets do you want?' said Tom Ogilvie. 'We've got all your records.' I gave the numbers of three targets, including our old friend Monkey 34, and asked for them to be engaged at noon, one after the other.

The Liaison Officer then took me aside and most agitatedly begged me not to point out the target until the shells had fallen. 'They would be terribly scornful if the shells were a bit outside the bull!' I did not deign to answer that, just staked my all on the accuracy of 126's guns. At noon precisely I pointed at 'Monkey 34', and as I pointed the top of the hill suddenly erupted and the smoke curled gracefully upwards from twenty-four shell bursts. That was something that even Monsieur le Commandant could not criticise.

After handing over to the French we moved nearer to the enemy hills and went into action near Enfidaville, a pretty little French town in the foothills surrounded by acres and acres of olive groves. The First Army were doing their best to close their end of the trap, but just couldn't quite shut it, so for some days there was a sort of stalemate. The enemy were hemmed in on all sides in the Cap Bon Peninsula and the end was in sight.

For political reasons it was desirable that the First Army should share the glory of the 'kill', so Montgomery was ordered to reinforce them with two of our Divisions, and the final thrust was made by the First Army. Any attack from our side would be very difficult and costly in men, so we did not grudge sending the reinforcements.

In these last few days of the campaign we had a feeling like that of the last week of term. One could not help feeling 'How ghastly to be bumped off now, right at the end of the show!' It even made me get up one night when a shell fell in the distance and pull my bedding off my comfortable camp bed into the slit-trench ... just in case! Signalman Knowles was killed in those last days. An 88-mm shell landed right by his truck. He was a fine type of soldier with years and years of service with the Territorial Army behind him.

At last, after a busy time firing for all and sundry divisions, we got the order to pull out of the line and go to Algeria, rest, refit and train for another campaign elsewhere. We were not to see the crowning of our efforts – the surrender at Cap Bon – but I do not think anyone was particularly sorry. We had pulled our weight to the best of our ability and were quite ready to let others finish the job. As we pulled out of action, for the last time in North Africa, 307 Battery were smartly shelled, so the enemy had the last word. Happily, there were no casualties.

There was a great feeling of elation when the final crushing victory was announced. We had taken part in the longest and fastest advance known to history: over two thousand miles in something like eight months, against a stubborn and skilful enemy. From the time of his defeat at Alamein he had been so harried that only once was he able to strike, except in defence.

The victory was won by a splendid team: the RAF, the Navy, the Tanks, the Guns, and the Infantry, backed to the hilt by the Supply Service. A break in any one of these links could have lost us the campaign. Because it was a team effort, it is impossible to say that any one arm made the victory possible, but most people will agree that never before had the Artillery been so effective or so well handled. I prefer to leave to others the assessment of its value. Perhaps it will suffice to quote Montgomery. He said, 'The Gunners were terrific!'

Chapter 17

Algerian Holiday

Why should I keep holiday
When other men have none?
Why but because, when these are gay,
I sit and mourn alone.

Ralph Waldo Emerson

128 [H] Regiment RA, May/June 1943

We spent a few days resting in a camp from which we could hear the battle booming away, fifteen miles off. Then the trek to Algeria began. We passed through Kairouan, Tebessa, Sbeitla and Setif and stopped at a little town on the sea called Bougie.

The frontier between Tunisia and Algeria is reached by a steep and twisty climb to a pass in the mountains. As the road mounts higher and higher you come to a pine tree belt, very like the hills of Mumaon in India. The peacefulness and stillness of the pines was quite delightful. There was a kind of expectancy in the silence, fulfilled as a gentle breeze made the forest quiver with a muffled, distant roar that gently surged towards us until the treetops swayed and bent, and peaceful silence reigned again.

And as we topped the pass, the countryside lay spread before us like a Promised Land; a land of hills and downs, and trees in leaf, and great swathes of scarlet Flanders' poppies, like bloody gashes in the growing corn. The local Arab seemed a better type, and herds of well-bred horses grazed the fields. No more dusty desert trails for us. We'd left its sands a thousand miles behind.

The Arab children shouted *'Huitième Armée! Armée huitième – sigrette? Une petite sigrette? Chocolat?'* A pretty French girl driving a nice pair of cobs in a buggy at first looked coy and turned away, then turned again, smiled and waved a *'Bravo! Armée Huitième!'* French children crowded round us, questioning us about the sand leaking from the mine–protective sandbags in our trucks. 'From Tripoli'? they asked. 'No, from Libya',' we said. Then they fell upon it and took great handfuls home to keep.

After Setif the road led us through a deep and twisty gorge, round hairpin bends, through tunnels and along the edge of many a precipice with a rocky stream below. It was a land of oak trees, mostly cork oak, and the soft leafy green was a delight to eyes used to wrinkling against the desert glare.

Then came the sparkling blue of the sea as we reached the coast road, here marked '*Route Corniche, Etroite, Sinueuse, et Dangereuse*'. And so it was. We first saw Bougie when we were still some miles away, creeping along a twisting shelf, the sheer side of the hill above us and the wavelets creaming far below. Most attractive it looked, set in a little bay with white houses standing row upon row on the steep side of a hill, their red roofs contrasting with the green of the trees.

We settled down to a life of comparative luxury in a camp among green bushes on some rough ground well clear of the town. Our Mess tent was set up again, embellished with an awning of scrim that gave it a kind of veranda – somewhere to sit with the sea breezes cooling the heat of the sun. The rations were still the old bully and biscuit and M&V stew, but we managed to buy some eggs and fresh vegetables and sometimes some bread, so we almost began to live for eating instead of eating to live. There was plenty of work to be done, but there was bathing as well. Bathing was as perfect as anywhere in the world: the water was so warm that one could stay in it all the afternoon and then lie in the sun to dry.

There was an aircraft landing ground right by us that often brought visitors. One of these was an American in a light plane of the Auster type. He greeted us with, 'Say, fellas, is this Algiers?'

We told him it wasn't.

He replied, 'Gee! I thought it looked kinda small, but that goddam hill looks just like what they said I'd see ... Well, s'long fellas, I'm on my way!'

He was only 200 miles out in his reckoning.

One day a really big plane landed, so big that it only just managed to stop short of a vineyard at the end of the runway. Thinking that it might be the Colonel hitchhiking back from a week's leave in Cairo, we hurried down to meet it. The door opened, and out stepped Vivien Leigh, Beatrice Lillie, Dorothy Dickson, Dorothy Hyson, Kay Young, Leslie Henson and several other stage celebrities. We were the only reception committee. They explained that they were a travelling company putting on shows for the Forces. As a rule, they travelled by road, but the night before they had dined with General Eisenhower and he had lent them a plane for this stage of the journey. It was soon obvious that no one in Bougie knew of this change of plan, and that no one was coming to meet them, so we delightedly stepped into the breach and invited them to lunch.

How 'Ossy', our catering member, managed to eke out a lunch for seven to feed seventeen only he knows. It was very tasty too. We had tinned salmon and salad, meat sandwiches intended for a training scheme, and tins of peaches. For drink there was beer, lemon squash and gin. The only thing we did not put before them was our last half bottle of whisky, which we were keeping for when Jerry returned. But old Leslie Henson sniffed unhappily at the beer and gin and suddenly disappeared into the curtained-off back of the tent, where the stores were kept, and bless me if he did not rout out that half bottle and place it triumphantly on the table! He was so amusing we did not begrudge him it.

The party went with a swing. We were thrilled at entertaining such company out of the blue, and they were intrigued to find themselves in such primitive society, eating off a strange assortment of tin plates, plastic plates and chipped china ones with cracked tumblers and handleless cups to match. They found it difficult to understand that our homes were the little bivvies that had to be entered on hands and knees and that the raggedy Mess tent with the sacking awning was our only other shelter from the elements. They were pleasant and interesting people, and a welcome change from our own company. They gave us special tickets for their show, which we should have missed otherwise because of a hush exercise, so altogether it was a most pleasant interlude.

*

So far it must seem that we were purely on holiday, but actually we were working to a fairly intensive programme. We were refitting and re-equipping and preparing for a landing in an unspecified country. We had the deck of a ship with all its fittings marked on the ground on which to practice loading and stowing and lashing our guns and vehicles. When we were competent at that, we did it over and over again on a real landing craft. Finally, we embarked everything and tried our hand at getting it ashore on a shelving beach.

All that was interspersed with normal training and work. One day I went out to find a place to calibrate the guns (i.e. to compare the shooting of each with the standard gun of the Regiment). We drove along a little mountain track and really seemed to get to the top of the world. We were two or three thousand feet up and could look down on the tops of hills that had seemed enormous from below. Little villages directly beneath us were so far down that they were hazy in the distance.

It was soon obvious that a calibration shoot was out of the question in such country, so we stopped and just admired the view. I have never seen anything like it. It was not the craggy massifs of a mountain range, nor was it the slopes and valleys of down land: it was just hill after hill after rounded hill in all directions, purpling into misty haze in the distance, spreading before us like the waves of a monstrous, petrified sea. I could have stayed there forever, just gazing.

As well as practising the practical side of the landing, we refurbished old skills and trained for fitness – mostly by mountain hikes – and we attended lectures and demonstrations on models. We soon knew the landscape of the invasion country almost as well as if we had been there, though only the Colonel and I knew the secret yet – that it was Sicily we were to invade. Many deceptions were practised, for the benefit of possible spies. One of these was the attachment of Greek Army Officers to some units in the hope that this would get round to the enemy and make him jump to a false conclusion. It is said that one of these Greeks was so convinced that we were going into Greece that when the coast came in sight he started recognising landmarks of his own country – in Sicily!   A convincing proof that the secret was well kept.

Some of the lectures were at Djelli where Divisional HQ was, twenty miles away – two and a half hours, that is, by the Route Corniche. One lecture started early in the morning so that the Colonel and I decided to go the night before and stay at a little auberge called the Hotel du Cap, about halfway. We were surprised, and rather annoyed, to find that in the bay below the hotel – which was open to anyone – all our latest top-secret landing craft and other devices were being tested for all to see. In fact, I was introduced to the latest amphibious lorry by the daughter of the house, a pretty and charming young lady of six years, whose name appeared to be 'Mercredi'. She took me under her wing – or to be more exact, parked her bottom in my lap and told me all about it. '*Voila! C'est un auto-bateau, il court sur la terre et flotte sur la mer.*' She was a pleasant child. Never shall I forget her look of amazement when I got my genders wrong. She would firmly correct me: '*Le bateau – pourquoi dites vous la? Ce ne'est pas la!*' Perhaps I might have learnt to talk a little French if I had stayed there a little longer.

During this rest period I was lucky enough to be sent to Porte-aux-Poules, close to Oran, to watch an American Combat Team (Brigade Group) demonstrate a beach landing. It was a journey of 150 miles, so we expected to go by air from Algiers, but there was no plane available so we did the whole trip by car. Tom Ogilvie of 126 Regiment, Donald McKelvie of the Seaforth and myself formed a party and travelled together.

The country we passed through was breathtakingly lovely and some of the little villages were most picturesque and attractive. One of these had the lovely name of 'Tizzy Ouzu', which I shall never forget. I must admit to getting tired of a long, long stretch of very narrow twisty cliff road. There was barely room for two cars to pass, and it really was hair raising when you met another car on a corner, particularly as we were on the side nearest the cliff edge. But not until we were nearly there did we meet any trouble. When it did come, Donald was lucky to get away with it: a huge American ten-tonner brushed his truck over the edge without even noticing it. He and the driver both jumped clear, but he got a nasty knock on the knee. Then my car broke down, so we all crowded into Tom's and finished the journey without further incident. Our introduction to our American allies was rather spoilt, though, by having to ask for a doctor for Donald and a recovery truck for two of our trucks.

We were then given pages and pages about the next day's scheme. Such is the difference between our two languages – particularly our military jargons – that I could hardly make sense of a single sentence.

The landing itself was interesting, but we did not learn much from it, chiefly because the commentary was unintelligible to our un-Americanised ears. Also, the Staff Officer looking after us was a very bad type of American – not a common type, I'm glad to say. He could talk about nothing but his own importance and the wealth of his ''ole man' ('makes shirts in Chicago – got more dough than he knows how to use'). He had one other topic: the inferiority of British equipment, our worn-out cars being the only examples that he had ever seen.

We were surprised and intrigued to find that none of them had heard of the Eighth Army. They had a vague notion that the British had been doing some fighting somewhere in Africa, but didn't know where. For our part we felt a bit scornful of their green-ness as they were newly arrived from Texas and had never heard a shot fired in anger. All except that one Staff Officer were nice enough fellows, so we parted good friends, each scratching his head at the idiosyncrasies of the other.

On the way back we decided that we would have a full day in Algiers and also that we would not stay in the awful transit camp that we had been pushed into on our way down. So we went to see a gentleman called the 'Town Major' and refused to leave his office until he had billeted us in the plush Aletti Hotel, which was reserved for Colonels and above. It did us very nicely. Four of us shared a room, but Tom and I each won the toss for a bed, so we were comfortable enough.

We had a most excellent dinner at the famous Oasis restaurant and then strolled round looking for something to amuse us. In particular, we thought a nice quiet drink would be most acceptable. The town was dead. I think there must have been a curfew in force. So we wandered about rather hopelessly until suddenly we met a British Military Policeman – they always seem to appear when I am in any sort of distress! 'Let's ask the Copper where we can get a drink,' said Tom. The Red Cap was most helpful. After scratching his head and looking thoughtful for a bit he said, 'The only place I can think of is the Sphinx: it's a licensed brothel, but they keep good whisky there.'

Thanking him, we went off to investigate. After passing through some twisty, dirty lanes and dark alleys we clambered up some broken stone steps and eventually found ourselves in a comfortable room with a well-stocked bar. 'Madam' was just closing, but she gave us our drinks – at a pretty stiff price – and we settled down to enjoy them.

Not for long. A door burst open and '*les girls*' came bouncing in, and tried to bounce us away with them, but we weren't having any and managed at last to convince them that we intended having our whisky in peace, do what they would. At that they all sat down, chattering like mad, most carefully adjusting their skirts so that no one could be unaware of the underwear they didn't wear. One or two were quite pretty and attractive, but not so the rest. They never stopped talking, and we were hard put to keep pace with the mixture of rapid French and broken English. Donald was a great source of interest because of his kilt. The prettiest of them questioned him at length about it, to no purpose because he couldn't talk French. At last she leapt to her feet and exclaimed: 'Ah! Me ondestand – you wear skirt because you same as me under 'eem – like dis?' Up came the skirt, and to be fair to her her beauty lost nothing by the display. Quick as a flash, she grabbed at his kilt with 'Me see, eet is true?' Doubtless she would have disproved her theory in no uncertain manner, but we dashed to Donald's rescue and hustled him safely home.

Back at Bougie we had a most harassing time re-equipping. I used to think that the time before a military operation would be one of rather breathless apprehension, but believe me, the administrative battle – the struggle to get what you need for the real thing – is usually such a strain that the start of the battle itself is a positive relief. Not that there is no apprehension in the last hour or two before zero. There is plenty. A Jock I met just before Alamein summed it up with: 'Och, 'twill be a'reet at tha time – but there's a mony willna live to tell tha tale ye ken.' It is a great moment when one has done all that can be done and there can be no more changes. Then one can stop worrying, put everything else out of mind and concentrate on the battle itself.

This particular administrative battle was one of the worst of its kind. We had to have new guns, new stores of all kinds and all vehicles not in first-class order were to be exchanged for new ones. That sounds very nice, and so it would have been if we could have drawn from the First Army base of Bizerta. But our supply line still went round the Cape of Good Hope, and the pipe had to be emptied before we could change over. That meant getting everything from Tripoli, when it had arrived there from Cairo, and Tripoli was 1,000 miles away at the end of a most indifferent road.

Nothing came according to plan in spite of the superhuman work of our Ordnance Chief, who travelled so much that he never knew whether he was in Tripoli, Bougie or Cairo. We got rid of our dud vehicles ... and then no replacements arrived. We sent parties to Tripoli to fetch the new guns ... and they came back empty handed. In the end we had to take the guns of a First Army Regiment, and was the Regiment angry? We nearly came to blows. Other Divisions were combed to find vehicles for us and gave us far worse ones than the ones we had given up. In fact, when we embarked we were far worse off than when we left Enfidaville, except that we had nearly new guns.

At last the time came to leave lovely Algeria, its idyllic bathing beaches, the Route Corniche and the glorious ever-present hills. Great secrecy was imposed. Only the Colonel and I knew where we were going: back to the dusty olive orchards round Sousse. We had still not been told the port of embarkation. This time we took the coast road past Djelli and went as far as Philippeville before turning inland to Constantine. The latter town is a most impressive sight as you approach it from below. It is built on two hills, joined by a great high single-span bridge over a deep chasm of a ravine. In the past it was an impregnable fortress, and I'm glad we did not have to storm it, even with our modern weapons.

Near Tebessa we were reminded that not even war could keep some locals from their pastime of stealing. Two of our men had blankets stolen from under them while they slept. Herbert Tree, the Brigade Major RA, had all his kit stolen except one shirt and a pair of shorts. These got steadily grubbier and grubbier until at last we could bear it no longer and clubbed together to provide him with a change of clothing.

At last the day arrived, and we loaded everything into LSTs (Tank Landing Ships). These had doors at the bows that opened like clam shells. The idea was to run them aground, as near the shore as they could get. Then the bows opened, a kind of drawbridge was lowered and the vehicles trundled ashore. Each engine was made waterproof so that it could go through four feet of water, though we hoped the ships would take us further than that into the shallows.

We left behind us the warfare of open space and limitless room for manoeuvre and were to meet the exact opposite – narrow wall-sided lanes, terraced vineyards and cramped fields, and, above all, people to get in the way and get hurt. We would no longer have the whole country to our warring selves. There would be refugees to pity and burning houses and all the horrors of war to cope with. If we had to go to war, we would have preferred to fight in the desert, but for all that there was a thrill in the knowledge that we were at last going to attack the soft underbelly of Europe.

Chapter 18

Into Sicily

All through the windless night the clipper rolled,
In a great swell with oily gradual heaves,
Which rolled her down until her time-bells tolled
Clang, and the weltering water moaned like beeves.

John Masefield

128 [H] Regiment RA, July 1943

Our flat-bottomed ship rolled and bucked like a bronco. Hyocine tablets protected us from seasickness, but it was a restless night as the movement at times nearly threw us out of our bunks. All that was forgotten when the coast of Sicily appeared like a cloud on the horizon.

We arrived off the extreme south eastern tip of the island at 11.00 am on 10 July 1943 and looked in vain for signs of war, but a miracle had happened. Instead of a beach made crazy with bursting shells and palls of smoke we saw a peaceful Mediterranean bay with hardly a soul in sight on the shore. The landing there was unopposed.

Anchored all round us on a glassy blue sea was a huge fleet of odd-looking ships, landing craft of all types, with a few orthodox vessels intermingled to give tone to the scene. Eagerly, we searched for landmarks – and there they were, as familiar as if we had seen them before, so well had we been briefed on models and air photos and maps. The lighthouse at Portopalo on the right hand and a big factory chimney on the left framed the picture for us, and we could even pick out the spots we had tentatively chosen from the photos to use as collecting areas for the trucks and guns when they rolled away from the beach.

About 4.00 pm we went in to land. The Captain said he would land us dry shod or bust the ship, and he made a very fine attempt. He got the little vessel going at about ten knots and simply charged the beach. I was up in the bows, holding on for dear life, but the shock when it came was a slight one. The ship slid up the sand of the shelving shore and came – quite literally – to a grinding halt. As she stopped, the drawbridge crashed down,

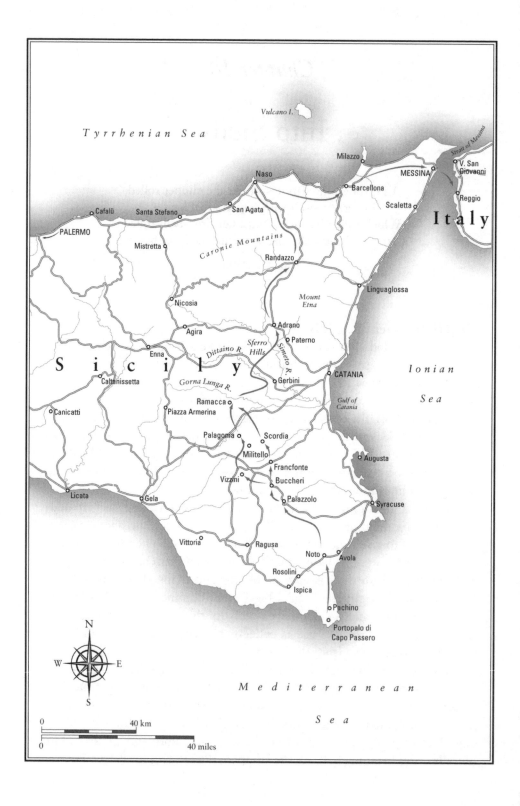

and the first truck rolled down the ramp, hit the water with a slight splash and growled through to dry land.

The light vehicles were on the top deck and had to be lowered to the hold by a lift, so we had to wait for our turn. It came at last. My jeep ran down the rather steep ramp, dipped its bonnet under the water – like a bather reluctantly getting his head wet – and levelled off in about two foot of water with twenty yards to go. In no time at all we were ashore and speeding off to the collecting area. It was a grand moment! We had arrived. Whatever might happen later, we had got ashore and could compete with the enemy in the way we now knew so well. He had missed his chance of catching us at a disadvantage.

For a time we stayed in a tomato field awaiting orders, and the tomatoes were ripe and excellent. Then Jerry came back from 152 Brigade and gave us the form. 492 were to go ahead with the 5th Camerons in the Advanced Guard and the rest of the Regiment would follow later. The Division was to advance parallel to the east coast, aiming for Catania.

It was dark when our turn came to move, and the first event of the moment was the loss of the bowl of my pipe, somewhere in the little town of Pachino. Cigarette smokers were well catered for, but NAAFI did not stock pipes, so the outlook on the new campaign was bleak as far as I was concerned.

While still musing on my unhappy future, I got the order to bring the Regiment into action, so could forget about it for the moment. The order called for a moonlight reconnaissance under quite new conditions. One had no idea what the land was like: was the ground hard or soft? What crops were there? What effect would growing vines have on our progress? And many other questions. This meant doing most of the job on foot, so that one could get the feel of it, but all went well, and soon the muzzles were stretching out towards the enemy as good guns should.

The night passed peacefully and in the morning we were able to take stock of our surroundings. The island seemed to be used to us already and our lorries cruised about as if they had been on the Sicilian roads for years instead of hours. The farmers and peasants were going about their affairs as if there had been no invasion. The men touched their caps politely and said '*Buon giorno*' while the women took a quick side-long glance, smiled and passed on. No one was in the least frightened of us.

Soon our Infantry met the enemy and we opened fire, but not for long. The order came to advance and for the whole day we pressed forward. Noto, Palazzolo and Buccheri were passed with hardly a halt. The only thing that delayed us was the narrowness of the roads and lanes.

We came upon some abandoned horse-drawn guns – most amateurishly sited – and in a hollow behind them were their wagon lines. The sight took one straight back to India in pre-war days. The picketing ropes were stretched between wagons or limbers just as ours used to be, and the horses were tied to them with the same old clove hitch. As soon as they saw us, the horses started whinnying and telling us it was long past feed time. The pity of it was that some of them were lying there dead from our shell fire and others had nasty wounds, though they did not seem to notice and were not the least backward in calling for food. It made one glad that we did not take horses to war.

Further on we found that an old soldier of the Seaforth had selected a pair and harnessed them to a wagon with most of the Battalion's kit on board. It was so enterprising of him that we almost forgave him for causing one more bottleneck to delay our guns.

We struck the first real resistance at Viccini and at Francofonte there was a pretty tough engagement with some German Paratroops. Our reconnaissance parties were strafed from the air near the latter place and when I came to the gun area-to-be I found the dry grass was burning furiously from the effect of our shelling.

I wirelessed the Colonel that only salamaders could live there, and he gave me another place, much further forward. In fact, this was the kind of place that you sense as not very safe; the kind of place where there is a feeling of being overlooked, in which nothing moves. Smoking debris shows that the battle has not long subsided and there is a kind of unfriendly silence there. There seemed no reason for not putting guns there, though, so I went on with the reconnaissance.

Presently I met 'Babe' MacMillan, the Brigadier who had relieved our much-liked George Murray. With him was the Brigade Major Harry Cumming-Bruce. They looked a bit surprised to see my party wandering around, and Harry asked what I was up to. 'Choosing gun positions,' was my answer.

Said the Brig, 'Don't you think this is a bit far forward for them?'

I told him that Jerry had given me this area, so I presume he had a reason for it.

'Well,' said he, 'we would love to have you, but this position is a bit uncertain. We've cleared the enemy off that ridge for the present, but we are very thin on the ground, and can't guarantee that he won't slip back in the night.'

I called up Jerry and told him, 'Our friends don't advise us to come here, what do you say?' The outcome was that we stayed where we were until next day.

That was almost my first meeting with MacMillan. He was quite a different type from Murray, much more highly strung, very efficient, more ruthless perhaps. No better as a Brigade Commander, I should say, but probably fitted with a better brain for higher command. We found him easy to get on with, but we missed old George a lot. He was invalided home from Algeria.

The next meeting was a few days later. The Colonel and I were scouting ahead one early morning in a very narrow walled lane, just behind the infantry Carrier Platoon that was in the lead, with the rest of the Brigade strung out behind us. The Carriers were feeling their way very cautiously and finally halted and stayed still for a long time. 'Come on, let's have breakfast!' said Jerry. So we got the little cooker going and made a jolly good job of frying the bacon and boiling the kettle. Just as we were finishing the Carriers moved on, leaving us as the cork in the bottle of the Eighth Army's progress. While we were frantically packing the stores away – it is unforgivable to block the road – up came Brigadier MacMillan.

'Jerry, what *are* you doing?' said he, obviously near the end of his tether from lack of sleep and ready to get really annoyed.

'Oh, we're just moving, Sir,' said Jerry. 'The carriers are only just ahead!'

He looked urgently round for something to distract the Brig's attention, and his eye fell on my kettle steaming gaily on a little fire.

'Have a cup of tea – Dick's got a kettle on the boil – we shall only be in the way if we tread on the carrier's heels!'

MacMillan's face broke into a smile. 'That would be just marvellous,' he said.

Now, that kettle was boiling for a purpose. You may remember that I had lost my pipe in Pachino – well, the night before, the Sergeant Major in charge of our LAD (vehicle repairers) had given me an old pipe of his remarking that he couldn't bear any longer the sight of a pipe smoker without a pipe. The boiling kettle that Jerry saw was hard at work sterilising that pipe!

What would *you* do? I made a quick decision: if I threw away that water it would take ages to boil some more, by which time all Jerry's pacification would be undone, so I made the tea. In self-defence, I must add that I tasted it before handing over the steaming mug, and there was only a slight taste of nicotine. Said MacMillan, 'Best cup of tea I ever tasted!' Some years later, when he was GO Commander in Chief Scottish Command and I a Staff Officer in Northern Command, I found myself showing him round a training area in Yorkshire. I told him the story behind the mug of tea in Sicily and he was most amused.

A mere five days after the landing, the Division was holding a line from Scordia to Palagonia – far better progress than had been expected. From there we advanced and by a series of bold moves seized first the crossings of the River Gorna Lunga, and then those of the Dittaino. The General intended then to capture the village and airfield of Gerbini and form a bridgehead across the River Simeto into the Catania Plain.

At Gerbini we struck unexpected and determined resistance from hard-fighting Germans. In the words of Douglas Wimberley, 'Emboldened by the speed at which we had gone forward we were now too hasty and took rather a bloody nose.' The battle was tough, and lasted several days, during which the Germans were gradually pushed back into the Sferro Hills. There the fighting was, if anything, more fierce: one of the Black Watch Battalions had a particularly sticky time when our gunfire set fire to the ground where they were pinned down by Spandau fire.

Another Black Watch Battalion, the 7th, suffered heavily when the Artillery of another Division mistook them for enemy troops and shelled them. It was one of the terrible mistakes that sometimes happen in spite of every care, but it had a sequel in one of the rudest episodes I have ever witnessed.

At that time we were supporting 154 Brigade, which included the 7th Black Watch. A little time after the shelling incident a new Major of ours went to their Battalion HQ for the first time, having just taken over the Battery. There he was greeted by their Second-in-Command with 'Who are YOU? Get to hell out of it! We don't want any more of your bloody Gunners shedding our Highland blood!'

I was so furious when I heard of this that I said to Jerry, 'For heaven's sake let's ask to be relieved from supporting these so-and-so's!' His blood was boiling too, but he realised that the war had to go on. It's no use fighting your own side, and feuds between Gunners and Infantry just can't be allowed. So he went and somehow got it all smoothed over. The remark was inexcusable, but very forgivable when you remember the strain under which the Infantry were working. For instance, the Argylls at Gerbini had 18 Officers – 50 per cent – killed, wounded or missing, and 160 other casualties. To be shelled by your own side at such a time might well be the last straw that breaks the barrier between sanity and hysteria.

As resistance was so strong on this side, Montgomery recoiled a bit and shifted the pressure to the left. Accordingly the Highland Division pulled back from Gerbini and held on to the Sferro bridgehead while the pressure was exerted by the Divisions on our left. Eventually we were relieved there by the 5th Division.

For some reason the Colonel and I had to make a reconnaissance in 5th Division's territory, and we had a most unhappy experience there. We passed their gun positions and entered the OP area when the Colonel must have suddenly got the sense of danger that I have mentioned before. At any rate, he then made the only mistake I have known him make – he stopped bang on top of a hill and started to sweep the plain in front with his glasses, remarking that he thought we were a bit far forward.

He was right. Before we had been there half a minute there was a tremendous bang and we leapt out of the jeep and flung ourselves into a little hollow. One has a very quick eye for the slightest depression in the ground at such a time. A shell had burst just by the back wheel of the jeep.

Then we saw that Ellis, the driver, was not with us. He had been sitting in the back as Jerry was driving. Providentially, something seemed to distract the attention of the German anti-tank gunner, and that was the only shot he fired at us, though we heard him 'pomping' away at something else.

Seeing that all was quiet on our front, I crawled through some damnably prickly thistles and brought the jeep into the hollow under cover. Poor Ellis was terribly wounded in the head but still alive. We bandaged him and set out to find a Regimental Aid Post and a doctor. The RAP should have been discreetly but clearly marked and arrowed from the main track and easy to find. But 5th Division were new to war and had not learnt the importance of good signposting. Worse still, no one could tell us how to get to the RAP. Everyone we asked either did not know or directed us back the way we had come.

At last we set out in despair for our own RHQ and RAP, ten miles away over a rough track. It was a terrible drive. Holding the poor chap, mercifully unconscious, I felt every bump for him. We got him a hospital, but there was obviously no hope for him, and he died that night. He was such a cheerful chap: everybody liked him. A tailor in ordinary life, he always found time to do little repair jobs for any and everyone. I believe he was more missed than almost anyone we lost in the whole campaign.

The push on the left continued and we shot for other Divisions most of the time, though still ready to support our own people in case of need. Then came the time to clear the Sferro Hills. This was carried out by 152 and 154 Brigades. The fighting was heavy and much complicated by enormous olive orchards, where both sides were so mixed that neither knew where the others were, and the OPs found it hard enough to see them let alone distinguish friend from foe.

The Divisional history pays the Gunners some nice compliments for this, the 'Battle of Sferro Hills':

> For their excellent shooting on every one of the Battalion fronts in this battle great credit goes to the Divisional Artillery. The 126th Field Regiment actually fired more than 2,000 rounds per gun in support of the 7th Black Watch ... the counter attack on them (5th Seaforth) and the Camerons by German tanks and lorried Infantry was smashed up by the Divisional Artillery and in particular by Colonel Jerry Sheil's ever ready guns of the 128th Field Regiment.

That was the Highland Division's last real battle in Sicily, though they still had some rearguards to deal with, but the Divisional Artillery continued to be more than busy shooting for other Divisions, particularly the 78th, which was operating on the west side of Mount Etna.

This volcano now became part of our daily life, an enormous massif to the north with a curl of smoke peacefully ascending by day and sometimes a little fiery glow by night. The lanes got narrower and stonier as we approached it and the dust was a dirty black from the lava soil. This soil is excellent for vines, and indeed Sicily is a country of vineyards and oranges and lime groves. The oranges were deliciously refreshing on a hot dusty journey, fresh picked from the trees when we halted. The grapes too were a delight. I remember waking up one morning, after a night move, to find I had been sleeping in a vineyard. The early light came kindly through the pattern of the green leaves and just above my head was a prize bunch of ripe Muscatels, all ready for breakfast.

The fields were nearly all terraced with stone faces and would have been nearly impossible for mechanised Artillery but for the bulldozer. With that excellent machine we would first knock down the wall of the lane and clear the debris, then a track was made at right angles to the stone faces so that the guns could easily get from one terrace to another. One could not help being sorry for the unfortunate farmers whose fine handiwork was thus destroyed.

The Sicilians were a dirty, cheerful lot, miserably poor and clearly showing the mixture of Arab or Moorish blood in their past. In fact, they looked like Arabs in dirty European dress, or perhaps Levantines. As for the dirt, I once stepped into a shack to read my map out of the wind – never again! Within two minutes I was out of it and stripped to the buff, the doctor pouring DDT powder over me. They may have been animal fleas, but never have I seen so many, or had to many bites in so short a time.

The children were attractive little imps. They had a most appealing cry of '*Caramella, una cara-mella!*' About a dozen of them would surround one's jeep, but would desert it in an instant when an American car appeared on the scene.

Perhaps the most notable things in Sicily were the carts. These were real craftsmen's products, beautifully painted – sometimes with really good pictures – with carved spokes and all kinds of fancy, decorative work. One wonders how the owners could bring themselves to use them for dirty labour when new and shiny.

Meanwhile, pressure was being exerted over the whole island. In the west Palermo had fallen to the Americans, and with all the allies converging on Messina in the east, resistance crumbled and then ceased entirely. The Regiment's last action was at a place called Linguaglossa, where we saw an eclipse of the moon. The whole campaign had taken thirty-nine days. But in case it seems to have been 'too easy', let me quote some of our Infantry's casualties:

2nd Seaforth	14	Officers	194	Other Ranks
5th Camerons	12	Officers	68	Other Ranks
5th Seaforth	13	Officers	132	Other Ranks

We ourselves had four Officers wounded, four Other Ranks killed and nineteen wounded.

After Linguaglossa we rested for a day or two and then were called forward to Messina to support the landing in the toe of Italy that followed at once after our victory. The Germans were on the run and the Italians were on the point of surrender, so it was essential to keep the impetus going. Any delay would allow them to reinforce and reorganise resistance.

Chapter 19

Messina and After

The harbour-bay was clear as glass,
So smoothly it was strewn!
And on the bay the moonlight lay,
And the shadow of the moon.

Samuel Taylor Coleridge

128 [H] Regiment RA, August/September/October 1943

We drove to Messina by a road that seemed to traverse the backbone of the Northern Cape. It wound its way along a ridge above a pine tree belt with on every side a lovely view. In front, the hills of southern Italy rose palely in the distance, and on either side, blue beyond belief, lay the sea.

The town starts on the side of a steep hill and slopes down to a flat foreshore where the principal parts of the city centre and the port lie. As we were descending the hill some airburst shells suddenly appeared from nowhere with a nasty crack. I don't like airbursts – you can generally hear the ordinary shell coming and have time to lie flat until it has burst, but the other is like a sudden whip crack just above you and startles you out of your wits.

We chose as our RHQ a magnificent building, some sort of research institute or laboratory. The doctor was delighted to find a skeleton: he set it up with a Red Cross flag in one bony fist and the other pointing to his consulting room. It gave people quite a turn when they were looking for him and came face to face with this apparition.

The gun positions were actually in the streets. We were to fire across the straits into Italy and had to get as close to the shore as possible so as not to waste our range. I did not like the idea of moving into such a confined space. Memories of Plymouth under aerial bombardment were still fresh in my mind, and I think in the minds of others. To us, safety lay in the wide-open desert. Here in Messina we thought we would be shelled and bombed to hell itself. Our fears were groundless. In the event, nothing came near us.

Lieutenant Richmond
Gorle, 1935

Home leave cut short

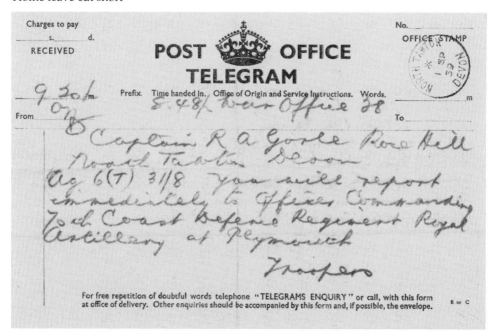

H Field Battery (Ramsey's Troop) RA. Runners up, Lucknow Horse Show, 1937

Djuliket hounds, 1938 (RA Gorle centre right of picture)

HMS *Newcastle* (launched 1936, decommissioned 1958) (courtesy of Naval-History.net)

HMS *Courageous* (launched 1916 as a large light cruiser, converted to an aircraft carrier 1926, sunk in the Western Approaches 17 September 1939 with loss of 518 lives out of a complement of 1,200) (courtesy of Naval-History.net)

Damaged HMS *Exeter* returns to port after taking part in the sinking of the German Heavy Cruiser *Graf Spee* (courtesy of Naval-History.net)

The author,
Richmond Gorle

Lieutenant Colonel
WA (Jerry) Sheil in
1941, as a Major
(By kind permission of
Anthony Sheil)

Officers of 128 (Highland) Regiment RA in 1942

Back row: 2 Lt OW Tilley, 2 Lt RW Lindsay, Lt JR Henderson, 2 Lt JH Inglis, 2 Lt JL McInnes, 2 Lt IS Beaton, 2 Lt LG Stephen, 2 Lt JB Cameron, 2 Lt N McL Miller, Lt RP Jack, Lt JH Trapnell, 2 Lt DR Paton, 2 Lt F McKenna, 2 Lt RON Williams, RCOS

Middle row: 2 Lt DD Ridley, Lt TG McInnes, 2 Lt AM Horne, 2 Lt JG Webley, Lt & QM BC Willoughby, Capt AL Aitkenhead, 2 Lt W MacDonald, Lt JL Grant, RAMC, Capt JD Inglis, Capt J Connel, 2 Lt JD Robertson, Lt JEA Blatherwick, Lt WB Smith

Front row: Capt HJ Wilcox, Capt IK Munro, Capt DH Johnston, Capt DOR Noble, Maj R Gordon Finlayson, Maj RA Gorle, Brig CB Findlay, CBE, MC, Lt Col WA Sheil, Brig GM Elliot, MC, Maj FCG Naumann, MC, Maj WN Owen, Maj A Field, Capt HJ Decker, Capt PM Leach, RAChD, Capt JT Lang

The *Duchess of Richmond*, passenger liner converted to troop ship, disembarking troops at Algiers in 1942

Table Mountain with its tablecloth of clouds

Steamer Point Aden, late 1930s, with county-class HMS *Kent* in the foreground. HMS *Kent* survived the war. Her sister ship HMS *Dorsetshire*, after an illustrious first half of the war, was the first ship, with HMS *Cornwall* to be sunk in the Pacific following a Japanese air attack

Dummy tanks being transported before El Alamein and an assembled *Grant* tank

A 25-pounder firing at El Alamein (IWM E18470)

The Qattara
Depression

Italian prisoners at El Alamein

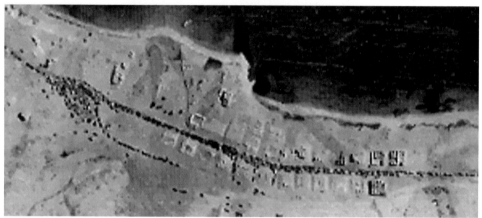

Traffic jam at Sollum

Arco Philaenorum (pulled down by Colonel Gadaffi of Libya in 1970)

Leptis Magna today

Claiming the
territory for the
51st Highland
Division
(IWM NA1918)

The Tripoli parade

A troop of 128 Highland Field Regiment in the Tripoli parade (IWM E4145E)

Takrouna. The fortifications are visible at the top of the hill

Home leave. This is what it was all about! The author with two of his children, Rosemary and Peter, in Devon

Brigadier Dick Bethell
(By kind permission of Hugh Bethell)

Some characters from 181 Regiment RA (By kind permission of Don Neal)

Captain Nigel Winter Prutton

Captain RG (Ray) Bristowe

Captain Philip Attewell

Captain Philip Mulholland

Lance Bombardier Howarth

Sergeant Tunnicliffe

Schans from the air. A scaled and annotated air photo used by the author in the battle

Party after the second liberation of Tilburg
Livie, ??, Gorle, Reit Siegers, ??, ??, Tomlinson, Walter Matthews, ??, Signals, ??
Anna and Deryck, The Doctor and Lucy
Padre Cairns, Annie Siegers, Villi, John Shaw

Crossing the Rhine in a Buffalo (IWM BU2057)

Hauling a 25-pounder off a Rhine crossing raft (By kind permission of Don Neal)

25-pounder, after crossing the Elbe

181 Fd. Regt. R.A.
BLA.

30 Apr. 45

Dear Peter,

I am writing to wish you luck at school. If you find it a bit strange at first, don't worry, as you will find you soon get used to it and will find a lot of boys that you will like.

The other day we watched an air fight over our heads. It was most exciting to see the German planes racing across the sky with British ones hard on their tails. We heard bursts of machine gun and canon fire from the British spitfires – ratatattattat! and down came two German planes, bursting into flames as they hit the ground. A little later one Messerschmidt appeared and all the Ack-Ack guns fired

at it, and down he came too – the third plane in five minutes!

We've been pretty busy lately. One night we were hurrying along to get ready for a battle, next night we fought the battle, and the night after we were chasing the Germans again, so I am a bit weary tonight and am looking forward to sleeping like a top tonight.

Lots of love, and good luck to you,

from

Daddy.

Letter home

Wotersen billet, after the war had ended

Other Divisions carried out the invasion of southern Italy, but we sent some OP parties over to cover the initial bridgehead and fired a programme lasting all night. For us in the Regiment it was quite uneventful, just hard slogging to keep the shells moving.

In the early hours the Colonel and I were talking together in the Command Post, remarking how well things had gone at our end – a fast rate of fire all night and not a single gun with mechanical trouble. Then the phone rang: it was 308 Battery. 'We've just had a gun blow up – no casualties!' As we were asking for details, he said, 'Wait a minute – I believe another's gone!' A loud boom confirmed him as he spoke. The Colonel seized the phone.

'How many more are loaded?'

'Three, Sir', came the answer.

'Tell them to open the breeches and stand clear, they'll all go!'

They did. The barrels were nearly red hot from the night's firing so if the shells were not fired within a few minutes of loading enough heat reached the fuses to set them off. In all, five guns burst that morning, without a single casualty. The trouble arose through an OP Officer giving the order to stop firing without first emptying the guns. When the Command Post Officer realised the danger and asked permission to fire, the Infantry had advanced beyond our extreme range so the OP could not let him fire. The CPO thought of the sea, but there were too many ships about. So he gave the order to unload by hand, but by that time the heat had swelled the shells and they were immoveable. Providentially a cook arrived with a can of tea at that moment and they broke off, leaving the breeches open. If they had left them closed, there would have been a shambles. As it was, the main force of the explosion went out at each end, merely bulging the barrels instead of bursting them into death-dealing fragments. A very lucky escape. Those were the last rounds 'fired' by us in the campaign.

After the wild night of bangs and crashes it was strange to see the townspeople going about their business as usual. Neatly dressed girls tittuped along the pavements at 8.30 am, so the offices were working as usual, it seemed. There was a man selling papers, and at a corner a barrow boy took up his usual standing selling 'prickly pears', the fruit of the cactus. As a customer gave his order, the boy slit the prickly skin lengthways and drew the segments back so that the buyer could take the pulp and eat it. I saw one old man take seven, one after the other. As fast as the boy peeled one the old man was ready for it: his only breakfast, I suppose, and not a very filling or appetising meal with which to start the day.

We had a little time to look over Messina and found it an attractive place, but the sight to be remembered was the beautiful deep blue of the straits. When we saw them, they were full of ships of all descriptions, crossing and re-crossing. Even 'ducks' (amphibious lorries) were crossing in flotillas. There is a story that the leader of one of these, a Subaltern of the RASC, was horrified to find a Destroyer signalling to him with a lamp. Wondering which rule of the sea he was breaking, the Subaltern tremblingly acknowledged the call and slowly deciphered the message. It was simply 'Quack quack!' Naval humour.

Our work finished, we pulled out in the country and camped. The local people treated us as tourists rather than enemies. They have no love for Italy and their hearts were never in the war. In fact, so unwarlike were they that we never bothered to keep any Sicilian prisoners. We just took away their arms and told them to go home. When next we saw them, they were thumbing lifts from the 'conquerors'.

Certainly, the villagers had no rancour against us. In fact their friendliness was almost a nuisance. I remember once when we had a concert party to amuse us, the villagers seemed to think it had been arranged for their benefit. At any rate, they got there first and pinched all the seats! The troops had to squeeze in as best they could, but somehow no one thought of turning them out. One tiny boy even wandered on to the stage, where he made an excellent foil for the funny man of the party.

Having time on our hands, we decided to move by the sea and settled into a lovely olive grove on Cap Faro, on the north coast. The only snag was that there was a steep cliff path down to the sea so that by the time we had climbed up it again we were ready for another bathe! The beach was delightful, the warm calm water just perfect.

It was so secluded that no one ever dreamt of wearing any trunks or costume – the naked state seemed the right and natural one. It is quite the nicest way of bathing – so free and comfortable in the water, and so pleasant to have nothing clinging and clammy on you when you come out, and you bake a nice bronze with none of the white segments that look so comical after normal sunbathing. If only Adam and Eve, when they invented clothes, had forborne to introduce all the taboos and complexes and petty pruderies that now go with them.

While we were waiting for the boat at Cap Faro, with Stromboli smoking in the distance, leave seemed hardly necessary in that peaceful atmosphere, but it was offered and quite a number were able to see a bit more of the island. Catania was our official leave centre, but the Colonel knew of a better place. Palermo is a much nicer city, and it had been hardly touched by the war. It was the American official centre, but he did not let that worry him. An Officer was despatched with a small party to commandeer a house by the sea a little way out of the city, and to get American approval for us to use it. This they did, choosing a nice place called the Villa Mondina, and each week we sent off a party of a dozen or so soldiers with a box of rations and instructions to enjoy themselves.

One of these parties experienced real and typical American hospitality. They arrived in Palermo in the dusk and asked the way from a 'Snowdrop' (US Army Police). 'Say, we're just goddam traffic cops – we don' know nuffin! Come back with us an' we'll fix you up.' Not only did they fix them up, but they treated them as guests for the whole of their leave, and gave them a thundering good time! As a result our chaps came back confirmed friends of all Americans.

The officers of the Divisional Artillery also went to Palermo, to a place that the CRA arranged for with the Americans privately. I had a very nice week there. The only snag was the American insistence on parking efficiency. It was just too efficient. A car could not even stop in the main street without a Snowdrop bearing down on it and sending it miles out into the suburbs, whence the occupants had to wend their way back on foot.

Apart from the trip to Oran, this was my first experience of Americans. I found them generally pleasant, but rather baffling. One day in the Officers' Club with George Eliot, the CRA, and some others, I heard a little group discussing me quietly.

'Is that guy a Major, or a Secund Lootenant?'

'I guess it had better be a Major.'

'Say Major, you're goin to have a Scotch!'

I told him that I had already ordered a round of drinks for my own party, but he waved that aside.

'Major, you's gonna drink with us furst!'

That was that: I smiled and gave in. Then followed: 'See you's a Cannoneer [this after reading my shoulder-title almost letter by letter]! I guess that's what we are too. We think our 105 Howitzer's a better gun than your twenny-faive pounder – shoot!'

That started a heated discussion, mostly among themselves. The 25 pounder was not doing too well at first because the 105mm is a bigger piece, but luckily our gun was found to have the longer range, so that balanced the other's heavier shell. I think the final result was a draw, and I was left wondering at their memory for little details in the construction of their piece, which I had long forgotten in ours.

Some of their nurses joined us later: very charming, but a little outspoken, and their voices seemed a little strident. Then one of our party lost his red and blue side-cap. It tickled me a lot that when one of the girls was found to be sitting on it she was not in the least abashed and declared openly that she had intended appropriating it as a souvenir. It would not surprise me now that I know them better, but it seemed very strange behaviour then.

*

November/December 1943

Soon after my time in Palermo we moved to Syracuse and embarked for home in the *Dunnottar Castle*. After a pleasant trip we arrived at Gourock, on the Clyde, on a shivering winter's day. There – to the horror of the Scots – we were put into a train to England, to Berkhampstead of all places. One couldn't help being sorry for them ... they had so been looking forward to being feted in their own Highlands.

In spite of attempts to keep our arrival secret, Gourock Station was festooned with flags and streamers saying 'Welcome Home, Highland Division!' so no one could help guessing our identity and all were most kind to us. The nicest welcoming touch came from the driver of our train. In the middle of the night he poked his head into the carriage and asked if we were warm enough. 'If you feel it cold,' he said, 'shine a torch up the train and we'll push some more steam through.'

That was the end of the 'First House'. There was then an interval until the show started again, during which we moved to St Albans and the Regiment underwent many changes. Jerry got his thoroughly deserved promotion to Brigadier and succeeded George Eliot as CRA. I only met him once more – he was killed by a mortar shell side by side with Thomas Rennie, the new Divisional Commander, near the Rhine.

The Flowers of the Forest are a' wade away.

Richard Cobden

Pike got married to a pleasant, smiley young woman in St Albans. Bombardier Beales went on driving the successor to 'Ben Nevis'. After the war he became a long-distance lorry driver. He had started the war as groom to Major Jock Campbell (later Major General Campbell VC) then he became my batman at Plymouth and a trusted friend of the family. When I went to the Highland Division he came too. I trained him to drive and he proved one of the very few men with natural road sense, needing no instruction on that score.

Driver Taylor became driver to my successor, Norman Owen. Taylor and I never understood each other until we had a swearing match one early morning. We had been on the go all night, and just as he had settled the car under a thorn tree with a camouflage net draped over it I had to go off in a hurry. It took some time to get the net off the thorny branches and I thought he was being deliberately slow and told him to snap out of it. That was the last straw, and he let fly some real soldiers' language at me. I threw it back, added some more and closed the incident. After that, we got on famously.

George Eliot, the CRA, went to a staff appointment and was a Major General next time we met. He has not appeared much in this story, but he is none the worse for that. He was a fine CRA and a most humane person. He wore himself out with his efforts to ensure that everything possible was done for the Regiments to prevent casualties.

I was suddenly told that I should go to the Staff College.[1] It seemed wrong to do so when it was obvious that the invasion of Europe could not be far off, but it was my last chance because of my age, and I was persuaded that it was foolish to throw it away. I accepted the nomination and went.

It was a terrible wrench to leave. The Regiment was a team, and one felt part of it. Orders did not seem to be necessary – things just happened. One said 'Move at five o'clock,' and that was enough to set in motion the quite complicated sequence of actions that ended with everyone in their places in the new position and nothing left behind. No chasing or chivvying was needed. Each man knew his job and did it; the spirit of loyalty was marvellous. The wounded or sick always got back to the Regiment, walking and hitchhiking sometimes 100 miles or more to get there. Two young gunners, in hospital so long that they had been struck off our strength, heard that they were to be posted to another Regiment the next day, but were not standing for that. That night they took French leave from the hospital and walked until they found us. That was not an unusual occurrence: in fact, it was commonplace. They liked to stick to their jobs.

Once, Fowler the Mess waiter went sick. I thought he was rather a sourpuss and didn't like serving the Officers, so I took the opportunity to replace him. When he came back, he raised Cain. He came to me almost weeping: 'What have I done wrong? I've always done me best for my Officers; I couldn't help going sick, could I, Sir? I didn't deserve to be flung out, truly I didn't, Sir!' So he was reinstated.

The men in the Batteries were the same. They would spend hours digging the gun pits; then, just as they had finished, without rhyme or reason they would have to move in a hurry and start all over again. They never complained or sulked. Many times I told them I was sorry they had been so harried with moves, and always the answer was the same: 'That's all right, Sir, as long as it's helping to win the war!'

The men passionately wanted news, and news is one of the hardest things to get in a war. There is seldom time to pass on even what you have gleaned yourself, and you probably do not know very much. As part of my job, when I went round the Batteries I used first to prime myself with all the situation reports I could get hold of, and then set up a marked map and try and pass it on and explain what the Division was doing. A film star could not have wished for more rapt attention. I have seen men queuing for a meal, leave it to get cold, and rush to my map like stampeding cattle! I wished I could tell them more and put it across better. Loyalty and *esprit de corps* like this almost make war worthwhile. It is seldom seen in times of peace.

I left the Regiment at St Albans still preparing for the next bout, but I found when I got to Camberley that I hadn't quite lost sight of the Highland Division, for a new Commandant had just been appointed. It was Douglas Wimberley!

Notes

[1] Attending and passing the Staff College course is a prerequisite for further promotion.

Part 3

EUROPE

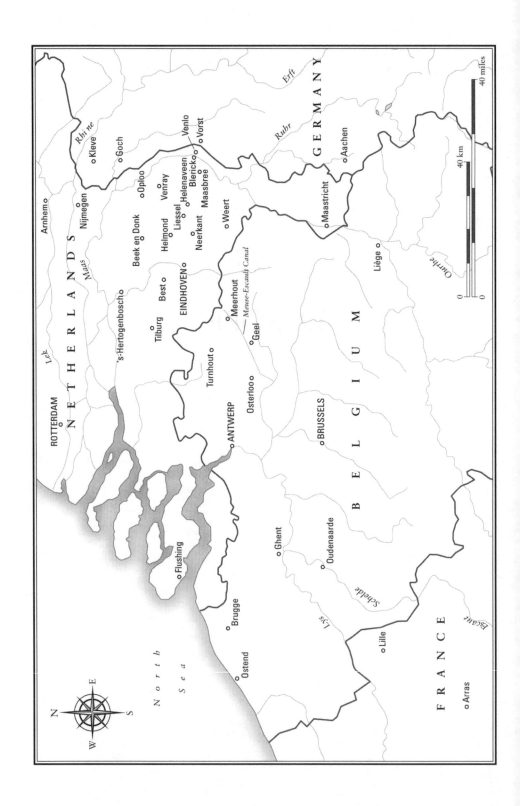

Chapter 20

Prelude to Action

They now to fight are gone,
Armour on armour shone,
Drum, now to drum did groan
To hear was wonder;

Michael Drayton

Staff College, January/June1944

I stood at the window of the Staff College anteroom. Overhead was a stream of almost countless gliders, in tow for Normandy. There were many of us there, and we watched in silence, for it was 6 June 1944 – D-Day for the Invasion of France – and we were ashamed to be mere students of war on the day of action. After that the schemes and 'battles' on the Marlborough Downs seemed pointless. The map of France with its daily moving red line absorbed our every interest.

For all that, we were getting valuable instruction in the art of war, which stood us in good stead afterwards. Apart from teaching of general subjects, the directing staff had correctly appreciated where the landings would take place – which was more than the Germans had! – and many of our schemes before the invasion followed almost the exact course that the actual battle afterwards took. Our training could hardly have been on sounder lines.

At last the course was finished, and after a spot of leave [see plate] I was sent for a fortnight to the School of Artillery to learn the elements of the Gunner side of staff work. Before I had been there a week an urgent War Office telegram was delivered to me in the very middle of a lecture. I was to report at once to a Reinforcement Holding Unit at Cooksbridge for immediate shipment to Normandy, but I was to go as an Anti-Tank Battery Commander! That was a shocking blow. It did not seem at all fair reward for the sweat of cramming an eighteen-month staff course into thirteen laborious weeks. I had expected a staff job or, a remote possibility, promotion. What I most wanted was to go back to a Field Regiment, but here I was, expected to learn a completely different way of soldiering in the middle of a battle.

It didn't seem sensible, so I phoned the War Office there and then and told them so. The wartime line was so bad that I could not hear what they said, but I gained the impression that they were telling me that some General or Brigadier has asked for me by name, so I dropped the protest. In war it helps a lot to know that someone values your efforts enough to ask for you on his staff or under his command. It was without foundation, but that impression buoyed me up for a long time.

In spite of the apparent urgency, it was four days before I saw the back of Cooksbridge – so much for War Office urgent telegrams. As I was on my way to the quay, who should I meet but my friend Jimmy Bingham. I just had time to ask him to be godfather to my daughter, Heather, then about minus two months old, before going up the gangway. This was a 'dry' ship – in the alcoholic sense – as it was American. The Yanks have a law that their Navy and Army may not drink at sea. I was, therefore, rather tickled when the Captain invited one or two of us into his cabin, locked the door, unlocked the steel safe and took out a bottle of whisky. 'Don't tell the boys,' he said, 'or they sure will be wild.'

Next morning we passed something like a big hotel being towed towards France. No one could think what it was until the Captain told us it was part of a 'Mulberry' harbour a hollow mass of concrete made in England, towed to France and sunk to make a breakwater. When we got to Avranches, near Bayeux, where we landed, we found that the harbour there was entirely artificial, made of these concrete blocks. These harbours were one of the wonders of the war, on a par with 'Pluto', the pipeline for petrol laid on the sea bed of the Channel.

I expected to find orders for an immediate posting when we landed, but no one had even heard of me. That was a bit of a damper. When nothing had come through after three days I began to worry. If I was 'urgently' needed I did not want to hang about at base, waiting to be discovered, so I managed to borrow a car and go to 2nd Army HQ to ask about my future. They didn't know what to do with me either.

My visit did speed things up, though. After all the waiting, I was woken at midnight and told to be at XXX Corps HQ by 10.00 next morning. That is typical of how things often happen in war. You kick your heels for a month and then have to do something by the day before yesterday.

Chapter 21

With the Desert Rats

When in disgrace with fortune and men's eyes,
I all alone between my outcast state,
And trouble deaf heaven with my bootless cries,
And look upon myself and curse my fate,

William Shakespeare

7th Armoured Division, July 1944

Many who fought in the desert called themselves 'Desert Rats', but the title belonged rightly to the men of the 7th Armoured Division only, for they bore on their sleeves and painted on their tanks and trucks the jerboa, or jumping rats of the desert. It was they who made this little animal famous, their prowess turned what might have been a derisory name into a title of honour, and all others who used the same were usurpers.

To this Division I was now posted, as Brigade Major Royal Artillery. My heart bounded for joy when I heard the news, for it was a plum job for a Staff Officer newly out from Camberley. But there was a catch in it that made me wary. I was told that my appointment was temporary, with a chance of permanency if my face fitted, but it was made clear that the CRA had asked for someone else. Therein lay my disillusionment: not only was I going unasked, but I was also a Leah in a Rachel's place. As I had absolutely no practical experience of staff work, the dice were loaded against me.

That was clear from the moment I arrived. The Brigadier made it obvious that I was not the man he wanted. It was soon evident too that he did not mean to take any trouble to train me. As we were going into battle the next morning I was definitely going to learn the hard way!

The Desert Rats were a very fine Division. They had fought together for a very long time and were a splendid team. Everyone knew just what to do in any given situation; in fact, as with my earlier unit, orders were barely necessary. However, they had evolved methods and jargon that were peculiarly their own, so it was terribly difficult for an outsider to pick up the threads, and an outsider I was.

The Division was very much a closed shop and very, very 'Cavalry'. To begin with, the dress of the Officers was a matter of individual taste, and very natty and sensible most of it was. Almost all wore corduroy trousers. If it was cold a golfing 'windcheater' replaced the normal battle-dress top, and some even wore coloured socks. Nobody dreamt of wearing anything so commonplace and ugly as a battle dress with boots and gaiters. The characters of the famous 'Two Types' cartoons were pure 7th Armoured, barely exaggerated.

Can you wonder, then, that the CRA was disappointed at getting a flat-footed Officer from an Infantry Division ... one he had never heard of, with no staff experience?

Our first battle was near Caumont, and we were directed to Aunay-sur-Odon, near Caen in Normandy – names familiar to me from our Staff College exercises. We moved off at 'tank light', which is the earliest time that a tank can see to move (as opposed to 'first light', about half an hour earlier, when a man can just see to get about).

My job was to sit in a Cromwell tank and keep track of all that was said on the wireless by the Regiments of the Divisional Artillery. This tank and two light armoured cars called 'dingoes' formed the CRA's 'Tactical HQ' ('Tac' for short), which he put just behind the battleground. Main HQ, run by the Staff Captain, was some miles behind and only joined us at night. Further back still was 'Rear HQ', which dealt purely with supply and routine matters.

Once one got the hang of it, it was intensely interesting. Quickfire talk was going on the whole time, giving an almost minute-to-minute story of the battle. I had to keep a log, scribbling down the gist of each conversation, keeping my map tidily marked with all the changes of position as they were reported, and reporting the salient points to HQ RA of the Corps at intervals. The whole story had to be arranged in an orderly form in my head for retelling to the CRA at a moment's notice. At the same time I had to know who did what throughout the Division so that I could get the Regiments any help they needed, and in the absence of the CRA, I had to be prepared to meet a sudden change in the situation with a decision in accordance with his plan. It was gruelling concentration from dawn to dusk, with hardly a moment's respite.

Night seldom brought much rest. Tanks do not do much at night, but the Infantry do most of their fighting then: an Armoured Division has one

Tank Brigade and one Infantry Brigade. Even if there was no fighting, there was a pile of routine work, to say nothing of the preparations and orders for the next day, and the Regimental Commanders usually came in to discuss this and that. By the time all that was finished it would be about 1.00 am and all except the Duty Officer would go to bed. He was lucky if he could stretch out by 3.00 am, and even then he would probably be woken up three or four times. Duty tour came round every third night.

At night we worked in the 'Armoured Control Vehicle' – the ACV – which was really rather a horrid contraption. It was a big steel box of a lorry fitted with tables and swivel seats for the Staff Captain and Intelligence Officer and me, with a spare for a visitor or the CRA. In it were the wireless sets to Corp HQ, RA and the Regiments, and two telephones that rang incessantly. At this time of day wireless reception was at its worst. Atmospheric and other interferences were deafening and continuous, a sort of 'juddle-diddle-juddle-diddle' on a high-pitch note. One or other of us would be shouting to try and get a message through, another would be answering the phone, while the third tried to work out a fire plan or strove to hear what the other wireless was trying to tell him. Nerve-wracking pandemonium is too good a description of it!

That first battle lasted for six days. I have a wonderful memory of slipping between blankets at 9.00 am when it ended. I heard my batman say 'What time shall I wake you, Sir?', but I was asleep before I could answer. Such are one's powers of recuperation that I was up in two hours' time as fresh as a rose – almost! I think that was because I made myself have breakfast before going to sleep. Food and sleep together are fine restoratives.

After a couple of days' rest, we were again in the thick of it, this time with the Infantry Brigade and fighting a night battle. For some reason Main HQ had not been able to get close up to us, so we were controlling from Tac. That is to say, I was battened down with a tarpaulin covering the tank to keep the light from showing. It was very hot and airless and the juddle-diddle was making such a fiendish row that one could hardly hear anyone on the net at all. In fact, there were times when one just could not get through with a message.

Suddenly through the chaos of noise came a faint cry from the 5th Regiment RHA – 'Medium apples falling!' That meant that the Medium Regiment was hitting our own troops and must be stopped until the reason could be found and corrected. I stopped them and sent word to the CRA, who had vanished without telling me where to find him. But the cry came again 'Apples – Apples – Apples!'

That put me in a nasty dilemma. The only people still shooting were the two RHA Regiments, which were firing a creeping barrage with the Infantry following it. One does not stop a barrage lightly because you cannot tell where your Infantry have got to when you want to start it again. So I struggled with the atmospherics to try and find out more about it.

All I could get from Bill Norman, the CO, were frantic wails that the 'Apples' were doing a lot of harm. At last, faintly but very clearly, I heard: 'The Brigadier wants the barrage stopped. He would rather have no fire plan at all than this!'

That was terrible: two RHA Regiments hitting their own troops. Apart from the casualties, they would have forfeited the Infantry's confidence and would not regain it, perhaps for years. However, the CRA could not be found and something had to be done at once, so I stopped the barrage.

When all was silent on our side the CRA arrived, wanting to know why the firing had stopped and very angry about it. However, when he heard the facts he agreed that there was nothing else that I could have done. Then the juddle-diddle quietened a little and the wireless said in a strained voice 'Apples still falling.' Then we knew the truth – they were enemy shells!

Very cleverly, the CRA himself restarted the barrage. Then the General phoned to know what it was all about. The Brigadier behaved splendidly. Though he had been nowhere near, he took the entire responsibility. 'I stopped it', he said, 'because I thought we were hitting our own people.' If anyone was to blame it was the Regimental Commander: he should have found out more about it before bellyaching like that.

But relations between us did not improve. The jargon was my worst enemy. I had to cudgel my brains for the meaning of it. If a Regiment tells you it wants some cigarettes it takes a moment or two to realise that the requirement is smoke-shell, not Players. And that was a simple 'cryptic'. My pauses to think irritated the Brig beyond measure, and it did not seem to strike him that I was getting into the swing of the super-excellent wireless 'drill' and improving daily. Nor did he seem to realise that I was doing for the first time things that he and the rest had been familiar with for years.

The upshot was that I soon realised that I should never gain his confidence and must take the first opportunity of asking to be relieved of the appointment. The climax came on the night of a big Corps attack. The fire plan arrived and I stretched out my hand to take it, it being the Brigade Major's job to distribute the tasks between the Regiments. Before I could grasp it, he snatched it away and started to work on it with the Intelligence Officer, completely shouldering me out of it. After two or three minutes of this, I asked if he was going to do the job himself. To this he snapped 'Yes!' and went on with it.

So there it was. A vote of no confidence, and given in the rudest way possible. That was one of the few times I have actually felt my neck swell with range, and for a moment I could see nothing. Happily, I remembered that personal feelings must never be allowed to interfere with the war. I kept silent and went on with some routine work.

Next morning I asked to go, and he said he had come to the same conclusion. He told me I needed experience with Armour to be able to do the job, and that I was deaf and couldn't hear the wireless. The last was completely untrue. I could hear as well as he could. It was a pity. I should have loved the job, and he was a first-class CRA. It was ironic that the General was sacked just then, and the CRA sacked himself in sympathy – and left the day before I did!

Chapter 22

Fortunate Journey

Here come I to my own again,
Fed, forgiven and known again,
Claimed by bone of my bone again,
And cheered by flesh of my flesh,

Rudyard Kipling

31 Reinforcement Holding Unit, 181st Field Regiment RA, August 1944

So, back to Bayeux in dejection. It's not pleasant to fall down on a job. It seemed an age since I was last there, but it was in fact only a fortnight, and many of the people I had met before were still around. Four majors who had enviously wished me luck as I went were even more fed up than before and welcomed me back with ironic cheers and real friendliness. We teamed up as the 'Five Unwanted' and spent the morning trying to teach a lot of mannerless Subalterns how to control a Battery. In the evenings we picked mushrooms and then gathered in my tent and groused at being left out of the war.

We were in a tremendous hurry to get killed, come to think of it. There were Officers in reinforcement holding units like ours who openly boasted of the time that they had been in situ and how they intended to spend the rest of the war there. I do not think any of us were particularly keen to fight: we merely felt that there was a job to be done and we should be doing it.

For three long weeks we picked mushrooms and complained, but then my posting order arrived. I was to join the 181st Field Regiment. No one had ever heard of it. Certainly none of the staff knew where it was. The Battle of the Falaise Gap had just been won; our Armies were sweeping across France and Belgium; communications were in chaos; and nobody had the slightest idea where anyone else might be. To add to our private confusion, we had just moved forward, to a place called Rugles. If I would wait a week or two, I was told, they would be able to find out where 181 was and send me to them.

A week or two! What would a short-handed Regiment think of an Officer who hung about at base for a week or two waiting for transport? Actually, they would not have noticed my absence, but one's self-conceit does not tell one that. Anyhow, I was sick of 31 Reinforcement Holding Unit and determined to leave it at the first possible moment. By dint of wide inquiries I discovered that this might be one of the Regiments of 15th (Scottish) Division. Someone suggested that they might be somewhere near Lille. That was good enough. I decided to hitchhike. I went to the Adjutant and asked for a small-scale map, but there was only one in the unit, and I couldn't have that. He let me borrow it and I sketched in the rough position of the main towns and made do. It would at least show me which direction to take and what towns to make for.

When the time came to start out, everyone was most helpful. The Mess Secretary gave me a big box of rations and John Harshort[1] undertook to drive me to Vernon-sur-Seine where the bridge had been blown up and a temporary one built by the Sappers was in its place. It was argued that the new bridge was narrow, so there was bound to be a bottleneck there that would slow the traffic and give me a chance to get a lift.

Just as I was leaving someone thrust two letters into my hand. They were from my wife and mother-in-law and conveyed the good news that there was a new arrival in the family – a charming little girl, the letters said, and mother and daughter were doing well. With that load off my mind, my spirits soared, and I felt that all was right with the world.

My friend set me down at a little *estaminet*[2] right by the bridge and I saw and surveyed the traffic over an aperitif. The whole Second Army was moving steadily forward. Column after column went by in a continuous roar and grinding of gears, stretching for miles, nose to tail with hardly a break. The German Air Force had been driven out of the skies; otherwise, to move thus would have courted destruction.

I contemplated a leap on to a slowly moving vehicle, but that meant abandoning my bedding roll and suitcase, and perhaps even my precious rations. It did not seem necessary to jettison every comfort so early, so I waited for a traffic jam. It came at last. The truck on the bridge stalled and all the others telescoped until they almost touched in the same old way that drivers are continually taught not to but always do.

I leapt to a truck. 'Where are you going?'

'To Amiens, I believe.'

A quick glance at my 'map' – yes, it was in the right direct. 'Can you take me?'

There were three chaps in the back, but they obligingly made room and I scrambled in. I found I was with an RAF Airfield Construction Unit – something I had never heard of before. My companions were good company, but the unit? Well, it hadn't started to be a unit! They had set out at 3.00 am and had made no arrangements for anything to eat after that. You can imagine how delighted those poor 'irks' were when I opened my box of food.

We flowed with the traffic stream until late afternoon before drawing out of it and parking on Amiens airfield. There we hung about in the cold wind for over an hour waiting for that apology for a unit to get organised. Then we got some musky tinned stew and lukewarm tea. No one complained, so I suppose they were used to feeding like that.

In the morning I came across a Scottish Staff Officer who as soon as he heard I was looking for 15th (Scottish) Division treated me like a brother. He got a seat for me in a jeep going to Arras, which made the second leg of my journey. We drove through country famous for battles of the Great War, making a pleasant tour, and got to Arras in the afternoon. We rattled into a most attractive cobbled square with a nice church and a rather ornate town hall, but I did not take much interest in the architecture at that time because we drew up right alongside a jeep bearing the Red Lion Rampant of the 15th (Scottish) Division.

15th (Scottish) Division order of battle

44th Infantry Brigade
8th Royal Scots
6th Royal Scots Fusiliers
6th King's Own Scottish Borderers

46th Infantry Brigade
9th Cameronians (Scottish Rifles)
2nd Glasgow Highlanders
7th Seaforth Highlanders

227th Infantry Brigade
10th Highland Light Infantry
2nd Gordon Highlanders
2nd Argyll & Sutherland Highlanders

Supporting Units
102nd (Northumberland Hussars) Anti-Tank Regiment, Royal
  Artillery
1st Middlesex (Machine Gun)
15th Scottish Reconnaissance Regiment

Divisional Artillery
131st Field Regiment Royal Artillery
181st Field Regiment Royal Artillery
190th Field Regiment Royal Artillery
97th Anti-Tank Regiment Royal Artillery
119th Light Anti-Aircraft Regiment Royal Artillery

Divisional Engineers
624 Field Park Company Royal Engineers
20 Field Company Royal Engineers
278 Field Company Royal Engineers
279 Field Company Royal Engineers
26 Bridging Platoon Royal Engineers

Divisional RASC
283rd Company Royal Army Service Corps
284th Company Royal Army Service Corps
399th Company Royal Army Service Corps
62nd Divisional Company Royal Army Service Corps

Divisional RAOC
15th Ordnance Field Park Royal Army Ordnance Corps
305th Mobile Laundry and Bath Unit

Divisional REME
44th Infantry Brigade Workshop
45th Infantry Brigade Workshop
227th Infantry Brigade Workshop

Royal Army Medical Corps
153rd Field Ambulance RAMC
193rd Field Ambulance RAMC
194th Field Ambulance RAMC
22nd Field Dressing Station RAMC

23rd Field Dressing Station RAMC
40th Field Hygiene Section RAMC

Machine Gun Battalion
1st Battalion Middlesex Regiment

Other Units
15th Recce Regiment RAC
15th Provost Company CMP
15th Divisional Signals Royal Corps of Signals

The driver was on the point of leaving, so there could not have been a more fortunate encounter. He said he would certainly take me if I would not mind chasing round the country, looking for some ammunition lorries that had got lost. He was a Corporal of the Royal Army Service Corps and good company. We hunted high and low for those lorries, without result, and although it was three days since the leading troops had passed through, we were greeted by cheering crowds wherever we went. At last he gave up the search and we set a course through Lille to a place near Oudenarde, about thirty miles beyond, where his Company was.

The Company Commander was most pleasant when we got there. He told me the Division was about ten miles further on, but as it was pouring with rain he suggested me staying the night with him, promising to send me on in the morning. I agreed, and he fed me like a prince and gave me the corner of a stable to sleep in. There, lulled by the munching of friendly horses, I drowsed into the sleep of satisfied achievement.

The feeling of 'something accomplished' was still there when I arrived at HQ RA in the Company Commander's own car. The seemingly impossible had been done. Following the slenderest of clues, I had found my new Regiment in two and a half days, and I went to meet the CRA – Linden Bolton – with a smile on my face.

It was soon wiped off. His first words were: 'I don't want you! I asked for a Junior Major. You're far too senior. There's a vacancy for a Battery Commander, but you are senior to the Regiment's Second-in-Command!'

On hearing that the Second-in-Command was Geoffrey Graham, whom I had known as a kid at Lapford, I said I had not the slightest objection to serving under him, but the Battery had changed Majors too often lately and Linden was afraid that I would be taken away from it for a staff job or promotion, making another quick change. At last he said I could stay if I promised to refuse promotion or a staff job for at least six months. That was unfair, I told him so, and stalemate was reached. However, I begged him to let me stay as an Attached Officer for a time – anything to avoid being sent back to base again – and that was allowed.

Well! I had some very bitter feelings as I hung about, trying to be useful without getting in the way. 'No more hitchhiking,' I said to myself. 'They can damn well come and fetch me next time!' It seemed that it was not possible to get a job unless a highly placed friend spoke for one – one had to be on the Old Boys' network; to have caught the eye of the Great in some way. I had never taken steps to catch the eye, so now I must suffer for being inconspicuous! These and other thoughts of despair and humiliation went through my mind. Coming on top of the loss of the Brigade Major job, this was a crushing blow, and the bottom of my morale fell out with a crash.

Although these thoughts were only the product of a mind suffering a temporary buffeting by fate, the Old Boys' net was – and always will be, at least in war – a very real thing. Generals and Brigadiers rightly had a big say in the choice of their Officers, and it was only natural that they should choose from among those known to them. The system had a lot of good in it. It gave many a young Officer who happened to be at the right place at the right time the chance to get on. 'On-the-spot' selections helped to make each Division a family affair and ensure good relations between staffs and Regiments. Yet the more senior but equally able Officer who did not happen to have a friend at court, or who happened to be in a military backwater for the time being, often lost out heavily through being overlooked.

My stay at HQ RA was enlivened by my first experience of the 'liberation' atmosphere when we moved from Oudenarde. That journey was fun. The route was lined with joy-mad, cheering girls, some of them exceedingly pretty. Fruit and flowers were thrown into the car all the way, though sometimes we got tomatoes, too soft to stand the flight. Girls stretched out to shake the driver's hand, or rather to make the two palms meet with a resounding smack as the car rolled slowly by. Sometimes he managed to hold on, and the girl was dragged along for a few yards, screaming with laughter. Others with a hint of mischief plonked an over-ripe tomato in the car and ducked away before he could throw it back. All were quite daft with delight that the occupation was over. They had kept these scenes going for days on end. It was said that they even came down in their nightdresses to cheer a column that passed in the night. Really, it was fantastic to be met like this, on the way to war!

The day after the move the CRA had a sudden change of heart and told me I was to go to 181 Field Regiment after all. Why, I do not know. Never was news more welcome: it was the change of my fortunes.

My first contact with the new Regiment was the arrival of the Commanding Officer's own car to fetch me, with his batman to handle my kit. That had a wonderful effect – I felt wanted again. There was no need for the CO to do this, but it was an extra courtesy that made one feel one was going to a unit that did things generously and properly. And so it turned out. That act was the keynote of the spirit in the Regiment. It so impressed me that I have always remembered it and tried to do the same for my Officers when I was in command.

Notes

[1] John Harshort in 1969 was running the Adventure Training Centres in Wales as a civilian.
[2] A small restaurant where drinks and snacks are sold.

Chapter 23

Flags and Flowers

Here come I to my own again,
Fed, forgiven and known again,
Claimed by bone of my bone again,
And cheered by flesh of my flesh,

Rudyard Kipling

181 Field Regiment RA, August/September 1944

181 Field Regiment was deployed round a farm and when I arrived the Colonel, Dick Bethell [see plate], was giving his orders for a battle. I found him in a small room crammed with people, competing for a hearing with a noisy wireless set that kept on interrupting, as wireless sets will.

He introduced himself with a friendly handshake and reeled off the names of half-a-dozen others, ending with '... and this is Philip Attewell [see plate], your Senior Troop Commander. He's just off on a Battery Commander's reconnaissance – unless you would like to go yourself? But perhaps you would rather meet your Battery first?'

And that was the start of a partnership I enjoyed very much. Dick Bethell was extraordinarily nice to work with. He never interfered, but he was always at hand to help or advise just when it was most wanted. 'I'm a terribly lazy man,' he said once. 'I sit back and make other people do all the work – but I'm quite honest about it!' Actually, he was the most conscientious man alive and never spared himself in working for the good of the Regiment and saving the rest of us trouble.

On leaving him I went straight to my Battery, the 179th Field Battery, one of the nicest crowds I have ever served with. They were mostly Shropshire lads, as 181 had been converted to Gunners from the 6th Battalion The King's Shropshire Light Infantry. A few others from London and elsewhere fitted in well with the kindly country folk without in the least altering the county spirit and character. It was amusing to find a pure English Regiment in a Scottish Division, and funnier still to find them all wearing the Balmoral bonnet and liking it! The rest of the day was a complete whirl for me as there was a battle starting at dawn next morning. Luckily it turned out not to be a serious one, but of course I did not know that at the time and had to prepare for the real thing. I started by meeting most of the other nine officers at lunch, then I had all the men on the parade and presented myself in a Balmoral newly drawn from stores and Scottish Lions newly sewn on my sleeves. 'Take a good look at me,' I said, 'and try not to shoot me if it's dark when we meet again!' Then I dashed off to meet the CO of the Royal Scots Fusiliers (RSF), the Battery's affiliated Battalion with which I should be in action.

The CO turned out to be Ian McKenzie, who had been one of my instructors at the Staff College, so we were off to a flying start. When he assumed command the Battalion was at a low ebb and his predecessor had been sacked. It was expected that a bit of a 'tiger' would be sent to pull them together. Instead, a little sandy-haired man from South Africa arrived and quietly took stock. 'What good can this little mouse do?' said the RSF. Nothing happened for three days and the pessimists congratulated themselves on being right. Then heads started to roll. The Second-in-Command found himself posted to a base job, the Adjutant was sent packing and two of the Company Commanders were replaced. It was not a mouse that had come to them.

I joined the Battalion at Malines and moved with them to relieve a Battalion of 50 Division across the Albert Canal, somewhere near Osterloo. My two Troop Commanders were Phil Attewell and Nigel Prutton [see plate]. The first I put in a windmill and the other in a church tower: splendid OPs, but terribly dangerous. Both sides did awful things to towers and windmills because they were such fine OPs, but we had to take the risk because there were no other vantage points anywhere near as good.

Phil was a handsome, apple-cheeked boy ... at first sight. Actually, he was much older than he looked, and a fine, reliable Officer, skilful and intelligent, and as loyal as they make them. Nigel was a bookmaker by trade, as sharp as nails and brave as a lion. He had a superstition that was almost an obsession. He was convinced that if he were not relieved from the OP at the time the relief was due his number would be up. So if he had been told he would be relieved at the hour, you could bet your last dollar that he would call up at four minutes to and ask if relief was on its way. Up to the hour he would die with the best, but then his contract ended.

They were a first-class pair. Both commanded Batteries before the war was over and Nigel was awarded the Military Cross for taking over a Company of Infantry when their Officers were all put out of action.

The night passed peacefully, which was just as well, as it gave me a chance to get into the saddle. I had never commanded a Battery in war, and besides, this one was a bit difficult at first because my predecessor was a man with ideas of his own, which he had put into effect. In doing so, he had changed the organisation, departing entirely from 'the book'. Everyone knows that 'the book' can be improved upon at times, but the main reason for having a standard procedure is to make it easy for a new arrival to take up the reins at a moment's notice in war and drive on as if there had been no change. Even though I had no idea to whom I was speaking on wireless or phone, there was plenty of cooperation, and I soon found things working as they should.

A Battery Commander's job is of course vastly different from that of Second-in-Command. As second in command I was the Colonel's deputy in the gun area. I had to choose and prepare the area and control it in action according to the Colonel's orders and directions. Now, as Battery Commander, my place was with the Colonel of my affiliated infantry Battalion. My job was to advise him on Artillery matters and to plan fire support for the Battalion to suit its varying needs. Under my immediate control were my two Troop Commanders, manning OPs in the forward Infantry Company areas on the Battery wireless net. I could speak to the OPs and the troops, the Battery Command Post and the Battery Captain, the latter being my deputy in the Battery area, though he did not deal with fire control, which was the job of the Senior Subaltern, known as the Command Post Officer or CPO.

I had another wireless on the Regimental net, by which I was continually in touch with the Colonel, the other two Battery Commanders, the RHQ Command Post and the other Batteries. When I was separated from the Battalion Commander I had a third wireless that I could tune to the Battalion frequency and speak to him and any part of the Battalion. In addition, whenever we stayed long enough in one place to lay a wire, I could telephone to any part of the Regiment. When we supported Tanks instead of Infantry, the setup was exactly the same.

The picture I have tried to conjure should show at every stage, from the Company of Infantry (or Squadron of Tanks) upwards, a Gunner and an Infantry (or Tank) Commander alongside each other, planning each operation together from the start and seeing it through together, while a beautifully planned wireless system enables the artillery plan to be quickly passed to the guns that are to carry it out. These may be not only the guns of one's own Troop or Battery, but those of the Regiment or of as many Regiments as might be required.

That was a digression, but I do not apologise, because knowing the background will make the story more interesting. The Gunners owed their success in this war mainly to three things: 'Ju-ju', the survey that enabled many Regiments to shoot together almost as one; wireless, which allowed the Artillery Commanders to control their units from almost anywhere; and the intimate liaison with the Infantry and Tanks – made possible by wireless – which made joint planning and mutual understanding possible. All this had been understood and striven for in the past, but our efforts had been dependant on signalling by lamp, a flag or helio, and primitive field telephones.

When it was barely light, a thrill of excitement stirred us. Nigel reported seeing a Belgian flag. Did it mean that the enemy had withdrawn? Then Phil saw one too – and another – another – more and more! Soon there was competition for wireless space to report them. It was clear that the enemy had gone, so Ian McKenzie decided to send out a Carrier Patrol to find out the form. I sent Nigel with the Carriers to bring down fire if they should bump into anything, and Ian and I followed. Phil came with me as a reserve OP.

First, we came to the little town of Willomsche, where the flags had appeared. The people were mad with joy, cheering, clapping and flag-waving. Fruit and flowers were thrust into our jeeps; lovely nosegays were tossed at us; one dear old lady stopped my jeep and insisted on Bull (my driver) and me eating a plate of peaches before she would let us go on. It was all rather harassing at this stage, as one wanted one's wits about one in case of ambush.

Having got thus far without incident, Ian decided to press on to the next little town, Meerhout by name. Here we saw a 'liberation' from the very start. We arrived just as the Carrier Platoon had passed through. The place was dead. Not a man was to be seen; not a dog barked. Then a few bewildered white-faced men appeared. Suddenly, the fuse lighted – it dawned on them that they were free! A cheer went up and an excited mob filled the streets like the breaking of a dam. Apples and peaches were thrust at us; the air was bright with Belgian and British flags. Men and women were laughing, crying, dancing and cheering, and trying to kiss us!

We came to the main square and Phil and I got out. In a moment we were thronged and hemmed in; everyone tried to shake hands and kiss us at once. 'Come and have coffee!' '*Non! Du vin! Venez, Venez!* ' 'Come home with me!' More flowers, more fruit ... I turned to my jeep in despair – this was no time to play. We had to catch up with Ian and find a rooftop to try spot the enemy. There, sitting demurely on the bonnet of the jeep, was a perfect fairy of a girl. She was dressed in a dark blue frock with a border of yellow and red – the national colours. In spite of the hurry I just had to stop and speak to her. I should have kissed her '*pour l'Entente*', but I was too pre-occupied to think of that.

Smiling and doing our very best to talk French, we pushed through the crowd. Rather, we did a sort of daisy-chain, shaking hands to right and to left, and both together! Behind us, our drivers were being mobbed: doubtless they enjoyed it.

Then another charming fairy, this time in a pretty white frock, was impelled into our path and presented Phil with a lovely bouquet. 'Phil!' I said. 'You must kiss her!'

'Don't be silly, Major!' said Phil, his apple-cheeks ruddier than ever.

'Phil, it's almost a military order!' I said, and at that he bent down and kissed her, raising the crowd's joy to an ecstasy of delight, with a crescendo of '*Bravo! Bravo! Bravo les Anglais!*' It was the most popular thing he could have done.

At last we struggled to a flat roof and joined Ian, but we couldn't see anything other than treetops when we got there. Many followed us and there was more shaking of hands while the owner of the house produced some most welcome beer. He was just in raptures because we had chosen his house, of all the town. Then Ian McKenzie got a message from Brigade that he had stuck his neck out too far and was to return at once. But Meerhout had had its liberation – nothing could take that away from it!

We got back to the Carriers to find them wreathed in flowers, so it was a carnival procession that withdrew from the town, and a slow one too, because people were still bringing out the fruit and blooms. We just had to keep stopping because they looked so disappointed if we seemed to be passing their offerings by.

What a pity we could not take the little jeep-fairy with us, as the Battery mascot!

Chapter 24

The Escaut Canal

Again the long roll of the drummers,
Again the attacking cannon, mortars,
Again to my listening ears the cannon responsive.

Walt Whitman

181 Field Regiment RA, September 1944

In mid-September 1944 XII Corps was ordered to open a route to
Turnhout, and as part of this operation 15th (Scottish) Division was told
to establish a bridgehead over the Meuse-Escaut Canal forward of the town
of Gheel. 44 (Lowland) Brigade were given the job, and they succeeded in
bouncing the Royal Scots across before the enemy could stop them.
However, the enemy then reacted strongly, and 'Pontius Pilate's
Bodyguard' was tightly hemmed in in a small village just the other side, so
it was decided to get the rest of the Brigade across and then break out (the
rest of the Brigade being the 6th Royal Scots Fusiliers [RSF] and the 6th
King's Own Scottish Borderers [KOSB]).

I joined the RSF for this attack in the afternoon of 14 September, in
Gheel, though the final decision to send us across had not yet been made
and we had time on our hands. The people were most friendly, but there
was a strained look on their faces and they were ready to scurry to the
cellars at the first sound of a gun. An occasional shot struck the church
tower, which had been knocked about a lot, and there was a very dead horse
by the church door. I was thankful to find that another Battery had put an
OP up the tower, so there was no point in us putting one there too. It was
a solid bit of masonry, but all the same one didn't relish being up there
when a shell hit it.

In the evening we heard that we were to cross in the morning, but the
plan was not finalised until very late, so I had to go down to the Battery in
the early hours and rouse the principal actors for their briefing. It was 3.00
am before I got to bed, with breakfast ordered for 5.00 am.

This is the cue for Lance Bombardier Howarth to appear [see plate].

Howarth was the driver of my 'Half-Track' – an armoured car with wheels in front and tank tracks behind. He was also the self-appointed cook and housekeeper of the Battery Commander's party. He was a 'character'. Short, fat and untidy, never without a patch of oil somewhere on his clothes, sharp tongued, quite fearless and very good hearted, in ordinary life he was a Liverpool docker. Army discipline left him cold and he was no respecter of rank. A former Battery Commander once chided him for running over a duck when driving a carrier. Howarth turned to him and said: 'Ah'd have thee know this isn't a mucking pram ah'm drhaving – and if tha don't lahk ma drahving, tha can drahve tha muckin' self – ah'm tired!'

His first appearance is in the role of cook. By 4.50 am I was up and shaved and looking round for signs that breakfast was underway. I found none. So I sent for Bombardier Dythan, my Signal NCO and Number One of the party. He heard me out while I expounded on the virtues of punctuality and obedience, and then said quietly, 'Well, sir, I think I'd better hand in my stripes. If you can make Lance Bombardier Howarth obey an order when he doesn't want to, good ... I'm afraid I cannot! I told him it was to be breakfast at five, and he just grunted.'

So I sent for Howarth. The pattern of his behaviour was becoming clearer: I remembered a half-heard remark of his the evening before – 'So it's all to be done through the 'usual channels', is it? We'll see!' Evidently he resented being given his orders through the Number One, Dythan, and was taking steps to teach the new Battery Commander a lesson. But I was puzzled at his timing. 'Bolshie' soldiers I'd met before, but never one who would take it out of his party by sending them into action without their breakfast.

When he came in his fate was in the balance. I had already been wondering why such a scruffy chap should have been chosen as the Battery Commander's Driver as it is a post of honour, reserved for a first-class driver and highly reliable man. I meant to try him, as my predecessor would obviously had got rid of him if he wasn't worth his keep, but I couldn't keep him if he did not accept me as the boss on my merits, leaving rank out of it. One has not time to spend in war on keeping one's personal staff in order.

The moment he stood before me I could see that he knew his bluff had been called because his knees were trembling. I took that as a sign that I should have no trouble in handling him and made a quick decision to keep him and not to punish him. So the conversation went like this:

'Why no breakfast, Howarth?'

'Well, Sir, there's no blackout to this house. You can't cook in the dark, can you Sir?' said he hopefully, but not very confidently.

It was a futile excuse, and he knew it, so he was taken aback when it was accepted at its face value.

'No, Howarth, of course you can't cook in the dark, but you could quite well have told someone about the blackout last night, couldn't you?'

He was then made to suffer a short homily on obeying orders – or explaining why they are impossible to carry out – and the incident was closed, with me wondering what the next move would be and just what was behind it all.

The answer came sooner than I expected. Just as we were on the point of setting out, a very apologetic Howarth came rushing out with – as it were – a stirrup cup. He dished out mugs of tea and packets of bully and biscuit like one demented. He was quite hurt when I told him to keep the bully. 'Ah never knew tha was going across t'canal!' he said. 'If Dythan'd told me that, we'd have had breakfast, blackout or not.'

So that was it. Dythan had listened to my order to the Battery, giving the whole story of what we intended to do, and he should have passed the gist on to his party. Instead, he had merely said to Howarth: 'Breakfast at five, Charley.'

'Who says?'

'The Major.'

'We'll see!'

It so happened that Howarth wasn't coming with me, as I was only taking the jeep, so the fact that something unusual was afoot passed him by, and he judged it as a good time to stage his protest at my apparent aloofness. Which seems to show that there is often more behind a 'military crime' than meets the eye.

It was cold and grey with mist when we arrived soon after first light at a big wood that ended on the canal bank at the place where we were to cross. There was a nasty silence broken by the fog dripping from the branches and the threatening boom of an occasional shell in the distance. The Sappers were trying to replace the bridge that had been blown up, but every time they showed themselves they got a good thumping, so it didn't look as if the bridge would be built in a hurry.

Ian McKenzie decided to do his reconnaissance on foot, so we left our small 'Tacs' and slipped into the wood with only his Orderly and a Signaller of mine accompanying us. Presently he asked me to collect his party and set up a temporary Tac HQ while he went to look at the proposed crossing place.

No sooner had I done so than the enemy seemed to guess where we were and strafed the place, hurting no one, luckily. Ian returned and moved us back a bit, and then we were well and truly mortared. Stevenson, my Signaller, had just finished a shallow slit trench for us, in which we thankfully crouched until it was over. The only casualty was my map case. I had left it on the edge of the slit, just by my head, and a splinter whizzed viciously through it.

Ian decided that we would be better off in a small bungalow in the middle of the wood. I reckoned that we would be worse off there because it was the only house in the wood and was marked on the map, thus an obvious target for the enemy Gunners to choose.

So it proved. We had not been there ten minutes before it was hit. Ian and I were down in the cellar at the time, looking at the Regimental Aid Post that the doctor was getting ready. Ian had a Signaller upstairs in the main room working a wireless, and my wireless was there too, but I had sent Stevenson to meet Nigel and some others to guide them to the house. Suddenly there was a crash and the whole building shook. Dust swirled from nowhere and enveloped us. We looked at each other with raised eyebrows – this was no way to start! Then Ian pounded up the steps.

'Where's Smith?' said he.

'I'm still here, Sir,' said Smith in a surprised but calm voice.

There he was, sitting on the ammunition box where we had left him, but looking as if someone had thrown a can of ashes over him. Three feet above his head was the hole where the shell had come in before bursting. It must have actually burst where Stevenson would have been sitting if I hadn't sent him away. At that moment he and Nigel came rushing in 'to collect the Battery Commander's corpse', as Nigel explained.

The plan was to cross the canal in collapsible canvas boats, taking only the minimum equipment, leaving the vehicles and heavy stores to be rafted over later. Being thus separated from our trucks presented the Gunners with the usual problem – that of carrying their wireless sets. These were heavy and awkward, and each set had two heavy banks of batteries to be carried as well. We had not the men to do the job without denuding the gun-detachments. True, we had some portable 'No. 18' sets, like those the Infantry had, but they were so unreliable that we never liked to use them except for very short distance.

On this occasion the Infantry promised to lend us men to form a carrying party for one heavy set, so we built our signal plan round that. It was arranged that I should bring it across and get it up to Nigel at the OP as soon as I could. That would give him communications direct to the Regiment. Before that he would have to pass his messages to me by portable set and I would pass them on. As an extra insurance we put my half-track with two big sets in it, with an Officer in charge, as a relay station at the back of the wood. So we had a fairly comprehensive layout. On top of all this, Philip Attewell was already deployed with a set on the flank, so our signal resources were used to the full and over.

The enemy knew that something was afoot and kept the wood under fire all the time we were preparing. He had one battery of fairly heavy stuff ranged on our house, but luckily his calculations were about a hundred yards out and he did not worry us too much – though we couldn't help wondering if he would find his error and make the necessary correction!

When it was getting close to the time I started to go and make sure that my party had collected the Infantry carrying party and their boats. Ian called me back and dissuaded me, pointing out that Dick Frisby, his second in command, 'had it all taped' and that the route to the crossing passed right by us so that I could pick them up without getting separated from him. A most unfortunate decision, as it turned out.

Ian jumped up and slapped the butt of his Sten gun. 'Now we can forget everything except the little gun,' he remarked.

We found that the chosen route was being shelled and Frisby had very correctly diverted the troops, but we caught up with the leading platoon just short of the crossing. All was quiet there except for a single spray of machine-gun bullets that dappled the smooth water. Back in the wood it was pretty horrible. The shelling had increased, after being continuous most of the morning, and the troops were not in good shape when they arrived.

The first two boats went over all right, but then people showed no inclination at all to move. They were disheartened for the moment, but Ian soon changed that. He was a real leader: he jollied and chivvied them until all was right again, and the place swarmed like an ant heap. He and I had a busy time helping to pull the boats to the edge and 'uncollapse' them, encouraging the chaps until they jumped in and pushed off. 'We must keep them moving,' he shouted, and with an 'I'm off now!' jumped in and paddled over.

Meantime, my party had not appeared. I stayed there for a bit, helping to launch the boats and so on, and then I completely lost my head in the excitement. Forgetting all about my party, it suddenly seemed wrong to shove people across and not go one's self, and I jumped in too. As soon as

I was across it struck me all in a heap that here was I, that most useless of all things – a Gunner without his communications to his guns.

It was done, so I had to make the best of it and hope they would catch up. Nigel was with them, so I was not too worried, and set about exploring. The Battalion was collecting in a large four-storied factory, actually a modern flour mill, and my first move was to see if 178 Battery had got an OP there, whose communications I could borrow to report progress. I found one with the Officer sitting comfortably in a window seat and soon let the Regiment know of our successful crossing.

By this time the mill was swarming with soldiers, making themselves far too obvious. A kind of reaction from the morning's shelling had set in and they were as light-hearted as a lot of children, firing rifles out of windows for no reason at all, not attempting to conceal their presence, in fact positively inviting the Bosch to take a hand in the game. I was as bad as the rest: I rushed up to the top floor to choose an OP, well knowing that top floors are places to be avoided in action. CRASH! A shell shattered a window.

I scuttled down a floor. Two more crashes, and I decided to postpone OP hunting until I had someone to man one, and went off to look for my party. I found them at the crossing completely left in the lurch and forgotten by the Battalion Second-in-Command. They had done a fine job, humping the heavy set and batteries unaided and commandeering a boat when none was forthcoming otherwise. In a very short time we were through by wireless to the Battery and Regiment from an OP on the fairly safe first floor.

When I found Ian again he produced a flask of tea, which we shared with great enjoyment. Hardly had we finished it when the enemy let drive at the upper storey in earnest from all angles. Shells crashed and banged above us, broken glass came tinkling down the stairs, and bricks and mortar fell all over the place. The Infantry were quickly brought downstairs, but there were a few casualties on the way. We were quite safe on the ground floor, it being a substantial building, but the noise overhead was not exactly restful. We were quite glad when it stopped.

During a welcome lull I was sitting on a corn sack trying to think out the next move when Nigel came in and shattered the peace with a few of his usual staccato phrases:

'Can't stay here, building's on fire! Quite a blaze – spreading – must get out!'

Get out we did, with flames crackling and roaring above us and smoke pouring out of the windows.

'D'you think it will spread?' said Ian.

I replied that the further away we went the better, having visions of the whole street in flames with the enemy stepping up the heat.

I was a bit pessimistic, as it happened: the mill was pretty well gutted, but nothing else caught. However, Ian agreed with me, and we moved to a little house some way off.

Our new home was a small house, which had the serious disadvantage of being only about fifty yards from the site where the Sappers were trying to build the bridge. All the shelling directed at them was equally unpleasant for us as well. However, Ian set up his Tac HQ in the cellar, and I took over the kitchen, which was at the side of the house farthest from the enemy.

In the evening Howarth and the half-track were rafted over, together with Nigel's OP carrier. The arrival was most welcome: now we could have a hot meal and get at our greatcoats and bedding, and above all we could re-organise our communications so that we were no longer dependant on improvisations. I had the vehicles most carefully tucked against the back wall of a house next to the canal and brought the wireless remote control wires into our Tac HQ. That gave us two safe harbours, as it were, but the seventy yards between vehicles and house was a regular 'mad mile'. No one dallied over the journey if he could help it, and Bombardier Dythan earned a Military Medal for many times repairing the wires under heavy shell fire.

That night was most unpleasant. To start with, there were far too many people in the small room. Then the bridge site was shelled most of the night, so we had bangs and crashes all round us, shaking the house. Sleep was very light and intermittent.

The RSF were to attack at 7.15 am, to break out of our small perimeter, and Nigel was to go with them, but the enemy spotted them forming up, and time after time the attack was broken before they could get off. Poor old Nigel had a most unpleasant time. Again and again he and his carrier seemed to be the centre of the target area. Eventually, the attack was abandoned. By then the whole of 44 Brigade – the KOSB having followed us across during the night – was bottled up in a small village barely large enough to hold a Battalion. Not a nice situation.

By this time the mill was a smouldering ruin, except for the ground floor, which was hardly touched. I put Jonah there to watch the right flank with an Officer from a Medium Regiment nearby to bring down the heavy stuff if needed. At any rate, they would be nice and warm!

While exploring the place I found one of 178's OPs and spent a pleasant half hour with the Officer. He spotted some movement in a field and gave it a burst. The effect was magic. A lot of men broke cover from a ditch at the back and ran for dear life to one nearer to us. That move did them no good, as the next burst landed slap on top of them – twenty-four shells in a salvo (all in one crash, that is).

Then we saw what they were up to. Before our eyes part of the hedge, about 1,000 yards away from us, started to move. Very slowly a gap appeared, and we saw that the moving hedge was in fact a beautifully camouflaged anti-tank gun. The Observing Officer let fly with all the Regiment's guns, but we could not see whether the anti-tank gun had to be abandoned or not. Anyhow, those Germans had something to write home about!

The lull in the shelling that persisted while I was on my rounds ended as I got back to our house. A shell landed right by the back door, just as Howarth was coming in with a mug of steaming tea in each hand. The blast made him move much faster than he intended, but he did not spill a drop: a cool customer, that man.

The mug he was bringing me had some tea leaves floating on the top, so he blew them off like froth from a tankard of ale. After his efforts in getting it to me I couldn't very well refuse it, so I made myself think of other things while I drank it. He had a foul cold at the time, and I got one shortly afterwards, so I can only suppose that, hot as the tea was, it was not hot enough to sterilise the cold germs.

During the day we had a Signaller killed and two others wounded right beside the trucks that I had hoped were so safe. A self-propelled (S-P) gun had sneaked forward and slipped a few shells along parallel to the canal, behind the sheltering houses. Such is one's luck in war.

The RSF sent out a carrier patrol, which met one of these 'eighty-eights' (S-P guns). I saw one of the carriers come back carrying a man with his roughly bandaged legs raised to rest on the front of the vehicle to help control the bleeding. Both of his feet had been shot off. He, poor lad, was quiet and resigned under morphine, but the Sergeant in command was completely unhinged for the time. 'It's murder!' he screamed. 'Bloody MURDER! Bloody murder!' Ian looked gravely and sadly at me and went to calm him and help him regain control. I felt so sorry for Ian that this should have happened in front of me – a comparative stranger from another Regiment.

However, Howarth had just brought me one of his so-welcome mugs of tea, and that was just what the wounded man needed. I had to go away before he had finished it, and the carrier crew left the mug for me, but someone else made off with it. Somehow, the little theft jarred – an example of how strangely some things can affect one in war. With all that physical and mental suffering, one seemed to have been in the presence of something higher than the ordinary run of daily life. The pettiness of it brought one back to earth with a jolt.

In a lull, Dick Bethell came to see us, and we had quite a bit of fun inducing him to put on his steel helmet. We had been wearing ours indoors in case the ceiling should come down on us. He well fulfilled the requirement that the visit of a Senior Officer in war should be as invigorating as a glass of champagne.

He soon made us realise that it was not raining everywhere because the sky over our heads happened to be black. Even if we were not making any headway, others were, and the pressure that we were exerting was helping the rest to push on. Next day he ordered our relief and Phil took over from me.

When we got to the crossing, where a boat was looped to a rope stretched across, we jumped thankfully in and gave a good heave – and nothing happened. We heaved again and again. Still no movement. I began to feel a bit panicky. Then we laughed a real 'belly laugh': in our hurry we'd forgotten to loose the painter!

Back at the Battery everything was delightfully peaceful. A farmer was taking out a horse and cart; his wife was feeding the fowls; some children were playing in the yard. It seemed unbelievable that the noisy place we had just left was less than two miles away.

However difficult things may have seemed, there were often some funny incidents. John Meredith of 178 Battery spent the night in a slit trench with the Company Commander on the edge of the village. Towards morning they heard shuffling footsteps coming. They kept silent until the wounded German – as they supposed – was nearly on them, then they yelled '*Hande hoch!*' There was a surprised snort in the dark and a body fell on top of them. John grabbed at what he thought was the man's ankle ... and found himself holding the snout of a pig!

Chapter 25

Woodland Battles

As soft lips that laugh and hide,
The laughing leaves of the trees divide,
And screen from seeing and leave in sight
The god pursuing, the maiden hid.

A C Swinburne

181 Field Regiment RA, September 1944

The operations of the next month will seem less disjointed and unconnected if we look at the 'big picture' for a moment or two.

At the beginning of September the ultimate aim of General Montgomery (who was commanding the Twenty First Army Group) was the isolation of the Ruhr Valley, Germany's main centre of industry. To achieve this he intended to force his way on a narrow front right up to Arnhem, on the far side of the River Nederrijn. He then meant to cross the River Rhine itself as soon as possible. Before this operation could be started, it was necessary to clear the Pas de Calais, to capture and bring into use the port of Antwerp, and to capture the airfields of Belgium.

At the time of the incident on the Escaut Canal described in the last chapter, the Second Army was roughly on the line of Escaut, with the First Canadian Army on its left and the American First Army on its right. The Pas de Calais was nearly clear and it remained but to clear the Scheldt Estuary to enable Antwerp to be used. The time was ripe for Montgomery's bold thrust to the Rhine, which, if it had been fully successful, might have brought the war to an end in 1944.

The plan was for the Second Army to 'lay an airborne carpet' over the river obstacles of the Wilhelmsvar and Wilhelmina canals near Eindhoven, the River Maas, and the Nederrijn at Arnhem and Nijmegen (on the Maas). The Guards Armoured Division was then to cut a narrow corridor, just a few miles wide, and join up with the British 1st Airborne Division dropped on Arnhem. The sides of the corridor were to be kept from caving in by VIII Corps on the right and XII Corps (in which was 15 [Scottish] Division) on the left.

XXX Corps was to operate the thrust and was to reinforce the Guards' armoured spearhead as fast as they could.

The American 101st and 82nd Airborne Divisions were successfully dropped on Eindhoven and Nijmegen on 17 September. On the same day our 1st Airborne and the Polish Brigade were dropped on Arnhem, but the fortune of war was against them. The Polish Brigade was dropped in the wrong place and was never able to make contact with the 1st Airborne. The Brigades of the 1st Airborne Division were more scattered than was intended, and they met very tough opposition from the start. To cap their troubles, bad weather intervened and made their reinforcement and supply drops largely ineffective. There then ensured a frantic race against time with everything depending on the Second Army joining up with the 1st Airborne before the latter were annihilated.

The Guards Armoured Division pressed on with all possible speed, competing with a dreadful road, full of bottlenecks, and meeting strong resistance at many points. 43rd (Wessex) Infantry Division scotched them up and cleared up behind them so that they could push on faster.

At one time the enemy cut the corridor in half, behind the advancing divisions, but the American 101st Airborne and a British Tank Brigade restored the situation. Meanwhile the 1st Airborne Division were living an epic of sustained bravery and effort. Hemmed in on every side, they fought one of the greatest losing battles of history.

Their most urgent need was artillery, as in those days only one Regiment of light mountain guns could be dropped with them, and three batteries of anti-tank guns. Many of these were destroyed early in the action and ammunition was scarce for the remainder. This need had been foreseen, and an Army Group RA of 'Medium' guns was well forward in the column. The story of their approach reminds one of the faint wail of the distant bagpipes foretelling the relief of Lucknow, only this time the relief was too late.

The gunners of the Airborne Division had wireless sets tuned to the frequency of the hurrying guns and the OPs were ready to direct their fire the moment they were within range. The plight of the Airborne soldiers was desperate: the enemy had penetrated deeply and most of the units were fighting battles on their own, cut off from their neighbours. Shelling was intense and continuous; on our side ammunition was growing scarce.

Suddenly the Airborne wireless signaller heard a Morse call sign – three letters of the Morse alphabet repeated over and over again. It was the call of the leading Medium battery. The call grew stronger and stronger until at last the Battery was close enough to switch to speech. Word went round that the artillery of the relieving Army was nearly in range. Hope ran high.

Then came the message that the guns could reach them – from nearly nine miles away. Quickly, the OP sent the map reference of the target, and just as quickly the Battery queried it – it coincided almost exactly with the reference that the OP Officer had given of his own position. 'That's just where we want it!' They preferred the risk of being killed by our own guns to the continuous strafing from German tanks and machine guns, and I have been told by those who were there that the shattering bursting of the Mediums' 'coal boxes' was a blessed relief.

The Guards linked up with the American 82nd Airborne at Nijmegen and 43 (Wessex) division passed through them to the Nederrijn. But the 1st had been fighting continually for eight days, against tremendous odds, and were no longer capable of continuing. On 25 September they were ordered to withdraw. The remnants were skilfully pulled out and ferried across the river in the dark, covered by a Battalion of Dorsets from 43 (Wessex) Division.

That is the bare outline of a brilliantly conceived operation. Montgomery estimated it as ninety per cent successful in that it disposed of three serious water obstacles and gave us a firm hold in Nijmegen. He was also certain that it would have succeeded entirely if the weather had not been against us, and if it had been possible to place the Polish Brigade properly.

Our job, then, while all this was happening, was to hold open the corridor and expand it as occasion offered. It was an unspectacular task, one might say, but necessary. In carrying this out, the general idea seemed to be to probe with small forces, recoiling if resistance was too strong and coming in again later with a full-scale attack.

We had a day of rest before starting the new phase and found ourselves – 179 Battery, that is – in the school buildings of a convent. We were on our own, so had to make sure that our defence plan would stand up to any surprise enemy penetration. When reconnoitring for the local defence plan, I found that one very likely way for the enemy to reach us could only be guarded against from a window inside the convent itself. That worried me quite a lot, as I thought that the Mother Superior would never willingly let me station troops inside the convent. She would be more likely, I thought, to say that Heaven was their defender, and that we would enter at our peril.

Never was an appreciation more wrong. She welcomed us with pleasure and was delighted that we were there to look after them. The upshot of it was that the Sergeant Major and I did a thorough reconnaissance of the place, followed by a bevy of nuns chattering away and pressing apples on us.

Our move from the bridge brings Howarth into the picture again. For some reason RHQ had insisted that tin hats should be worn, a thing we never did unless our heads seemed in imminent danger, as they were uncomfortable and heavy. Behold us, then, with the Battery lined up by the roadside waiting for the order to move. Up comes Howarth: 'Excuse me, Sir, this wearing of tin hats, are you expecting trouble – or is it just an order, because it makes my head ache!' It was rather fortunate that he was smoking before permission had been given, so I was able to maintain my composure by blowing him off the road for that, or I should have exploded with laughter in his face.

Many Gunner Officers never wore tin helmets, even in the front line, again mostly because of the discomfort but also because they interfered with the wearing of wireless headphones. I know one or two who definitely disdained to wear them because they found it had an effect on the morale of the people they met. I had proof of this one day, because we all were ordered to wear them as a matter of course by Dick Bethell, who gave out that if anyone got a tap on the nut that a tin hat would have prevented, that Officer was for it – if he lived. Soon after that order I met the Scots Fusiliers Padre. He said: 'My heart sank yesterday – I saw you in a tin hat; that made me think we must be in for a real thumping!'

That evening Ian decided to investigate a small chateau to see if it was occupied and we arranged a small fire plan to take the heart out of the opposition. Having sized up the strength of the place, he decided that it would be better to infiltrate quietly in the morning, to take the enemy by surprise.

So next morning a Platoon slipped silently into the early mist and disappeared among the trees that surrounded the place. Nigel went with them on foot with a Signaller carrying a light wireless. Soon we were biting our lips with suspense: there was not a sound to be heard, yet Nigel did not answer our calls for news. We thought his set must have broken down and began to wonder if the party had been scuppered. Then someone realised that after each of our calls there came a slight hum. At first we thought it was from our set, then it dawned on us – it was the carrier wave from his set; he was pressing his transmitter switch without speaking. Evidently he could not speak without giving the show away, but the hum showed that he was all right and could hear us, so we relaxed and awaited events. Suddenly his voice boomed through to say that they were safely there and the Bosch had left. He said afterward that the silence was so eerie that the slightest whisper seemed to echo in the mist and he dare not speak to us, so he hit on the idea of just pressing the switch to acknowledge our call. It was a useful tip, which we stored away for future use. As soon as they were there he caused quite a stir of admiration for his skill by ranging on to a small bridge very close to himself, so that he could block the enemy's passage if they should think of returning.

Ian McKenzie and I went to see the nuns in the evening and came away with a bag of some of the best apples I have ever tasted. I told Nigel to be sure and bring a lot back when he returned, but he forgot all about it. I wish I knew what sort they were.

I next found myself looking for an OP in a factory in a village nearby. Dead silence reigned there, though there was a Platoon of Infantry inside. The enemy had a post just across a canal, just fifty yards away, and neither side dared make a sound for fear of drawing fire. I met some Middlesex Machine Gunners there and was struck with the way their faces lit up at the sight of a Gunner cap badge. I had already found that the men of the Scots Fusiliers treated my men as if they were part of the Battalion, and this was further proof of the good feeling that existed between the two Arms. It was quite evident that the Battery – and, indeed, the Regiment – had completely won the confidence of the Infantry in the past, and that the latter believed them to be capable of anything. A proud – but very exacting – position to be in.

After I had fixed an OP for Phil I did some more creeping through the silent, deserted village, and from one vantage point saw a most extraordinary sight. I was looking at a British motorcycle standing by a bridge in no–man's–land when suddenly a Fusilier leapt from a ditch, kicked the machine into motion and rode back into the village without a shot being fired. From that day to this I don't know who he was, why he did it or how he got away with it.

*

Our next move was into Holland by night. For the first time we sampled 'artificial moonlight'. This was produced by a Searchlight Battery in a new role. It simply shone its beams on to low cloud and the reflected light was diffused over a wide area, giving a good imitation of moonlight and turning movement on a pitch dark night from a grope into normal travelling with a moon.

My first memory of Holland is of a narrow road with a row of gleaming silver birch trees on each edge. I remember thinking how clever of the Dutch to use trees to mark the verge and dyke beyond instead of putting white posts.

As we came nearer the source of the light, the bare flat fields were clothed in a beauty that they never wore by day, until at last we passed the projector itself, illuminating the little valley it was in so that it looked like a fairy grotto. The local people were asleep, but you could see it was a free country because every house had a flag flying from a pole in a socket on the wall.

We stopped at a pleasant farm where the people were most friendly, but the language was a terrible bar. In peace time most Dutch speak at least a little German, but they would not admit to it in the war for fear of being classed as collaborators. The ice was broken when someone suggested swapping ¼ guilders for sixpenny pieces. Even the shyest of the girls came forward with a smile to get her bit of English money.

Shortly after our arrival in the country 44 Brigade was ordered to advance on 's-Hertogenbosch and the Scots Fusiliers were put in the advanced guard, with my Battery to join them as soon as our Regiment could no longer cover them. I was delighted: one so seldom got the chance of having the Battery to play with on its own, right away from RHQ. It was not to be. Long before we were out of range we met stiff resistance and the guns never had to move.

As we started off we were with the Battalion in a tree-lined suburban road when a nice old Dutchman walked all round Ian's and my trucks, sadly shaking his head. We watched, wondering what it was all about. When he came to me he looked at me with such a comically sorrowful expression and said: 'What – no guns? No guns anywhere? You must have guns!' I could not help smiling as I thought how many my chuckling wireless could have raised for him if needed.

On our way we passed the Bata Shoe Factory, near Best, and when we were about 400 yards off all hell suddenly descended like the crack of doom on the wretched place. It was so unexpected that we nearly jumped out of our skins. It was an Uncle Target – all seventy-two guns of the Divisional Artillery's three Regiments were slamming into it. When we got over our first shock of surprise, it was thrilling. The noise was thunderous:

airbursts cracked overhead, great patches of roof suddenly disintegrated and smoke from the shells and burning buildings enveloped the place in a miasma of destruction. Then it stopped as suddenly as it began, leaving the factory a smoking wreck.

I called up the Adjutant and told him the fire was effective, but would he please give notice before he put one down so close to us without warning. I was never able to find out which OP ordered it, as we certainly had not.

Passing on from there, we came to a small village where Ian McKenzie set up Battalion HQ while the Companies probed the woods in front of them. Dick Frisby (Ian's Second-in-Command) and I reconnoitred the place together. On entering one deserted house I found an enormous basket full of eggs – just what the Battery wanted, I thought. Unfortunately I left them for a moment while I went to 'liberate' a roll of Bronco [toilet paper], which we happened to be short of. When I came back I found Frisby and his men shovelling the eggs into their haversacks. 'Hey! Those aren't yours,' said I.

'Well, they aren't yours either, if you come to think of it,' said he.

I told him, 'Finding's keeping!'

He capped that with. 'Possession's nine-tenths of the law!'

So we had a friendly wrangle, but all I got out of him was a couple of eggs apiece for my party.

One of the sad things of this part of the war was the number of fowls, tame rabbits, goats and even sheep left shut up without food or water when their owners fled. I spent a long time opening cages and doors, liberating a lot of captives who at once set to work on their owner's gardens with evident enjoyment.

Even worse was the number of cows with swollen, dripping udders, bellowing to be milked. Some of them came up to us and as good as asked for something to be done about it. We did our best, and relieved as many as possible, but we could not spend too long at the job as there were other things to do.

Meanwhile, the Companies were steadily probing the woods. That afternoon I scored a minor triumph. The Infantry had located a bazooka (small anti-tank weapon) at a track crossing in the wood. Phil could not see it and did not think it worth having a blind crack at, but Ian kept on muttering about this blessed thing, so at last I called for fire on the cross-tracks, and by sheer luck scored a direct hit. That stopped Ian's grumbling.

Later on we went to see Hugh Gow and his 'D' Company. He was in a dense part of the wood where there was so much undergrowth that the OPs could see nothing. The only sign of the enemy was the musical brrrr of his Spandau machine-guns, which just could not be spotted. Ian decided to withdraw the Company at dusk and asked for a small fire plan to keep the Spandaus quiet while this was done.

That set me rather a tricky problem. Nigel confirmed that they were impossible to spot, so the only thing to do was to put down a screen of fire in front of our own troops and hope that some of the shells would reach the Bosch weapons. So I pinpointed our Infantry positions as well as I could and drew up my plan.

Looking back, I just can't think why I did not have a test round or two to verify that I had not put the targets too close to our men. I took a fearful risk in not doing so. But my luck was in. The Company pulled out successfully and Hugh Gow was delighted with the covering fire. He said it was grand having our shells so close to them, almost putting a curtain between them and the enemy, and giving them a great feeling of confidence. I thanked my stars – and vowed never to take such a risk again.

The next day saw the KOSB in trouble. They always seemed to be in the mud. This time they attacked a little hamlet called Fraterhof and had many casualties. The ground was flat and partly wooded. Drainage dykes intersected the fields and seemed to offer the only covered approaches to the enemy position. But the wretched KOSB soon found that each of these was enfiladed by Spandaus and the attack failed.

The upshot was that the RSF were told to take on the job. The Divisional Commander, 'Tiny' Barber – tallest General in the British Army – came to Battalion HQ to give directions. I well remember him as he put a forefinger the size of a ham bone on the map: 'That's where you must get to,' he said. I also remember the uneasy look on Ian's face: he had summed up the difficulties in his mind and knew that it was a most unpleasant assignment.

At that moment Dick Bethell arrived and saved the situation. 'It's quite out of the question by day,' he said. 'I've just come from the KOSB and have seen the ground.' He then gave a most cogent exposition of why it was out of the question. The General heard him out and then cancelled the attack by day with no hesitation, telling the RSF to take it that night.

The postponement of the attack gave us ample time to reconnoitre and plan. We found the country flat and bleak. Large woods alternated with muddy, dyke-bordered fields, and there were no hills and hardly any rising ground. In default of high ground the farms and hamlets became strong points, because they gave a little concealment, and also a little height to give the OPs a commanding view over the surrounding flatness. In addition they were generally built at cross-tracks, and thus acquired an extra value as minor centres of communications.

The farm buildings also provided a screen to site Artillery behind. When there was no farm we put the guns in woodland clearings, or behind the woods themselves. The woods made fine tactical obstacles because you could never be sure just what was in them. The brushwood could be turned into a 'hell's kitchen' by anti-personnel mines, particularly by a new variety – the 'Schu'-mine – made of wood to defeat our mine detectors. The only way to find them was to probe gently with a pointed rod, which took time. Of course, a wood is also ideal for ambushes.

That description applies to the whole of the area in which we operated for nearly a month after leaving the Escaut Canal. We had no long moves, our activities being bounded roughly by the sides of a triangle with Eindhoven, Tilburg and 's-Hertogenbosch as the apexes.

The evening found us all ready for the attack to go in at 9.00 pm. Then, half an hour before it was due to start, Ian suddenly found it necessary to move his HQ. That gave me a lot of trouble. The move was only about a mile, but it meant that we only had fifteen minutes to get set up in our new place – time enough by day, but this was a dark and rainy night.

The Signallers' fingers became all thumbs and the wireless sets gave trouble. I dropped a heavy steel shutter of the half-track's window on a finger, which did not improve my temper. To crown it all, the Infantry managed to drive a carrier round the yard before we had made our cables and remote control wires secure. It is wonderful what a lot of damage to cables a carrier can do in a very short time. In fact, it was not my choice of how to spend an evening.

Punctually at 9.00 pm the guns opened fire and the attack started. Ian's wireless gave trouble, so for most of the time he was more than usually dependant on my set for news of the battle. It was a pretty good 'mix up' because of the dark and rain, and the difficult country. Nigel's reports were good at first until he got separated from the Company Commander. Then he could only give his own local picture, as he had no wireless to the Platoons. From our position we could only see an occasional flare and hear the noise of shell bursts and machine guns. At last came the news that they had reached the objective and were digging in.

It transpired afterwards that Nigel had put up a fine performance. Finding that all the Senior Officers of the Company were killed or wounded, he took charge and led them to the final objective and directed the consolidation on it. For this I am glad to say he was awarded the Military Cross.

Then, when I had arranged the Defensive Fire tasks with Ian McKenzie and Nigel and the excitement had subsided, Dick Bethell called us up to say: 'Jolly good show! I'm coming up to see how you are.' That was typical of his selfless outlook. He could not rest until he was sure that we had got all we could possibly want. I did my best to dissuade him. In war people just don't travel about the front at night unless they have to. To reach us he had two or three miles to go, during which he might bump into a enemy patrol, drive into an unmarked minefield, or he might spend ages trying to find us in the dark, in strange country. Apart from that, I wanted to get some sleep while all was quiet. After all, it was nearly 1.00 am.

Half an hour later he had not arrived and I began to wonder if something had happened to him. I got on the air and asked if any of the other Batteries had seen him, thinking that he might have called in on them on the way. All said no, except the Adjutant. He said accusingly, 'He left for your location thirty minutes ago!'

Then I remembered something and broke into a cold sweat. On our way we had come to a very sharp turn into a side-track. At that point an American soldier showed me a string of mines that he had pushed into the side, having no more use for them. It was a standing order that anyone who found mines was to broadcast the fact so that anyone likely to pass that way could mark them on his map and avoid them. In the hurry and bustle of moving I had forgotten to do that. Had I killed my own Colonel by my negligence? Do you wonder I sweated?

While I was still on edge with suspense, he rolled in, just as cheerful as ever, congratulating everyone on pulling off a difficult attack so successfully. Not until he had been with us for some time did he mention that he had had 'quite an adventure' on the way. He had overshot the turning, so got out to direct his driver. As the jeep backed into the hedge, off went a mine! The jeep went up with a roar and came down an untidy heap of twisted metal. The driver ended up thirty yards away, unhurt except for a cut on the arm. The Colonel himself was unhurt. What an escape! And what devil's luck that anyone should have had occasion to turn a truck at that point. But for that, the mines might have stayed there for years without harming anyone.

In the morning I sent Phil to relieve Nigel and took a walk round. Just as I was enjoying myself at his OP taking a pot shot at nothing in particular, I got a message from Ian to come back at once, as an enemy counterattack was starting. The guns opened fire as I hurried back to Battalion HQ and I found that Dythan had given Ian McKenzie an Uncle in my absence, which pleased me a lot, as a Signaller is not usually expected to be able to compete with fire control.

The attack did not come in on us, but hit the neighbouring Battalion, where Geoff Graham, the Second in Command, happened to be at the time. He was delighted at the chance to do some shooting and called for a 'Mike' (or Regimental) target straight away.

Now, part of the Second in Command's duties is to conserve ammunition by ensuring that people do not use the whole Regiment when a Troop or Battery would be enough. Before a Mike or Uncle is fired, the OP Officer has to give a description of the target. If the second in command thinks it is not big enough, he tells him to use fewer guns. At this time in the war we had ammunition to spare, so few people bothered to restrict the fire. But not so Geoff! He was a stickler for it. Time and again a Troop Commander would call for a Mike and forget to describe the target. Every time Geoff came on the air with: 'Give description of Target!' Naturally, this was most unpopular. It slowed down the rate of engagement, and anyhow, it is extremely difficult to see just what is coming at you. Usually an attack is announced by a furious outburst of gunfire from the opposing side and plenty of small arms fire. In answer to this you touch off what seems to be the nearest defensive fire task to the small arms, and then watch intently for a clue to the direction it is taking.

If you are lucky, you will spot some movement – little groups of figures, perhaps, hurrying from one bit of cover to another – and then you let fly with all the guns you can raise. That was what Geoff saw. He called for a Mike target and gave no description. Back at RHQ the Adjutant put his tongue in his cheek: 'Give description of target,' he said, and all the OPs on the wireless net chuckled.

'I can't see what it is,' said Geoff. 'All I know is that it needs a heck of a lot of fire!' He got the target at once. Never again was he finicky at releasing guns to an OP Officer who needed them in a hurry.

After that I went back to the Battery for a rest, leaving Phil with Ian McKenzie. They were in a little village, pleasant but rather cramped. I slept in the kitchen of an elderly Dutch woman who was very kindly disposed. She carefully made up the fire in the little goblet-shaped stove before she went to bed, smiling and making signs that I should be nice and warm. Next morning she was rooting about very early. She kept her Sunday finery in a chest in the kitchen and had forgotten her headdress. I saw her in it as she went off to Mass, a fine handsome figure in black, a bit austere and stiff, with a lovely lace crown and veil that reminded me of the Duchess's cap in *Alice in Wonderland*.

I used to enjoy coming back to the Battery. Everyone was so pleasant and friendly, and Ray Bristowe (the Battery Captain) [see plate] always had the domestic side so well organised.

As a rule the first thing I did was to have a quick walk round to see how everybody was. Then I would go to the Mess, usually the front room of a farmhouse. There, Bombardier Dodd would appear with a stiff whisky and soda as I settled by the fire or roaring stove. 'Nice chicken for lunch today, Sir,' he would say.

Dodd would have made a perfect butler. He really enjoyed looking after the Officers: 'Only I must have a good place to work in, Sir; I can't do nothin' proper if Cap'n Bristowe don't pick a proper billet for us.'

Then my batman, Gunner Bain, would appear and take me to my room and a boiling bath, and a clean set of clothes. A discussion would follow on the latest news and what had happened in the Battery, and I would give an account of our doings with the Battalion. Then a meal, and bed. In war it is sleep that one needs: sleep, and more sleep. More than half one's work is done at night, and when one does get to bed there are sure to be interruptions. One is always close to the wireless in action, and, personally, I always had half an ear open, and was always fully awake the moment it said something important, or if someone came into the Command Post, slipping back into sleep as soon as I heard that the right action was being taken by those on duty. Only when the Battery or Battalion was away from the fighting zone could one relax fully.

I never took Bain forward with me. Howarth or Bull fed me and produced the shaving water and looked after my blankets and small kit, which was all the 'batting' I needed in action. It did not seem right to take an extra man into danger when there was no other job that he was needed for. Bain was a big, quiet man with a nice sense of humour, and absolutely reliable. He could be outspoken too: almost his last words to me when I left the Regiment were 'We didn't think you'd be much use when you came – you was so *quiet*! We'd been used to Major Keenlyside: he was always shouting' an' creatin' about sumthin'!'

This time he produced me a bath in a hen house, boiling hot and very refreshing. Though I did not know it, I was washing off the last dirt of this phase of the Campaign. We had finished with the enormous woods and bleak, flat fields of this part of Holland. Next day 15th Scottish handed over their sector to the Highland Division and pulled out for a rest before starting a new thrust. We were relieved by our old friends of 126, 128's sister Regiment.

I had then been with the Battery exactly nineteen days, and fourteen of those had been spent with the Scots Fusiliers, in action. So the rest period was just what I wanted, and the opportunity to really go through the Battery and get to know everybody in it and everything about it. I had been in the saddle, it is true, but we went straight off at the gallop, and this was my first chance to fit my stirrups and alter the fit of the bridle.

Chapter 26

Rest and Repair

181 Field Regiment RA, October 1944

A thoroughly happy Battery pulled out of the muddy fields and jolted contentedly as the speedos clicked up the miles. The Gunners were dreaming of nice billets and bright streets, lovely Dutch girls to walk out with them and all the delights that civilisation seems to offer when one has long been away from it. A very surprised Battery found itself allotted one small farm near a tiny village called Beek en Donk. The village was nearly as small as the farm and there was no decent-sized town for miles.

My first reaction was to jump into a jeep with Ray Bristowe and prove that he was right in saying that there was just nowhere else to go within the area allotted to us. That done, we settled down to make the best of it. A fair-sized loft and stables gave the men some rather cramped quarters and a shed provided a cookhouse. The Officers' Mess was in a kind of scullery: small, dirty, uncomfortable and smelling of sour milk. It would have been passable as a shelter during a battle but it was definitely not fit to be a rest billet.

The owner was a decent elderly farmer. His wife looked as cross as two sticks, but actually she was quite a nice old soul. The language bar limited our conversations to smiles and grunts, except for the odd word of Dutch that we had picked up on our travels. We sometimes had a cup of coffee with them before going to bed, to show friendliness, and then we put our full knowledge of the language into action with the words sounding like '*Kommen schlapen camra – ouden nacht.*' Everyone would make a move at that, so I suppose that it was a fair approximation to what we thought we had heard others say.

The next two days were spent in cleaning and overhauling every bit of equipment. Guns were stripped and cleaned, wireless sets checked and repaired and every inch of signal cable examined for bares in the insulation, and of course all the car engines were serviced. Howarth and I had a friendly passage of arms when I found the half-track with the original mud on it still at the end of the second day. 'Between you and me, Sir, ah don't hold wi' cleanin' trooks. If t' trook's alright under tha bonnet – that's good enough for me!'

It is queer how fate – or Providence, call it what you will – sometimes takes a hand in one's affairs. One of our Sergeants decided that he wanted to transfer to the Infantry and asked to go to the Scots Fusiliers. In the process of arranging the transfer, we took him to be interviewed by Ian. Ian accepted his request and that cost him his life. While he was still only attached to the Fusiliers, waiting for the transfer to be put through, he did splendidly and was recommended for the Military Medal. Before the award reached him, he was killed in action.

The Battalion very comfortably ensconced in Helmond. They invited Phil, Nigel and me to a party, which turned into a dance, and was the first time we met any Dutch girls. They are honest and reliable, and most pleasant. By comparison, the Belgians, the most sparkling of our allies, were vibrant and friendly, but some were found to be untrustworthy opportunists. The difference was most noticeable on our reconnaissances.

One day, instead of the usual sullenness that we had grown used to meeting in Holland when we told a farmer or his wife that we were moving guns into their fields and should need some accommodation, the farmer's wife was all over us. Coffee was served in the best room, all was smiles and nothing was too much trouble.

'Do you know why all this is happening?' said Bob Livie, the Survey Officer. 'If not, look at your map!'

I looked at it and saw that we had crossed the frontier and were back in Belgium. But make no mistake – the Dutch were by far our staunchest allies.

When we had been out of the line for a few days the Colonel told me to take a truck and a couple of officers and have forty-eight hours in Brussels, so Phil and Moss Waters and I hit the trail. We found it a nice city, hardly touched by the war. The shops were full of good things – at a price – and the people seemed delighted to see us. Special leave arrangements enabled us to be billeted in a very comfortable hotel for five Francs a day: half a crown [25 pence]. In the evening we went out to dine. To our annoyance we were joined by a young Belgian who offered to be our guide and just would not be shaken off. Seeing that nothing but force would get rid of him, we gave in, and agreed to pay for his dinner if he showed us a good place. He seemed a nice enough chap, and was good company, but we rather wondered where we would end up.

We needn't have worried. I don't know whether he was a tout for a restaurant or a genuine anglophile. At any rate, he played no tricks and took us to a nice little place where we had one of the best 'black market' dinners ever. At a screened-off table we ate delicious clear soup with sherry, plump roast pullet about the size of a partridge, with green peas and all the trimmings, all cooked to perfection. There was a good wine, everything was of the best, perfectly served, and the proprietor presented us with an excellent brandy to crown it. It was the sort of dinner that leaves one in the mood to unbutton one's waistcoat and settle down to a good cigar. When the bill came it seemed an awful lot of francs, but in trying to work out the sum in my head I really wasn't sure if it came to five pounds or five shillings. In the morning I found it was twenty-five shillings, remarkably cheap for the black market.

After dinner we told our friend, Georges, to take us to Maxine's night club, steadfastly refusing his more lively suggestions. There the waiter promptly asked fifty shillings [£2.50] for a bottle of champagne, but Georges took him aside for a minute and the man came back with the bill altered to a pound. By this time two or three quite nice girls had joined us and the party looked like starting. One of them looked Argentinean, but she swore that her mother was English, and she was born in Manchester. She pretended to be most hurt at the suggestion that she must have left England at a very early age to have lost her north country accent so completely. She soon recovered when we all assured her that her present accent was quite charming.

We danced a bit, until the floor became too crowded, and then had a lot of amusement watching some American soldiers on the dance floor. Many of them still kept on their comical little side hats – nearly as silly as those we wore in the early years of the war. They looked as if they had strayed into civilisation by mistake, and had not the foggiest idea what to do now they had arrived there. They circled the dance floor with grim, set expressions, hugging their partners in a 'surfboard' grip, doing the most fantastic steps, and the concentration their faces expressed gave no sign of enjoyment of the dance but simply of a pressing need for feminine contact. Their women were not partners in entertainment: they were just vehicles in ... well, call it emotion.

Late the next afternoon we got back to the farm to find that we had narrowly missed the father and mother of a 'flap'! While we were in Brussels the Regiment had been put at half an hour's notice to move back into the line and a jeep had been sent to recall us. How fortunate that it failed to find us. In due course the flap died a natural death and all was peace again.

Ray now decided that it was time to tackle the farmer's wife about her vacant front room. We could not stand that horrid little scullery a moment longer. For a time she ranted and raved and then suddenly gave in, so in we moved. It was a typical parlour, shiny as a doll's house and used twice in a lifetime – once for a wedding and once for a funeral. Varnished oilcloth on the floor made it smell unused. Every picture was a religious one. A large statuette of Our Lord stood on the sideboard, and nearby was a smaller one of St Theresa. There were artificial flowers in a vase in the corner and the window was covered with heavy gauze curtains. Some stilted family groups of the year 1910 or thereabouts completed the adornments.

The room was a bit small for the eleven of us, but an improvement on the scullery. It was obviously the woman's pride, so I am glad to say that we left it as we found it, save for one or two unavoidable scratches on the floor cloth.

Soon rumours of moves and warning orders began to plague and disturb us, making it impossible to plan ahead, or to know how much equipment we dared take to pieces to overhaul. From one day to the next we never knew whether we would be there the next day or not. Such uncertainty is one of the most wearing aspects of the war. At last we were told that there was no possibility of a move for a week or ten days, so we could relax completely. We were called into action the next morning at 9.00 am.

Chapter 27

Holiday Tasks

Then came a bit of stubbed ground, once a wood,
Next a marsh, it would seem, and now mere earth
Desperate and done with; (so a fool finds mirth,
Makes a thing and then mars it, till his mood
Changes and off he goes!) within a rood—
Bog, clay and rubble, sand and stark black dearth.

Robert Browning

181 Field Regiment RA, October 1944

When a Division is resting, envious eyes are cast upon its guns by those still in action. You can never have enough guns, so the legend has grown that Gunners don't need any rest and they are pressed into service as much as is humanly possible. That is what happened to us at Beek. We were brought back early to add to the fire power of other Divisions, though I forget which they were.

We came into action near the village of Oploo in country as dreary and flat and waterlogged as any in Holland. It was just impossible to find good troop positions: one just chose a field with rather less water in it than the others and got the guns in as best one could.

Not being in support of our own Division, we had no OPs out. We just went where we were told and fired when we were told, leaving their Gunners to do the observing and planning. It was rather dull, but it gave one a chance to watch the Battery at work and correct any faults that became apparent.

For three days we had no shooting, which was just as well, as it rained like in the days of Noah. All the gun pits were flooded and had to be floored and riveted to stop them from collapsing altogether. The respite gave us time to conquer the elements and make ourselves fairly comfortable and shipshape by the time the fire plan arrived. The first programme was fired at night, and is perhaps interesting enough to deserve a digression.

*

We will go first to the Battery Command Post – the brain and computing centre of the Battery. Here the records and data are kept of every important target engaged by the Regiments of the Divisional Artillery. Fire plans are received here, to be broken down into data to set the sights of the guns. Corrections for wind and weather and many other sums are worked out here too, and it is the communication centre of the Battery. It is a place where the pressure of work is normally intense. Many calculations are in progress simultaneously, dovetailed to fit into the next series. The governing criteria are accuracy and controlled, unhurried speed. Every measurement and every sum is checked by someone working independently. Mistakes may costs lives, so there must be none.

Presiding over this centre of clear thinking concentration is Philip Mulholland, the Command Post Officer, or CPO. He looks like a schoolboy and is in fact little over twenty-one, but he is cool, clear headed and an excellent organiser. If he were not, he would have a nervous breakdown. He is only a Subaltern, but he is the keystone of the Unit. With a bad Battery Commander and indifferent Troop Commanders the Battery could still function, after a fashion, but if the CPO should fail there would be a ghastly catastrophe, and very soon. Tonight the Command Post is in a barn. The glare of a petrol lamp blinds us for a moment as we enter, then our eyes adjust themselves and we take in the scene.

Philip is standing between two white-topped tables – the 'Artillery Boards' on which the switches and ranges are measured. Grouped so that he can look over their shoulders are the men who do the sums. At the moment he is talking to one of the Troops on the phone. Another phone whirrs at his elbow and he quickly answers it. That is the 'Battle Phone', through which the Second in Command and Adjutant send their orders. It is only used for vital messages, so there is a rule that it must be answered by an Officer within twenty seconds. This time it is the Adjutant giving the time of the attack. Close beside Philip is a whirring wireless set. We are working by phone at the moment, but the wire may be cut, so the wireless is standing by ready to take over. In the corner Jack Porter, the Assistant CPO, is snoring gently. It is to be a long show, so he and Philip will split the night between them. Jack is a schoolmaster by profession and a very witty man with a great sense of humour. He is rather older than the rest, but very fit and active in spite of a balding head.

The least concerned of those in this room of tension is Polly, a nondescript and undersized fowl. She has been on the strength since the Battery was at St Etienne in Normandy. So popular is she that once, when she was left behind in a quick move, Ray had to go back thirty miles to fetch her. Tonight she has chosen a perch above the Artillery Boards and sits there unmoved by anything. Occasionally she opens an eye, blinks stupidly at the Tilly lamp for a moment, and then returns her head to its place under a wing.

The time has nearly come. Bombardier Westwood and his mate Bombardier Brooker sit back with a sigh of relief as the last sum checks out correctly. Westwood pulls out a packet of fags and Brooker feels for the matches. Philip has the battle phone to his ear and his mouth at the Troop phone.

'One-oh seconds to go', says he. 'Five ... Four ... Three ... Two ... One ... FIRE! Roger shot on Serial One.' The last remark tells the Adjutant that 179 Battery ('R' for short) has started on the programme. The building shakes. Polly looks annoyed for a moment and goes to sleep again; a gentle snore comes from Jack's corner. Droves of shells from other Regiments whistle and screech overhead and the lamp flickers with each nearby bang. The Corps Artillery is at work.

Out of doors the sky is lit by continual flashes and the air pulsates with the rhythm of unceasing distant booms, into which the sharp bangs of our Battery's guns interpolate themselves with a crack that makes one's eardrums throb. We pick our way through the wet, dyke-bordered field until we come to 'Easy' Troop command post, where Jim Boyd is in charge. As we arrive, he remarks to his microphone: 'Change to Serial 2, zero four degrees, angle of sight two-oh minutes elevation, six two hundred.' One by one four tiny bulbs glow in front of him as each gun acknowledges the orders. There is a short pause while the sights are reset, and the banging starts again.

Jim is a comparatively elderly, slow-speaking Lowland Scot, loved by his men. He is most amusing when he thinks he has a grievance, arguing solemnly about it until suddenly the humour of it strikes him, when he slowly starts to laugh – and no one who is near can help but join in. He stands where he can see all his four guns.

A dark hump reveals itself as Number One Gun as we edge our way along a wire fence. Its shield and barrel and the six figures of its detachment appear as fleeting dark silhouettes in the flickering brightness of the barrage. An intense flash from its muzzle illuminates the men's white faces and the whole Troop position is shown in relief as we approach. 'Load,' says Sergeant Boughey. There is a sound of metal on metal and a dull 'zonk' as the shell is rammed home. The brass cartridge is slipped in with a 'clitter-clink-klip', and the breech closes sharply. A feeble glow from a shaded torch glints on moving brass-hand wheels as the layer aligns the sight on a pin-point of light in front; a slight pause while he levels the range bubble, then, 'Ready! Fire!' and one more twenty-five pounds worth of destruction hurtles away to the enemy. A saw-edged roar tells us where the shells are bursting on the Bosch, nearly four miles ahead. We listen and thank our stars that he is short of artillery and can only send back a single shell for every ten that we pour on him.

October 13 was an unlucky day for us. Twice we got the order to move; twice it was cancelled. The second time we did not get the cancellation until the guns had been pulled and winched out of the pits, churning the place into a morass into which they had to return.

That evening Dick Moorshead and his Captain, Peter Sharp, paid us a visit, Dick being the Commander of 178 Battery. The weekly NAAFI ration had just arrived, so we had a pleasant evening over whisky and poker dice. Next evening we returned the call and drank their whisky. For some reason, these evenings stand out in my memory as delightfully friendly affairs. One so seldom had either the time or the inclination to go visiting in war that it was a real pleasure to forget events for a bit and become almost civilised.

Our next position was in a dreadfully desolate (Venray) area, flat and wet and with whole woods practically reduced to stumps by shell fire. And it was pelting with rain to boot! There was one ruined roofless house there, which we made the best of by tying a tarpaulin over what rafters remained. That gave us shelter enough to produce a mug of boiling tea laced with rum when the guns arrived at midnight in the pouring rain. Rum in tea is wonderfully comforting on such occasions. Just as we were settling in, a big fire plan was flung at us for 6.00 am. That kept us busy all night, drawing ammunition and otherwise preparing for it.

At 6.00 am precisely we opened fire and the wires became red hot with people telling us to stop. The attack had been postponed an hour and no one had told us. When we did start we found ourselves in the front row of a great collection of guns, which up to then had been hidden in the mists that had succeeded the rain. The din was tremendous and the mist held the smoke until we were lost in a smoggy inferno of sound that was deafening and most oppressive. Thank heavens the enemy did not shell us as well: after our wretched night that would have been the last straw.

After a couple of days back at the Beek farm we continued to act as reinforcing artillery and had our first experience of refugees. They came straggling back from the German side in their hundreds. Their carts, piled high with what they had been able to save of their belongings, blocked the roads and made movement very difficult. When the weather was fine they were cheerful and gave us the 'V' for victory sign as we passed. When the rain fell it was a harrowing sight to see grandmothers and children perched on top of the load in wet misery, with fathers leading the horses and mothers carrying the youngest on the seat of a bicycle.

One place, Loosbroek, was full of them, undernourished and starved. Quite a lot of our men's rations went to them – the British soldier is a very kindly person. The woman of the farm that we occupied was most kind too, but found the refugees a sore trial. It was the last straw for her when one of them started to have a baby in the night. 'She's forty, if a day,' said our friend, 'and it's her first.'

The first I knew of this was being woken up in the night and asked to give up my bed for a confinement. They also asked for a doctor, so I rang up RHQ and got hold of the MO, Stuart. He was horrified. 'Why, I haven't had a confinement since my student days!' he said. Then he became quite enthusiastic at the experience to be gained and by morning there was another little Dutchman in the world, named Stuart after his Scottish godfather. It is sad to have to say that Stuart was killed the next day. He took his half-track into a minefield to help a wounded man and was blown up.

It was now that eyes started to turn towards the town of Tilburg. On 24 October, when we were in the middle of a move, the order came for the OP parties and myself to join the Colonel in new country twenty miles away at once, near Sint-Oedenrode. We went flat out – or at least as fast as the road allowed – and met the Colonel, to be told to join the Scots Fusiliers at once.

I dashed on with Phil and Nigel to find the Scots climbing on to the tanks of 6th Guards Tank Brigade with orders to go and occupy a town called Oirschot on the route to Tilburg, which the enemy had been seen evacuating. We entered it at dusk and found it practically deserted, so we chose the best house and broke in, greatly helped by an officious young Dutchman who cut his hand breaking a window and bled like a pig. In spite of his injury, he managed to find us a couple of bottles of good wine buried in the garden, which went down very well. One almost forgave the poor chap for making a beastly mess all over the place. In case anybody thinks I am being unkind to him, I should mention that there was no cause for him to break a window and get cut.

On we went at first light, and for a time the Battery shared a farm with the RSF. I invited them to go round the guns, and I think both sides enjoyed themselves – our men had a very high opinion and affection for the Battalion, and I think the feeling was reciprocated. By a series of coincidences the Battery followed the Battalion into several locations after this, which seemed to make the affiliation a very real thing.

We had now come almost within striking distance of Tilburg and there was a slight pause while we gathered the intelligence to find whether it would be a fierce battle or a walkover. In either case, 15th Scottish had been promised the run of it, and there was considerable excitement afoot, as it was the first large town that had come the Division's way.

Chapter 28

The Liberation of Tilburg

Everyone suddenly burst out singing;
And I was filled with such delight
As prisoned birds must find in freedom,
Winging wildly across the white
Orchards and dark green fields, on – on
and out of sight

Siegfried Sassoon

181 Field Regiment RA, 27 October 1944

The capture of Tilburg was the last task left in the clearing of the enemy out of south-western Holland. With that completed, the Allies could be free to concentrate on pushing the Bosch right over the River Maas. Our progress was therefore watched with considerable interest by the rest of the Army. We were to act with speed, but there were to be no mistakes: a setback here would delay the general plan considerably.

Early on 27 September the Scots Fusiliers moved its HQ to a nice half-timbered house surrounded by big woods in the north east of the town. It was what we had come to know as a 'smashing billet' (a nice place to be), but we only stayed there just long enough to get ready for the attack. We had arranged quite a big fire plan to smother the edges of the town, but it was not intended to shell the town itself if it could possibly be avoided. Nigel and Jack Porter were with the forward Companies and I was in my usual place near Ian. The other two were on foot, and I sent them with the No. 18 portable wireless set, as distances were not great that day. They were to speak to me and I would relay their messages.

At first light everything was still and expectant. A slight mist caused people to vanish in the gloom of the wood as soon as they left you. The only sound was the gentle tap of water dripping from the branches. Then we started our engines and Ian's carrier moved off. At that precise moment my wireless to Nigel and Jack broke down. The wretched No. 18 set again. For a moment I was flummoxed. But while I was wildly racking my brains for a solution, the Signal Bombardier said he believed our frequency might be in the part of the band that overlapped that of the No. 22 set.[1] I jumped at that straw and yelled for Driver Bull. 'Turn the set on', I said, 'and try and pick up the OPs.' Breathlessly, we waited while he tuned. For a few moments there was not a sound – then Nigel's voice suddenly crackled in the headphones. We were saved! The crisis was over.

But there was another one brewing. My communications were now split between two vehicles, so these had to be next to each other. Unfortunately Howarth for once was a slow starter and the Machine Gun Officer and three or four other carriers slipped in front of him. I could not drop behind because I had to be up with Ian, and the track was too narrow for them to overtake. So there was I, a hundred yards separating my two sets. When I might be speaking to the OPs, up would come a panting Signaller from the half-track – 'Colonel wants to speak to you, Sir!' – and I would dash back to the jeep, and all the time the column was slowly winding forward, so I was covering quite a lot of ground. I had to keep an eye on Ian's movements too in case he should dash off somewhere. By the time the half-track managed to catch up I was a very hot and breathless Battery Commander!

Dick Bethell wasn't any help either, for once: he was rather trying. Everyone was so anxious to know whether the Germans intended to hold the town that they kept badgering those below them for news. Dick was the one who had to extract it from the man on the spot. Hence a continual stream of questions.

'Where have your friends got to?'

'I don't know – I haven't had time to ask them.'

'Have they struck any opposition?'

'Not yet.'

'Are they likely to?'

'I don't know!'

'Well, find out!'

So I had to puff up to Ian McKenzie and ask him, did he think the enemy was likely to make a stand?

Ian smiled and remarked: 'How the devil can I tell what the enemy's going to do? We haven't even bumped him yet – tell Dick not to be so impatient!'

By this time we had reached the edge of the wood and the outskirts of the town were in sight. We passed one of the Regiment's targets and Ian commented on the accuracy of the fire. It was good, too. The ground in and around what had been a Platoon post was pitted and pock-marked with shell holes. Nearby was a factory, looking rather sorry for itself, with great holes in the roof and smoke pouring gently through the gaps. One or two houses near it had caught some 'overs' from it; otherwise the town was untouched.

As we pressed on we caught up with 'A' Company and found Jack Porter enjoying himself on his first job as Forward Observer. He and his party had seen a couple of Germans running for dear life. One fell to a Bren gun bullet and the other got away. Otherwise there was no sign of opposition.

On into the silent, deserted streets we went, until Ian settled for a while in a large house. Some Germans were rounded up and brought in at the double for searching. This was to the huge joy of the large family in the house, except for one old lady. She evidently thought they were to be shot on the spot. That was too much for her and she burst into tears.

Finding we were to stay there for a bit, I set about house hunting, to be met by Howarth with news of a smashing billet. Having learnt that his judgement was good in such matters I told him to lead on, and soon we were installed in the house of a friendly doctor.

By now the people were becoming aware that they were free. They started milling about the streets waving flags and a few cheers were raised. There was still a strained, uncertain look in their faces, but it was the nearest that I had yet seen them to looking happy. The doctor was delighted we had come, put us in the best room and brought out the wine. Thinking of the possible counterattacks, I said he must on no account make my soldiers drunk, as the battle was not over yet. At this everyone applauded – including the soldiers. In the excitement the doctor's son, a young man of eighteen, quietly fainted. Howarth at once cottoned on to the reason: the whole family was suffering from starvation. Without a word to anyone, he collected all the spare rations that we always carried against emergencies and cooked them the best meal they had eaten since the occupation. They were almost in tears with gratitude. I expect the funny little British soldier with the abrupt manner and kind north country heart is still remembered there to this day.

Outside the house a crowd was admiring our trucks and asking all who appeared to sign their autograph books. There was not a suggestion of begging for chocolates or cigarettes, but when a packet of fags was produced it was emptied before you could wink. It was a real pleasure to see what enjoyment those cigarettes gave. Unlike the Belgians, the girls did not attempt to kiss us: they were just decorously and blissfully happy. A smiling request for an autograph was the nearest they came to making any sort of advance. One old man came up to me and pointed to one of the party playing the fool and stunting on a Dutch bicycle. 'German, like bicycle, he take it away,' said the old boy. 'Tommy, take bicycle, he play with it, and he bring it back – Tommy, he nice!'

After a while, we got news that another Brigade was entering the town from the south. This put Ian on his mettle. He was not an attention seeker, and he was far from being a jealous fighter, but he was quietly determined that the Scots Fusiliers should occupy the town hall. Without more ado we got the whips out and crashed through to the centre of the town, where he staked his claim. The Royal Scots Fusiliers now owned the town. Other people could come in if they wished, but the Scots Fusiliers were there to welcome them.

I at once settled my Tac into the best house visible. It was very nice and comfortable – so comfortable that a message came from Dick Frisby saying did I think it would be a good thing if the Battalion took it over from us? I said that I thought it would be a very bad thing, reminding him also that there were other houses about the place. They chose a comfortable, less showy place and left us in possession.

The town now gave itself up to the luxury of 'liberation'. As I passed through the streets every soldier was being mobbed by joyous crowds. The people were cheering and shouting and waving flags in a regular 'Mafeking'² of delirious delight. In fact, the 200-yard journey to Battalion HQ was really some experience, though even they were not quite as boisterous as the Belgians.

The RSF were now in reserve and no more was required of us that night, so I closed down the Battery wireless net and got permission to close my set on the Colonel's net. At the Battery, I was told later, they correctly interpreted this as meaning that we were in the lap of luxury and getting into carpet slippers – and they weren't far wrong! The family were charming and did everything they possibly could for us. Candles were lighted all over the house and we were given a roaring fire in the sitting room. Beds with sheets were provided, and they just would not listen to us when we said we were far too dirty to use their nice clean ones and would stick to our own. They shouted us down and said it would be an honour to wash our bedding.

As Nigel, Jack and I sat sleepily by the wood fire, Howarth appeared and told us that the ladies of the house wished to lay the Officers' table. Hard on his heels came two smiling girls and drew up a table by the fire, spreading a beautiful lace cloth and setting sparkling silver and cutlery on it, and a bottle of wine. Then Howarth took over and produced a sumptuous meal. He had obviously been swapping rations for flour and set some quite excellent pastry before us, whether made by him or the girls I never knew. All the while, he hovered round with the utmost pride and delight, asking us did we like this? and was that to our satisfaction? We began to wonder if we had strayed into the Ritz in our dreams!

After dinner we went to see the family and found them sitting at a long table, reading or sewing, or just talking. The owner was another doctor. He spoke a little English, and his son-in-law spoke a little French, so by hammering away at both languages we managed to thank them and carried on quite a nice conversation. Then we turned in early to revel in the joy of real beds and sheets, being sure that this was too good to last.

And so it was.

Notes

[1] The 18 set was used as a portable transceiver, developed for 1940. The frequency range is 6–9 MHz. Operational range is quoted as up to ten miles. The 22 set transceiver developed in 1942 was used as a general-purpose low-power vehicle and ground station with facilities for man pack. The frequency range is 2–8 MHz in two bands. The operational range is quoted as up to 20 miles (Green's Radio).

[2] The siege of Mafeking in 1900, in the Boer War, was notable because the garrison was commanded by Robert Baden-Powell, who later established the Boy Scout movement. When the tow was finally relieved, the news caused great celebration in Britain, out of proportion to its importance. The term Mafeking took on the meaning of excessive celebration.

Chapter 29

The Liessel Battles

The tired air groans as the heavies swing over,
The river hollows boom;
The shell-fountains leap from the swamps,
And with wildfire and fume
The shoulder of the chalkdown convulses.

Edmund Blunden

181 Field Regiment RA, October/November 1944

Next morning at 7.30 I was told to get the Battery to the north-western outskirts and we were there by 8.00 am. There were no orders when we got there, so the guns were brought into action in some allotments, and we spent the day trying not to cannon into small boys and girls who would get under our feet, doing our best not to be seen pouring away glasses of hot milk that the kind people would keep bringing us. Then we went like scalded cats down to Asten, where the Americans had taken a bit of a knock. They were saved by the 25th Field Regiment RA and our sister Regiment 131. 131 arrived to find the American Brigade almost finished after a most doughty fight and the 25th holding the front almost by gunfire alone. They deployed next to them and those two Regiments fired concentration after concentration. At the end, their OPs were the only troops in front of them, but they held the line until our 44 Brigade was able to fill the gap and drive the Germans back. It is an axiom that Artillery cannot hold ground by fire alone, and this engagement is the exception that proves the rule.

The Regiment took over from an American Artillery Battalion, and I was sent to the US 7th Armoured Division to gather some information. They were very pleasant people, and their coffee was excellent, but they did not seem to have a clue as to what was going on. It was ages before they were able to extract the news I wanted from one of the Battalions and all the time the dusk was falling, threatening to make me a night wanderer in a strange country, which is a thing to be avoided. This time I was lucky and safely in camp before it was quite dark.

In the morning the RSF advanced a bit and found they were overlooked by the Liessel Church spire wherever they went, so the spire had to go. A 17-pounder anti-tank gun was inched forward and shot after shot pumped into it, making a sorry mess of the spire so that it could not have been any more use as an OP. The first time that gun fired it gave my party a nasty fright – it crept behind the cottage we were in and loosed off without warning us. A 17-pounder's cartridge is nearly as big as the gun, and when it fires all the world knows about it. We thought we were done for. The ceiling came down, the room was filled with dust, and our ear drums ached from the concussion. We rushed out and said, 'Go away – you've brought our ceiling down!'

'Sorry,' said the Number One, 'we thought the house was empty!'

Later on when we passed that spire it was a mere skeleton.

In the afternoon two Companies were infiltrated into the town. Phil Attewell was with one and had a very sticky time. He and his Signaller, Foster, put up a very stout show bringing in a wounded RSF Sergeant under heavy machine-gun fire. Foster was recommended for the Military Medal. He only got a mention, though, as decorations were seldom given for rescues for fear of encouraging foolhardiness.

The Scots Fusiliers were given a Squadron of tanks from 6th Guards Tank Brigade and told to complete the capture of Liessel at dawn, it being conjectured that the enemy would have left by then. He wanted an OP with the tanks as well as the usual two with his own Companies, so I took on the job and was lent a Churchill tank, the bad old days in which a Gunner OP was expected to use his usual light armoured car in a tank battle now being over. It was now accepted that they must be mounted [in a tank] the same as everybody else, to avoid drawing fire on to themselves.

There was the usual morning mist when I collected my charger, but there were tanks warming up all round me, so I did not see how I could fail to notice when they moved. My only worry was that I should not be able to pick out the Squadron Leader's tank, as they all look alike to the uninitiated, not used to their markings.

I had been asked to keep off the air unless it was essential to speak, and for a long time I kept quite silent. As time went on, and there was still no sign of a move, I got restless and at last called up.

'Hello Victor one-six, when are you going to move?'

Back came the answer. 'Victor one-six, we moved ten minutes ago!'

In a flash it dawned on me – the tank I had borrowed belonged to another Squadron; one that was not going out. That was really most annoying – I had so wanted to start off in the correct place, being new to tanks and their ways. Then I asked where he was on the map and ran into the second bit of trouble – the Squadron Leader had not given me his key to the simple code using for passing map references. Each unit had a different one, so what he sent was a mere jumble of letters to me. All I could do was to go and hunt for him. We ploughed through a wood for a while. There were tank tracks and turnings everywhere, but not a sign of a tank. It was like trying to find hounds again when you have lost them. Then, quite suddenly, we hit the edge of the wood and at that precise moment the mist lifted, leaving us silhouetted against the trees and in full view of Liessel and any anti-tank guns that might be there. Even I knew that it was no place to be, and we scuttled back under cover and crept along just inside the trees.

At last we came upon a tank whose Commander was able to direct me to the Squadron Leader. He came on the air just as I had identified him and was getting the hang of our dispositions, asking for a small fire plan. That was easy to arrange now that I knew where we all were, and after that we manoeuvred uneventfully into the town.

Liessel was deserted and silent. One or two houses were smoking through holes in the roofs, and there was one of our reconnaissance cars lying in the road, blown up by a mine. 'Does one walk? Or does one crawl?' I asked a Fusilier I met. I had left my tank and was looking for my OPs with the Infantry. He replied that it was better to crawl, as they had not yet located all the snipers, but he showed me a covered way that saved a lot of hands and knees work, and after a while I found Nigel. He was quite comfortable and told me that there were only a few scattered posts of enemy left, which would soon be cleared up, so the town was ours. With that knowledge I left him and my steel charger took me swiftly and comfortably back to Battalion HQ.

We now had to clear some small villages to the south of Liessel. The first was a little place called Slot, which we entered next day. It was unpleasant there as there was a lot of mortaring and shelling. We set up shop in a dirty ruin with two dead horses in the stables and tried to forget the noise all about us. That night Ian McKenzie gave out his orders [briefing] very late, and after that I had to go to Dick Bethell's orders some miles away, so it was after 2.00 am when Bull and I got back, with a 4.00 am start ahead. You can imagine how grateful we felt as we wearily dragged our feet into the room to find Howarth heating some soup for us. He had heard that we would be late, so had given orders to be woken as soon as we were seen returning. Not only that, he woke me up with a mug of tea at 3.30 am. How things had changed since the Gheel days! We were a team now.

During the morning's advance I had a good chuckle at Ian's expense. There was quite a lot of shelling at one place where we halted, so the Infantry went to ground like moles – as we did. It was the best thing to do, only they made the mistake of not looking where they were siting their slit trenches. When Ian wanted to move in a hurry he found his carrier completely encircled by trenches and had to wait until they were filled in before he could get out.

The next place we came to was Neerkant, where we had another ruined house base and plenty of shelling, though none of it was close enough to be really uncomfortable. An American bomber, a Liberator, was shot down over our heads there. We saw two of the crew escape by parachute. The others are now just names carved on memorials, presumably.

We were preparing for an attack on Schans, but that was put off for a day, so I had time to amuse myself choosing a good OP and taking a couple of shoots myself. In the evening I had dinner with the RSF – roast chicken. The attack went in next day and was the only failure that the Scots Fusiliers had while I was with them.

Schans was a collection of groups of farms isolated from each other on a low ridge. The KOSB were on a similar ridge opposite Schans, forming a firm base from which we could stage our attack. The plan was quite simple: 'B' and 'D' Companies, supported by a Squadron of Grenadiers from 6th Guards Tank Brigade, were to seize the first groups of farms, and 'A' and 'C' were to pass through them to the final objective. Phil was to observe from a tank while I kept Murray with me as a reserve OP on foot, in case of need [see plate].

Our guns hammered the objectives and the advance began. Almost immediately Phil reported that the tanks had struck an unsuspected minefield and were held up on the start line. Several were disabled at once. The others tried to find a way round and ran into boggy ground, where many of them stuck. The Tank Commander – Major Pike – was at Battalion HQ with me when all this happened. He looked at me with something like despair in his eyes. 'The Battalion Commander tells me we must push on – but I've lost half my tanks already! You can't just barge through a minefield or through bogs either: what can one do?' At that he leapt into a 'Dingo' and dashed off to see for himself. That was the last I saw of him – he nearly collided with a mortar bomb and was brought back very badly wounded.

There was, in fact, nothing the tanks could do, though I wonder why their reconnaissance parties did not discover that minefield the day before, right on the start line as it was. They had just to sit there all day, under continuous heavy mortar fire, and give what fire support they could.

Ian seemed to be nearly always unlucky with his tank support. 'The Armour is a most unsatisfactory Arm,' he said to me one day. 'You never know whether they will do what they say they will. The Gunners are the people, you can rely on them always. If they can't do what you ask they'll tell you there and then; if they say they can do it, you can take it as done.' I think he was too severe in his criticism of the tanks, but it was a nice compliment to us. I can only hope we deserved it.

The first two Companies stoutly fought their way to their objectives, but were pinned to the ground there by fire, and in the afternoon it became clear that there was no hope of the other two Companies passing through them. At last Ian warned me they might have to pull back the first two. On hearing that, I told Phil to abandon his tank and find a ground OP from which he could cover the withdrawal. His tank would be a handicap with its mobility hampered by the mines and soft ground. This he did, choosing a window in a house where the KOSB had their HQ. It was right in the centre of the worst part of the shelling, but it was the only place from which the withdrawal route could be effectively covered.

Then I found that he had no light wireless with him and would have to manhandle one of the tank's heavy sets if he did have to take to his feet. I wirelessed that I would bring a couple so that he could leave one in his tank and pass his messages to it to be re-broadcast on the long-range set.

Said Phil, 'Is your journey really necessary?' Looking in his direction and seeing the vicious black and brown fountains of smoke and earth there, I heartily wished it were not. It was a two-man job, so I took one of a pair of identical twins, the Deverel brothers. I do not know which, and I do not expect anyone else does either! They just could not be identified individually. They were never allowed to be in the same part of the Battery together, partly because of the difficulty in knowing which was which and partly because my predecessor thought it would be too great a tragedy for their mother to bear if both should be killed by the same shell.

We each took a set and soon saw the point of Phil's question. The atmosphere was most unhealthy. Time and again we flattened ourselves on the ground as the screech of a shell came rushing our way, to burst with a horrid crash near enough to be alarming, its mates hurrying after it to prolong our misery. When the storm let up, we would peer at each other – and each time young Deverel's first words were 'I'm still through on the wireless, Sir!' The way that boy stuck to his job, his first time under fire, and thought of nothing else but his duty as a Signaller to keep the wireless through was a wonderful thing to see.

Phil got out of his tank and came to meet me, so we left Deverel in a ditch and went forward to see his OP that he chosen in the house. We met Dick Moorshead there. 'Hullo!' said he. 'This is a bloody awful place – shouldn't stay here if I were you!' Phil pulled me behind a wall just as the Bosch gave point to Dick's remark by landing a particularly vicious crump just the other side of it. That shelter was a regular haven, so we sat there and discussed our plans. The house was so obviously the centre of the enemy's target that we did not go upstairs, and I devoutly hoped that Phil would never have to use it as an OP. My wish was granted, though not in the way I would have chosen. The poor chap was hit in the back by a shell splinter soon after I left him. It was a nasty wound and I never saw him again. I shall never forget the time on this day when he forgot to switch his set to 'intercom' to speak to his driver and his words were broadcast on the net instead of into his driver's earphones: 'Go right, drive, right! RIGHT, for heaven's sake! You're going slap into the mine …' And then he realised that the switch was not over. All the strain of battle was in his voice: he was like a man in a nightmare, dreaming that he is on the railway lines with a train rushing at him and his legs won't move. He recovered, however, and lived to command a Battery before the war ended. We missed him a lot, and he had done splendidly by the Battery.

Deverel and I bounded from ditch to ditch and soon reached the comparative safety of Battalion HQ. There we found a 'shell happy' pig. Every time a shell burst the poor animal rushed madly round in circles, grunting and squealing. Then it found its way into the kitchen, circled the floor three times and fell down the cellar steps. There it grunted with surprise and lay down and went to sleep. I have often wondered how they got it out of that cellar. Then a sheep wandered in and looked questioningly at us with nostrils quivering, and eyes like dark glass marbles. When it saw that we did not object to its presence it shuffled into a corner and quietly chewed the cud. Animals do not like war – they see no sense in it at all.

That evening the Scots Fusiliers had to give up the attack and were withdrawn to Liessel. They pulled out at last light and it was dusk when the files of dusty and exhausted men passed us and embussed for the rest area. Ian had a friendly word and a smile as he met the eye of almost every one of his men and the Company Commanders paused to tell him who was missing and how the day had gone with them. Then we too started on the trek back.

The eight-mile drive seemed endless. The road was narrow and full of bottlenecks that kept interrupting the flow of traffic. There was a light fog at first that made it very hard to see over the half-track's great long snout to the edge of the road. We were, of course, driving without lights.

When we arrived at last, looking forward to a roof and a hot meal, we found that Dick Frisby had forgotten to allot a billet to my party. He came up to me, full of apologies, and took us to a ruined butcher's shop. The windows were out and there was not much roof. A cold meat slab of marble filled most of the room and a narrow, drafty passage offered the only possible shelter for the ten of us. It was cold, and the sky had the blue, frosty look that foretells a freezing night. We were hungry and very weary. I was prepared to settle down in the discomfort and make the best of it, but the men looked at me and grinned. The look implied that they were confident that I would produce something better than that, so something just had to be done. I went out to look for 'a better 'ole'.

Every house I went to was full. 'Sorry, we're packed like sardines!' 'Very sorry, no room at all ...' And so it went on. Then, when I had almost given up hope, I found great kindness among the Medics. I had come, without knowing it, to the billet of our Field Ambulance Unit. A soldier met me at the door: 'I'm sure we've got room, Sir, come with me to the Officers' Mess.' Before I could see properly in the glare of a Tilly lamp, someone had pushed me gently into a chair, and I found I was holding a steaming mug of sweet tea. 'You look about all-in' said my friend. 'Of course we can fix your party – how many are you?'

We found ourselves allotted two rooms, each with a stove lighted for us by our hosts. 'We had your Troop Commander Philip Attewell through this afternoon,' said one of the doctors. 'He's seriously wounded, but he'll be alright: we rushed him straight through to Helmond. It's a grand hospital, and you can be sure they'll pull him through.'

Those kindly actions will remain fresh in my memory always.

Chapter 30

Tunnicliffe's Pig

Revile him not, the Tempter hath
A snare for all;
And pitying tears, not scorn and wrath,
Befit his fall!

John Greenleaf Whittier

181 Field Regiment RA

Sergeant Tunnicliffe [see plate] was a very good-looking golden-haired giant, Number One of a gun and fully conscious of his fine appearance. When Moss Waters amused himself choosing snatches of verse that seemed to epitomise various members of the Battery, the one he chose for our friend was 'The Golden Vanity', and it was singularly apt. In ordinary life he was a butcher and one day when we were on a farm in action, but on a quiet part of the front, he found a pig that he considered had reached its peak. He said it would go downhill if left alive until its Dutch owner returned. So he killed it, and we all enjoyed the pork. So excellent was the pork that I even forgave him when I found that the reason why Bain could not explain the delay in bringing the bath tub I had acquired was because Tunnicliffe was using it to hold the chitterlings and so on while the pig was being prepared for the table. Next day, Battery Sergeant Major Milner, nicknamed 'The Grappler', informed me that Tunnicliffe was under arrest for disobeying Battery Orders 'in that he, contrary to Battery Order Number so and so, did slaughter a pig, the property of an allied national'. Of course I told Milner that this was all nonsense, but he smartly cut the ground away under me with the news that the Battery Order had been published only the day before the deed, under my name. True, I had not signed it, or even seen it, but naturally the Battery Commander is responsible for Orders published in his name.

'Sir,' said old Grappler, 'an order is an order. You publishes Battery orders for to be complied with – not for no pickin' an' choosin' which nor what they'll obey!'

He had me in a cleft stick: one has to back one's Sergeant Major, though the fresh pork was just what the Battery wanted. Very reluctantly I took my spoke out of the wheels of justice. The prisoner was marched smartly in, cap and belt off, as custom decrees, with another Sergeant as escort. The charge was read and the evidence heard and then I asked Tunnicliffe what he had to say. Never have I had greater difficulty in keeping a straight face than when his answer came: 'Well, Sir, Sergeant Major killed six turkeys a little while back, so I didn't think there'd be no harm in killin' the pig.'

Poor old Grappler was aghast. Discipline went by the board – Battery Commander's Office hour is a solemn affair, during which people do not speak unless invited to, but he burst out with: 'That was back in Normandy! Before this order were published! And you well knows it, Sergeant Tunnicliffe! Sir!' The last exclamation was accompanied by a rigid stiffening to attention in acknowledgement of his breach of military etiquette.

That was almost too much for me but I managed to keep a poker face until I had adjured Tunnicliffe to kill no more pigs until Germany was reached, and dismissed the case.

The 'Pig Position' was one of super luxury. We knew that we would be there for at least a week and we had no OPs out, the Royal Scots Fusiliers being out of the line, so we made a really good job of a gun position. The guns were dug in as usual, and in addition a deep dugout was made for each gun detachment. Steps led down to a sizeable underground room, and there you found a stove, or a fireplace contrived from old ammunition boxes, built-in bunks for the six men, boxes to sit on, and perhaps even a small table. This was no 'fad': the weather was getting really cold, and warmth and comfort was very important when it could be managed, to keep up morale. The British soldier will bear anything if he knows everything that can be done has been done to improve his lot. In the front line one hot meal a day is a luxury, and the soldier is happy because it is as much, or more, as he expected. Where more can be done, he expects more. He is at his happiest when he has done something for himself. Our chaps were as proud as Punch of their dugouts and each detachment vied with the others to produce the best design.

Everything was beautifully camouflaged and all the spoil removed from the diggings. In fact almost the only indication of a Troop position was the strange sight of four short pipes sticking out of the ground, pouring out smoke. It can be imagined that timber for dugouts and gun pits, stoves and suchlike were most valuable possessions, once scrounged: indeed, they had to be taken with us when we moved, so the Battery lost all pretension to smartness, and when on the move looked more like a gypsy caravan than a Battery of the Royal Artillery. At such times warmth and comfort are more important than appearances. Provided the body is clean, and the face shaved when humanly possible, and the guns and vehicles thoroughly serviceable, the rest can go hang.

What is important is to know when the need for untidiness is past. If the outfit does not go back to something like peace time standards when the reason for untidiness no longer exists, then personal and corporate pride are lost, discipline slackens and the unit becomes a useless crime-ridden rabble.

During our stay here I got rid of the Signal Sergeant. He was a pre-war regular and a nice enough and hard-working chap, but he could not make the grade. He had no drive or organising ability and the simplest plan had to be worked out for him in detail. Worst of all, there were continual grumbles from the Signallers because he did not organise the reliefs properly. His replacement, Sergeant Nicholson, was a gem. The first time he functioned as Signal Sergeant, he came in while I was shaving.

'Good morning, Sir. I've worked out a signal plan for the attack. I'd like you to see if it's what you want.'

I looked at his bit of paper and saw that there was not a fault. 'That's fine,' I said. 'Carry on!' I felt a glow of thankfulness that here was someone that I could rely on to get the answer without needing to breathe down his neck while he tried to find it. So it turned out. There were no more signals worries, no more moans from the Signallers for me to sort out.

More than once in action, while we were still cowering in slit trenches after an advance, Nicholson would appear from nowhere: 'Ah, there you are, Sir, I've got a line on its way – you would like a phone, wouldn't you?' That would never have happened with his predecessor. I should have had to send for him, and probably send someone to guide him into the bargain. Before his arrival the Signallers were in two hard-and-fast divisions – those who 'went to the OP' and those who did not – and there was quite a tendency towards what might be called 'battle snobbishness'. The OP people thought they were heroes and the others went slightly in awe of them. I had already arranged for all the Officers to take their turn, instead of only the two Troop Commanders, and now I got Nicholson to arrange definite teams of Signallers, which changed when the Officers changed. I am sure this caused a better spirit in the Battery. Certainly, it did a lot to train the officers, and it spread the risk of being killed considerably wider, at the same time diluting it.

Anyhow, with Nicholson in charge, life became so much easier. Communications are a Battery's life blood, if they fail all your efforts go for nothing.

Chapter 31

Helenaveen

Helen, thy beauty is to me
Like those Nicean barks of yore,
That gently, o'er a perfumed sea,
The weary way-worn wanderer bore
To his own native shore.

Edgar Allan Poe

181 Field Regiment RA, November 1944

In mid-November I took over responsibility for the OPs near Kostdijk, where the Scots Fusiliers had relieved the KOSB. Dick Moorshead, their affiliated Battery Commander, had his Tac HQ in a poky little room with smoke pouring out of a broken stove. The furniture consisted of one bench, and there seemed to be telephones everywhere, their leads and wires lying in a tangled jumble on the floor that tripped one at every unguarded step.

As soon as Nigel and Philip Mulholland were off to their OPs I took stock of the situation, decided it was just too depressing, and that something must be done. Apparently, all the phones were needed, but there seemed to be no reason to force us to bear the tangle on the floor. After vainly trying to tidy the mess, I suddenly remembered that there was a portable ten-line exchange in the Battery that we never used. Now seemed to be the time to see if it worked. A word to Nicholson and the exchange appeared, and the tangle disappeared like magic. It was definitely the answer for a 'static' position, and we used it after that every time we had a comprehensive phone layout. We managed to block the hole in the stove, found a box or two for seats, and things began to look much better.

Next day the RSF started clearing a huge wood called Vierutsen. The enemy were very little trouble, but mines slowed them a lot. They were mostly the wooden 'Schu-mine' that were so difficult to detect. We went in considerable fear of them because the blast was said to be so great that, if you trod on one, the rush of air would enter the bowel and blow you to pieces. An old wives' tale, possibly, but it made people tread very warily. Certainly there was very little left to bury in the case of some mine casualties.

Philip moved into a cottage on the southern edge of the wood and registered a target on the far side of a canal that flowed about 1,000 yards away. He was not quite clever enough and the enemy spotted him and gave a nasty dose of shell fire. I took a walk with him to find a better place and we quite enjoyed ourselves creeping and crawling along the wood's edge. Eventually we came to a small house where we thought one of the Scots patrols was lying hidden. We were not quite sure, so we did some pretty careful scouting in case there were Germans in it. Suddenly, a Jock wandered into the yard, dispelling our fears, but when he saw us move to show ourselves he thought we were the enemy and ran for his life. We leapt to our feet to save our lives. We knew the rest of the patrol would be pretty trigger-happy and had no wish to be mistaken for enemy in our turn.

After settling Philip, I went on to see Nigel, and found him comfortably installed where he could observe from a bedroom window. I spent some time trying to convince him that a telescope is ideal in such a place, but I think he still preferred his binoculars.

A day or two later we started to do a flank move on to the village of Helenaveen, circling a large wood, with the Carrier Platoon going round the other side of it. It was a nasty, wet afternoon and progress was very slow, with long halts while the leading Company probed the wood.

Just at dusk, Jonah [Lieutenant EWK Jones], who was with the leading Company, came on the air with: 'I have reason to believe I am in a minefield – there is a blown-up armoured car in front of me, and one of my friends' carriers has just exploded behind me. I propose continuing on foot – do you agree?'

Good old Jonah! Nothing ever shook him. I told him certainly to abandon his carrier, so he took his wireless with him on foot, and had a chance to do some useful shooting before the light went entirely. It was a ghastly situation to be in: carriers were only armoured on the sides – and lightly armoured, at that – and the bottom was just thin metal, worse than no protection at all against a mine. If a mine went off, the occupants had no chance of survival.

That night the situation was rather eerie. Each Company was in its own defended perimeter, as was Battalion HQ, but in between, anything might happen. We rested in a small village and I arranged a fire plan with Ian

McKenzie for the morning. John Murray, the OP with the Carrier Platoon, came in to report and found me by a tiny red and blue light that I had got Howarth to fix on the half-track. He said it was like a 'welcoming beacon', which pleased me a lot, as that was what I intended it to be. When you are trying to find someone in the dark in dangerous country, it is pleasant to know that there will be a sign to tell you when you have arrived. Without it, one truck looks very like another at night.

The 'juddle-diddle' on the wireless net was the very devil. We were a long way from RHQ and could hardly hear each other through the atmospherics. In fact it took all but three hours to get a simple plan through. At last it was all settled, and at 2.00 am I stretched out on a sofa for a little reviving sleep. An hour later I was woken up by the wireless to be told that our plan was unsafe and could not be fired. That, to me, was earth-shaking. Actually, the reason was that our own troops had moved into the target area from the other side, so our fire was not needed, but the 'juddle-diddle' was too intense for the Adjutant to get that through to me. I had to go and wake up the exhausted Ian and tell him we could not give him any support.

He took it very philosophically, merely remarking that they would have to do without, but it worried me a lot, as I thought I must somehow have let him down. One might think that he would have heard the news on his own wireless, from 44 Brigade, but if our wireless could not get through, you could bet your shirt that no Infantry set could manage it. Their communications never approached the efficiency of a Gunner net, partly because our Signallers were better, but also because they had to rely mostly on the portable sets, which we never used unless we had to. On at least one occasion I lent him my wireless net and he called his Company Commanders to the Gunner OP sets to get their orders via it because he could not get through on his own.

Early in the morning we set out for Helenaveen. When patrols drew no fire, a Company, accompanied by our John Murray, went to occupy it. In the distance it looked most attractive, a sort of miniature garden city with red roofs and cream walls in a setting of evergreens.

We caught up with Jonah at a halt and arranged for him to recover his carrier as soon as the Infantry Pioneers had cleared the mines round it. When he had been gone a little while, there was a sudden explosion. It came from the direction of the carrier, and I felt cold all over – it could only be Jonah. I started to run to him. A Gunner Officer from a Medium Regiment thrust a box into my hand. 'Morphine,' he said. I ran. Others followed. By the carrier I found a blown-up jeep with Jonah bending over a man sprawled on the ground. I saw there were two bodies on the road. A glance showed that one had no need of morphine. The other was just conscious; how badly wounded one could not say. Donald Gray, the Company Commander, arrived. I gave him the morphine, but he said he did not know how to give the injection. I knew how, but for some reason I shied off the job, so I showed him how to gather up a fold of skin and he actually did it. We wrote the dose and time on the man's forehead with a red chinagraph, wrapped him up and sent him back on a stretcher. I am glad to say he re-joined the Battalion some months later. He was probably saved by having sandbags on the floor in place of the seat.

After that Jonah and I went to look at the blown-up Infantry carrier. 'You know,' he remarked, 'the explosion went straight through the driver's seat – nothing was found of the poor chap: not a thing.' So you see why we dreaded mines.

Our chaps seemed to bear charmed lives that day, first Jonah missing the mine that destroyed the men behind him, then John Murray passing over the spot that got the jeep. Ian was not so lucky. In addition to his other casualties he lost Sturgeon, his own Orderly. We all liked Sturgeon. It was his duty to guard the Battalion Commander wherever he went. His silent figure with a grave face that surprised one by suddenly breaking into a smile of great charm was almost part of Ian's signature. I always felt safe with Sturgeon stalking alertly ahead with Sten gun at the ready. Fortunately, he was only wounded, and later recovered.

We moved back to where we had spent the night when Helenaveen had been occupied. Ian lead the way along a vile muddy track. He was on edge after these mine incidents, trying to go faster than the path would allow, continually chafing because my half-track was making rather heavy going of it. To his annoyance its front wheel slipped into a small ditch and slithered along it, unable to get a grip and steer out of the mud. I had just told Howarth to stop and reverse out, as the tracks could pull what they could not push, when Ian came dashing back. Against all military etiquette, he started to curse *my* driver – Howarth – for bad driving and not straightening his wheels. That he did such a thing shows how strained he was. Little did he know what a hornets' nest was waiting for him under that oily Balmoral bonnet. Like a rebound came the answer: 'A'hd lahk ta see thee straighten ta muckin' wheels! A'hd have these know this trook's got spring steerin'!' Without thought of being court-martialled for striking a subordinate, I seized him by the scruff of the neck. 'SHUT UP!' I said.

Ian looked flabbergasted and wandered back to his carrier in a daze with Howarth still muttering about 'spring steering'. What he meant I never found out. When I asked him what he thought he was doing, speaking to the Battalion Commander like that, he said: 'Well, Sir, he made me angry, he shouldn't have called me a bad driver ... there's not much I can do, but I can drive well, and I'm proud of my driving; I wouldn't have minded what else he said!' Of course, by the rules, I should have run him in, but one did not run Howarth in – he was too good a soldier. I apologised to Ian and he took it very well.

Back to the Battery for lunch. Old Bombardier Dodd met me with 'Roast beef today, Sir. And loganberry tart – you've just dropped in lucky!'

Chapter 32

Winter on the Maas

There are waters blown by changing winds to laughter
And lit by the rich skies, all day, And after,
Frost, with a gesture, stays the waves that dance
and wandering loveliness. He leaves a white
unbroken glory, a gathered radiance,
A width, a shining peace, under the night.

Rupert Brooke

181 Field Regiment RA, November 1944

'You are about to fire on to German soil for the first time!'

The announcement was electrifying. A spontaneous cheer burst from the throats of those that heard it and there was a rush of cooks and all sorts to be behind the guns when the momentous rounds were fired. Relief gun-layers suddenly became aware that it was time they were in the seats, and never have I seen layers more reluctant to be relieved. For a few seconds discipline ceased to be, but a quiet caution from the Command Post quelled the noise and the shells went off on time to the second.

We had come to a place called Vorst, arriving by a track that had been churned by tanks into an unbelievable morass. In places it was axle-deep in liquid mud and the vehicles floundered about in it like rudderless barges. We had also come by the route that the troops had used when trying to relieve the Airborne men at Arnhem. We appreciated their difficulties. It ran along a narrow embankment across a waterlogged country scarred with innumerable peat diggings. On each side was a dyke, and here and there a tank or heavy truck had gone too near the edge and slithered down the collapsing bank, leaving one more bottleneck to slow the passing traffic.

Our new home was packed with refugees, so, chiefly in our own interest, we organised for them to return to their homes, earning their gratitude by providing a shuttle service of lorries to take them there. One we kept. He was a big Alsatian dog that had been left tied up in the centre of one of our Mike targets. He was a living testimony to the efficacy of our shooting, having acquired an incurable dread of guns. Moss Waters took charge of him and named him Chum. For a time he was deeply suspicious of everyone else, even preventing the Battery Commander from entering his own Command Post one day. Kindness prevailed and soon he became very friendly. For all his friendliness, though, his strength and boisterousness was quite a trial, until we discovered that he had learnt some of our fire orders – in particular, which orders indicated that the guns would fire ten seconds later. On hearing the caution 'One-oh seconds to go' he would drop whatever he was doing and dash under the nearest table or shelf, staying there cowering until all was peace again. We soon cashed in on this. When he came unbearably obstreperous, someone would say, quite softly, 'One-oh seconds ...' The poor animal would efface himself with all possible speed.

He lost his good billet with us through this dislike of the guns. Moss usually took him out on a lead, but one day things seemed so peaceful that he was allowed to go free on his morning walk. Unfortunately, a whole troop fired just as he was passing behind the guns. He was off like a streak and for all I know is running still! At any rate, we never saw him again.

The weather grew colder, but there was still a sparkle of autumn in the sunshine, and Ray Bristowe enjoyed himself with a shotgun, after pheasants. He was a good shot, and one day his bag was enough to warrant unloading at his jeep before continuing his shoot. That was his undoing, as shortly afterwards he met the Dutch landowner and received a good drubbing down for poaching. He was told that 'an English gentleman should know better than to poach other men's pheasants'. This, in poor war-torn Holland, tickled Ray a lot, until he got back to his jeep and found that the keeper had appropriated the bag, leaving him just a brace as a courtesy to a visitor.

The last days of autumn vanished all too soon and winter set in in real earnest. The ground became like iron, ice was everywhere, and the trees, at first white with rime, soon had their twigs sheathed in ice. The men were nice and warm in their dug-outs off duty, but it was bitter on the guns and in the OPs.

By great fortune we found a warehouse full of cured sheep skins. A shifty looking chap appeared to be in charge and sold us enough to make a fleece jerkin for every man in the Battery. He may or may not have been the owner, but the price was ridiculously low, so we did not ask any questions. A Bombardier, a tailor by trade, made an excellent job of them, and we made everyone pay a little towards them on the grounds that people will look after what they pay for. The rest of the money came from Battery funds. We had a sudden mild spell in which the fleeces were not needed, but then the cold became more intense than ever. Imagine my fury when I found that half those improvident live-for-the-day-only idiots had dumped their jerkins in the warmer period. I was so angry that I told them that, as far as I was concerned, they could ... well, freeze!

Now the time had come to close right up to the River Maas. The enemy had been almost entirely driven across the river, but he still had a foothold on our side, in the little town of Blerick. This was really a suburb of the large town of Venlo, which the river cut into two parts. The job of clearing Blerick was given to the 15th Scottish. It was not one to be taken lightly – in fact it was a hard nut, requiring a 'set piece' attack, one calling for much reconnaissance and careful coordination.

We moved into out battle positions on 29 November, a mile or two forward of the village of Maasbree. There was plenty of time, and this was to be our winter quarters until the cold abated and permitted further large-scale operations. We settled in really comfortably and built even better dug-outs than in our last static position. A good farm made an excellent Command Post, with ample shelter for the Mess and Cookhouse, and for those not in the warm dug-outs. We took over the two front rooms and the pleasant Dutch family shared the kitchen with the Batman and Bombardier Dodd.

We had to be fairly alert, keeping patrols going and defence posts in position, as there was nothing between us and the river except a thick wood through which the enemy might well come upon us unobserved. In fact, when we arrived, there was an Infantry Company in the farm. They gaped when they found guns being put in front of their Section Posts, not realising that the tide of war had receded. It was interesting to find that they were a Battalion of the King's Shropshire Light Infantry. There was quite a bit of fun when they found we were the product of their former 6th Battalion and were wearing their flash on our sleeves. Unfortunately they did not stay long enough for there to be a proper reunion.

As soon as we were settled in we started preparations and rehearsals for the Battle of Blerick.

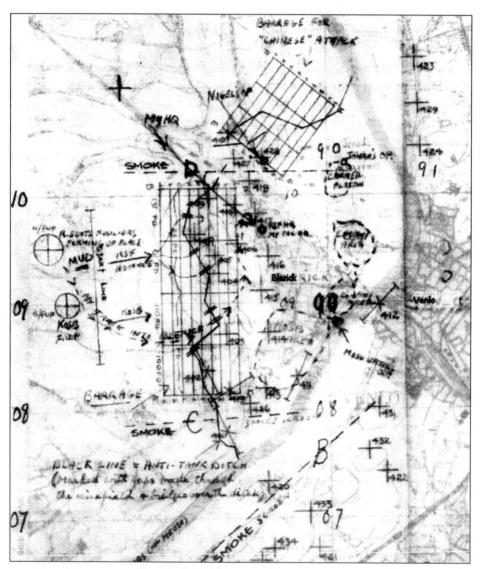

Battle Map used by the author. See page 204.

Chapter 33

The Battle of Blerick

And, little town, thy streets for evermore
Will silent be; and not a soul to tell
Why thou art desolate, can e'er return.

John Keats

181 Field Regiment RA, December 1944

The capture of Blerick, 3 December 1944, has been described as an operation 'perfectly planned and perfectly executed'. The town lies in a slight hollow in a bend of the river and the approaches from the west (our side) slope gently down from a low ridge situated some 2,000 yards from its western boundaries. Once an attacking force topped the ridge, it would be in full view from the tall buildings of Venlo, across the river, and from high ground in enemy country on either flank. About halfway between ridge and town was a deep steep-sided anti-tank ditch, quite impassable to tanks and vehicles, and the edge of a minefield had been located well to the west of the ditch. The extent of the minefield could be only guessed. In addition there were the usual barbed-wire entanglements.

The task was given to the 44th (Lowland) Brigade, now commanded by Brigadier Harry Cummins-Bruce, whom I had last met as Brigade Major of our old friends 152 Brigade in North Africa. In the early days of the war it would have been a formidable task indeed, even though the enemy had no tanks and was very much on the defensive. To have tried to breach the minefield and bridge the ditch in daylight would have been murder with the site open to direct fire from the front and from both sides. Even at night, the casualties would have been very high.

But there was a new factor in our favour. Throughout the war some of the country's best brains had been at work trying to find ways of dealing with mines, ditches and obstacles of all kinds. Many inventions had been tried, and the results had by this time been crystallised into an Armoured Brigade with Sappers specially equipped and trained to dispose of obstacles. This Brigade was placed at our disposal. In it there were 'Flail' tanks, with whirling chains in front that flailed the ground and exploded the mines; 'Scissors' tanks that carried bridges and lowered them into position with a device like a sort of lazy-tongs; 'Arks', tanks with flat tops that drove into the ditch and provided a steel roadway by letting other tanks drive over them; and 'Fascine' tanks that filled smaller trenches by dropping huge bundles of wood into them. There were tanks with the tops cut off, making armoured boxes to carry the Infantry swiftly across the bullet-swept slope, through the minefield gaps and over the newly made bridges, dumping them at the edge of the town. These were called 'Kangaroos' because we travelled in their pouches.

Nor did the Infantry have to depend on their own devices when they got there. The 'Crocodiles' were following on the heels of the Kangaroos. They were tanks equipped as flame-throwers, each capable of throwing a ghastly jet of blazing oil a hundred yards or more, setting fire to all it touched. One squirt made a pill-box an object of pity.

Those were what we called the 'Funnies'. They were grand, and saved hundreds of lives, and hours – perhaps days – of time. But they did not make the old and well-tried weapons unnecessary. The Royal Air Force was there with Typhoons to strafe the defence, especially his artillery, with screaming rockets. The Churchill tanks were there to guard the flailing Flails and bridging tanks and watch over the Kangaroos in case an anti-tank gun should try to bar their passage, and our Artillery was there in force.

We had our own Divisional Artillery, two Army Groups RA (called AGRAs) and perhaps another Divisional Artillery besides, and there was a new unit called a 'Mattress' Battery because it laid a mattress of a hundred rockets on the enemy in one salvo. What all these guns fired at can be seen by a glance at the map, which is the one I carried during the action.

The numbered crosses were drenched with fire from the Mediums and Heavies, and many were rocketed by the Air Force as well. On either side was a screen of drifting smoke, each laid there by a Battery, to blindfold the Bosch OPs and machine guns. In the centre were the barrage lines, marked as a grid. The guns lift from line to line, making a band, or wave, of bursting shells that swept over any hidden defence posts like a tide on the flow. Hard on the heels of the barrage came the leading Infantry in their Kangaroos, before the survivors had time to throw off the shock and try and bar their way.

That was Modern War. Nowadays nuclear weapons have made it seem ancient history, but in 1944 it was the very latest, and though Funnies had been used before, this was the first action in which they had been deployed in large numbers and their roles scientifically coordinated with those of the other Arms.

Methods of warfare change, but it seems the principles never alter. The introduction of Funnies changed the whole shape and course of this action, yet one of the greatest factors of its success was clever use of the old, old, principle of deception.

The map shows a smaller 'grid' north of Blerick. This was a barrage fired for a 'Chinese', or feint, attack. That was staged with all the noise and semblance of reality before the real attack started, to make the enemy think we aimed to cross the river and attack Venlo itself.

The feint was brilliantly successful. It so convinced the enemy Commander that he withdrew most of his best troops east of the river by the only connecting bridge. Once there, they could not get back again, because we kept the bridge under heavy fire throughout the day, so when the Infantry reached the town the resistance was negligible by comparison with what it might have been if the posts had been held by resolute veterans.

That is the plan in a nutshell. The efforts of man and machine were perfectly coordinated; in the view of the Staff it worked like a well-trained orchestra and the end was a striking success.

The day before the attack was, for me, a time of worry and anxiety. In the first place, we were allotted two Kangaroos to use as OP trucks. When we had tried them out, and found them excellent, we were told that we could only have them as far as the edge of the town, as they were needed to go back for a second load. That was quite impracticable, as we had no other means of carrying our wireless sets until our own carriers arrived when the battle was over, but it took a lot of breath to persuade the Infantry that you cannot change horses in mid-stream without getting wet. We carried our point in the end, but it took a lot of mental energy.

Then Nigel had to take a tank on another job, and no one could say when he would be back, or even whether he would be back in time for the show. As I had to provide a tank OP for the tanks protecting the Flails, his return in time was a matter of considerable importance.

The last big worry was an OP from a Medium Regiment who was to come under me for the attack. I expected him in the morning, and when he had not arrived by the evening I gave up hope. This was all the more trying because I had planned to use him as a substitute if Nigel did not return, and I wanted to take him round and let him meet the people with whom he would work. When he did arrive, the poor chap rolled in on foot, having ditched his carrier in the mud two miles away. I lent him my half-track to unditch it and bless me if he did not come back on foot again, having ditched the half-track as well. That was serious, because it carried most of our war stores, and all our food and blankets. But one's mind got pretty agile and inventive in war and I soon remembered that there was a Heavy Battery a mile or two away with vehicles capable of shifting Muhammed's mountain itself. So I sent the chap off to borrow one of their gun-towing trucks and washed him off the worry sheet.

Soon after he had gone, there was a clattering roar, and there was Nigel – and his tank! I could relax at last: it was the tank that I was most glad to see.

We had not finished with our Medium friend yet. He did not get back until we were all asleep and woke us up by tripping over us in a wet mackintosh. By the time he was fed and briefed for the morning there was not much of our night left. Nor was that all: I had just dropped off to sleep again when he came and shook me – his Colonel would not let him come on to my wireless net, as I wanted, insisting on him staying on his own Regimental one. So I had to alter my plan.

Then one final straw to test the camel's back: Dick Bethell called me to say that owing to the rain the Funnies might not be able to function, so we were to be prepared to do the attack on foot with no modern aids. There was little that I could do about that so late: I could only pray that our portable sets would not let us down. There was no time to get carrying parties organised, so I turned over and went to sleep.

In battle the only times that really matter are the rise and set of the sun and moon – the demarcations between the shades of light and dark – so it is of no importance that I forget what time we set off. It is enough to say that the moon was still in the sky and the east was beginning to brighten with dawn. It was damp and cold, but the drizzle showed signs of clearing. We were all muffled up to the eyes; I had on at least three sweaters, a fleece and a jerkin and must have looked a regular bundle.

Nigel was ahead with the tanks moving up to clear the minefield and bridge the ditch. Moss Waters was with the leading Company, ready to 'gallop' into Blerick with them. The KOSB were to attack on the right, with the Scots Fusiliers on the left, and the Royal Scots in reserve. For the moment the routes of the two Battalions were merged in one, marked 'Ayr' and 'Skye'. Soon they would diverge and we would follow the Skye signs to our forming-up place under cover of the ridge.

Slowly we clanked along. One could imagine the tanks and Funnies rumbling and clattering ahead of us at they moved into position. We were all segments of a vast steel snake winding its way relentlessly into the shell-shocked town. The sky paled to a light blue, the stars became fewer and dim, and the moon changed to silver. Already a glimmer of orange had appeared and the country was lightening around us.

Suddenly a whoosh and a roar made me duck with a start and the air seemed to shimmer with meteors and flame. For a split second I wondered what abominable weapon the enemy had loosed on us. Then I realised – it was our rocket Battery. The enemy was the sufferer, not us. In a few moments we heard the rockets popping and grating on poor old Blerick. Then the guns opened fire. After that the noise was continuous. Soon it became just an unnoticed background to one's thoughts.

It was now light and I saw we were passing a Battery of our Regiment. As I saw their steadiness and sensed the regular rhythm of their firing I felt suddenly elated and confident, no longer vague and unreal: these were something solid and friendly. I was part of their plan; through my wireless I was linked to my friends.

A little further on the column halted and a Jock came to wish us well. He started to brew us some tea, but we had to move on before the kettle boiled. Our next stop was by an LAA gun, and they did brew us some. Then we came to Dick Bethell's sign. We halted there, so I went in to see him and found him in a tiny dark cellar surrounded by Officers with whirring wireless sets. He was controlling the Gunner side of the battle, and had called in a set from almost every Regiment, so that if we called for a target he could put a Regiment on to it at once without having to wait for it to be relayed on other nets.

With his words of kindly encouragement still ringing in my ears, we moved on again and diverged to our forming-up place. As we arrived, Moss Waters called me to say they were just going in. He asked for Medium fire on a couple of targets and the Colonel produced it in a twinkling.

The soft, wet ground had given the Flails a lot of trouble, and many got stuck. Eventually the Churchills had to tow most of them into their flailing positions, thus themselves braving the minefield border. On either flank – a mile or two away – our smoke screens were in full blast and the two towns were almost hidden in a haze of smoke and dust. Thanks to the screens and the bombardment the minefield was gapped and the ditch bridged with few casualties. On the right the going was good, and the Battalion there got its troops safely into the town. But the Scots Fusiliers had great trouble on our side. Churchills were continually being called to un-ditch a Kangaroo and send it on its way.

The Forming-up Post[1] was not quite a bed of roses. Two or three Crocodiles were well and truly bogged there. Ian's Kangaroo got stuck on my right and then mine sank deep in the mud as I tried to get on to some firm ground. All the while some very angry shells were blasting the place and the air was full of bangs and the roar and stutter of tank engines.

Dick Bethell and I discussed this and that on the wireless. He particularly wanted to know how effective one of the smoke screens was, but was most sympathetic when I asked him to wait until we had unbogged the machine. I promised to let him know as soon as I could move again, and did so, getting Nigel's opinion as well, for good measure.

My tank men dug like mad to un-ditch us, but we had sunk too deep and had to wait for a Churchill to pull us. Meanwhile I was on tenterhooks that Ian would get his tank free first and go off without telling me where. We had walky-talky communication between us, so I called him and told his signaller to let me know the moment they were free. Imagine my annoyance when, sometime later, I found he had abandoned the machine and wandered off on foot – the Signaller hadn't told me because I had only asked to be told when they were un-ditched, which shows how carefully one should choose one's words. We went to look for him, but found he had thumbed a lift from a Crocodile and gone post-haste into Blerick without any of his HQ.

By this time the shelling had died down round us and there was some watery sunshine, so I took off a sweater or two. A Flail was milling about, flogging the ground. I got out to speak to someone and then stood, fascinated by this machine, quite forgetting for a moment the reason for its whirling chains. A colossal roar and a fountain of earth brought me to my senses with a jolt. I deserved to be hurt for my stupidly, but I was lucky.

We were now over on the right of the ridge and having lost Ian it seemed pointless to go back to Skye route again, risking getting bogged on the way, so I decided to use the Ayr route through the gaps and enter the town by the KOSB sector. There was an Officer of the Reconnaissance Regiment doing traffic control, so I asked him if there was any objection to our using their route. To my surprise, right in the middle of a battle, he snapped to attention and saluted smartly. 'No objection at all, Sir,' he said.

The RSF's doctor then came rumbling up in his Kangaroo to ask if I was going to Blerick: if so, could he follow me? I said he certainly could, though I had no idea how to find the RSF again. Looking past him, I saw that the whole of Battalion HQ was snaking after him. That was rather a nuisance. It is one thing to be lost oneself, but quite another to lose another person's Battalion HQ as well. Had I known that the reserve Company was tagging along behind them too, I might have been a bit worried.

Down the slope and into the minefield we went. The gap was well marked with red and white signs – 'Keep white on your left' was the slogan, the red being on the dangerous side. We took no chances and kept well in the tracks of our predecessors until we were over the ditch and well into the plain beyond.

A cluster of Nebelwerfer bombs burst on our right. I couldn't hear them above the noise of our engines and thought they were some of our smoke shells falling out of place, so I called the Colonel and asked if he was starting a new smoke screen there. That raised quite a hare on the net, with the Colonel asking everyone if their smoke screens were wrong, until Archie Browne of 177 cut in with a crisp: 'My screen is just where it should be – please leave it alone!' Then it dawned on me what they were.

At the edge of the town I paused to consider. I had intended going in and working left through the streets until I found the RSF sector. But the road was deserted and unfriendly, littered with bricks and debris, and there was no sign of our troops (the KOSB), so I changed my mind and decided to skirt the edge until I found the place where the Scots Fusiliers had entered. That seemed better than to go bald-headed into what might be a nasty trap. The disadvantage was that we should have to leave the marked route and might chance on a mine or two, but that had to be risked, and anyhow, our machines weren't as vulnerable as carriers and armoured cars.

Spotting a tank track going our way, I told our driver to keep on it, and on we went. A quarter of a mile on we came upon the maker of the tracks and halted. It was a Sapper in a Kangaroo who had stopped because he wondered if there were mines ahead. But for us, the die was cast: we could not go back, so we held our breath and took the plunge.

The scene was quite peaceful now. Except for the gentle popping of our smoke shells, the firing had stopped. An occasional rat-tat-tat from a Bren gun showed that the Infantry were still clearing the town, but there was nothing to be seen outside it except the long column of tank-like machines trailing away behind me. I was happier too because we had just passed a cemetery marked on the map, so I knew exactly where we were and could start looking for the Blerick end of Skye route.

Without more trouble we found it and started to turn towards the town. But as we breasted a crest and swung on to the road I spotted two soldiers in the distance, frantically waving at us. My first thought was that they were trying to give warning of a hidden anti-tank gun, so I took immediate evasive action. 'Back, Driver!' I shouted into the intercom, and he shot into reverse. With a clang and a jolt that hurt my ribs against the steel sides, we cannoned smartly into the doctor's machine – the silly ass had been riding in my pocket! While the drivers were disentangling, I focused my glasses on the waving figures. To my joy I saw one was Ian McKenzie, and he was waving us over to join him. Our troubles were over, and we rumbled sedately into Blerick.

Ian was delighted to see his HQ and gave me credit where none was due.[2] He had been finding it very hard to run the Battalion with only Sturgeon and two of his Provost Corporals.

That was the 'perfect attack'. To us microbes floundering in the mist it had seemed at times a ghastly mix-up, but that is how things do seem when one can see only one's own small part of the picture. The proof of perfection was the smallness of our casualties. By that standard the adjective was well justified.[3]

Notes

[1] FUP (Forming-up Post) is the place where the troops shook out into the order in which they were going to attack.

[2] The author was awarded the Military Cross for his actions in the Battle of Blerick. The citation is shown opposite.

[3] By the end of November the Germans had only three footholds on the west bank of the Maas. One of these was the town of Blerick, across the river from Venlo. The First Fallschirmjaeger Army had left a detachment of troops to garrison the town, which had been turned into a fortress complete with minefields, trenches and fortified buildings. Furthermore, an anti-tank ditch ringed the town. It fell upon the 44th Brigade of the 15th Scottish Infantry Division to wipe out this stronghold. After a night of rain, the attack opened at dawn with a tremendous bombardment of over 400 guns. The Scottish vehicles began to churn through the mud. There was hardly any dry ground anywhere in Holland. One whole squadron of Churchills and several Flail tanks bogged down even before making it to the starting line. With fire support from the Churchills, the Flail tanks blasted lanes through the minefields and the ditch was bridged and filled with fascines by engineer tanks. The infantry, due to murderous mortar, shell, and machine-gun fire, was under orders to ride the Kangaroos all the way into the town itself. The vehicles were then to drive back and load up the second wave. Although in places the attack went so poorly the ditch was not breached, in general the infantry, with armour and artillery support, cleared Blerick by the mid-afternoon, capturing 250 prisoners. Scottish casualties for the day were about 100.

Citations

London Gazette

War Office, 6 April, 1944

The King has been graciously pleased to approve that the following be Mentioned in recognition of gallant and distinguished services in the Middle East:

Capt. (temp Maj.) R.A. Gorle (44862)

War Office, 5 April, 1945

The King has been graciously pleased to approve the following awards in recognition of gallant and distinguished services in North West Europe:

The Military Cross

Major (temporary) Richmond Ambrose Gorle (44862), Royal Regiment of Artillery (Northlew Devon)

The Military Cross citation reads:

On 3 Dec, Maj GORLE was the arty rep with the 6 Bn RSF in the attack on BLERICK by 15 (S) Div. The objective lay beyond a wide stretch of open ground crossed by enemy dug-in defences and an A Tk ditch. This in turn was overlooked by the enemy located in the outskirts of BLERICK.

His position was one of great responsibility, involving the direction of many guns and the subduing of unlocated enemy positions. Moving to the attack with the leading infantry, Maj GORLE soon realised that the necessary recce for vital OPs could not be carried out in his vehicle in such open country. Major GORLE repeatedly left his 'kangeroo' in which vehicles the attacking troops were mounted, and well knowing the area to be mined, he walked under heavy fire to find suitable viewpoints and to keep in close touch with the operation. This he continued to do throughout the day. By his disregard of his own safety, and by his resource, he was able to continue to play his vital part in the battle until the objective was gained. He contributed materially to the success of the operation.

Brigade 9th Dec 1944, Division, 6th Jan 1945, Corps 15th Jan 1945, Army 17th Jan 1945

B.L. Montgomery, Field Marshal, Commander-in-Chief, 21 Army Group

Chapter 34

Life in Blerick

We were dreamers, dreaming greatly,
In the man-stifled town.

Rudyard Kipling

181 Field Regiment RA, December 1944

Now that we had closed up to the River Maas we entered on a period of relative inactivity while other parts of the front were cleared. Our job was to hold Blerick; a matter of keeping careful watch across the river, making the enemy's life a misery with artillery harassing fire and enduring a little shelling ourselves.

My Tac HQ went comfortably to ground in a barber's shop with a telephone line to every conceivable place, even including Howarth's cookhouse in the cellar next door. He prized that telephone tremendously, and it caused him to be dubbed 'Sunray Cookhouse', Sunray being the wireless code name for every Commander from the Commander in Chief down, the idea being to make it harder for the enemy to find out whom he was listening to by calling the corresponding Officer at each level by the same name. The sobriquet suited him, for besides being always cheerful, he was definitely boss of that cellar, and no one chose to dispute his sway.

One day the barber's wife came to see whether the shop was still standing. She was a very pretty girl, but we did not get a look-in as Nigel monopolised her most of the morning. When she was leaving I noticed, to my surprise, that she was wearing an Officer's cap badge. Later, I met Nigel, and was not surprised to notice that he had lost his!

My day usually started with an early morning walk with Ian round the forward positions and a visit to my OPs. Moss Walters had his in a house looking across the river and I went up into the rafters to see if we could make a better one by removing a tile, to make a peep-hole. On my way back I found I had to crawl down the stairs head first to avoid exposing myself as I passed a window. As I groped my way clumsily down, there was a chuckle from Ian.

'Are you a married man, Dick'?

'Yes, Colonel,' I replied.

'Well,' said he, 'your wife would laugh if she could see you now!'

Nigel was ensconced in a cottage on the left of the town with a wide open space between him and the river. It had been a small general store, which seemed to stock little else but rolls and rolls of super-fine toilet paper, which was most useful. In fact we became suppliers of it to the Regiment. It is surprising what a morale raiser such an 'unconsidered trifle' can be. We built Nigel a sand-bagged post on the first floor and nominated him paperboy to the Regiment.

These walks were usually not without incident. The Bosch used to fire off a couple of Nebelwerfers to wake us up. These used to catch us in the main street making our progress up it to take the form of a game of musical chairs, with house doors as chairs and 'Moaning Minnie' as the music. We would pause with a hand on the door handle, ready to dash in if the bombs seemed to be coming too near, hurrying on to the next inbetween bursts.

One day we were nicely caught between 'chairs'. The bombs came over like a coven of moaning witches and I felt their warm breath on my neck as we threw ourselves flat. I remember feeling rather jealous of Ian because he and Sturgeon had managed to get behind a wall, while I could only try and squirm under the kerb of the pavement.

We beat them to it next day by getting up earlier, and strange to say the Bosch for once varied his very regular habit and fired later. We were out on the left of the town when they did fire, and I could have kicked myself for not having brought a wireless set, because by following their trail of sparks backwards, I could see where they were hidden, so could have had great fun strafing them in their turn.

However, Nigel made up for it by spotting one of their self-propelled guns as it crept forward to annoy us and carefully watching it as it withdrew to its hide, in a garage. There he gave it the works. One can just imagine those Germans blowing on their fingers and stamping their frozen feet as they put away the gun and dismounted. Then – WHAM! The whole might of 181 Field Regiment descended on them. It must have spoilt their appetite for breakfast.

As Ian was a bit wary of the enemy trying to stage a comeback across the river on the Battalion's left flank, which he was holding with his Carrier Platoon only, I sited an OP there, to be occupied by Jonah in case of need. I was rather proud of that OP. I put it in a shed with reed sides. You could see through them when inside, while they completely hid the inside observer from view. We built a nice sandbagged post there by night so that the occupants would have good protection and yet be able to move about to their hearts' content.

The building of it gave the men of the Battery the chance of creeping about the front line by night, an excitement which they thoroughly enjoyed. Everyone likes someone else's job for a change. But one party nearly came to grief. Their lorry took the wrong turning and was heading for the river's edge, where they could have been shot to pieces, but a friendly Fusilier stopped them. 'Where you goin', chum? Looking for Jerries? There's bags of them over there! We'll look after the truck for you while you go and look for them!'

Others of the night birds had quite a bit of fun when Moss's carrier was put out of action by a shell bursting in a tree above it. We could not afford to lose such a valuable truck, so we had to, as the Army says, 'recover' it, even though it was in a street with only a single row of houses between it and the river. A gun-tractor was inched along there in the dark, as quietly as a truck of its type could be induced to move. With every joint creaking and squeaking and the engine popping like a pom-pah in the stillness, it was coasted up to the derelict carrier and hooked on. Then came the test: most of our 'Quads' (as the gun-tractors were called) required a fierce jab on the accelerator before they would move. Everyone expected a burst of fire when the truck let out its grumbling roar and waited tensely. To everyone's surprise, this one seemed to guess the danger, and she 'roared her as gently as any sucking dove'. Even the carrier's tracks didn't clatter too much – though to those on the job they sounded like an avalanche. In a very short time the recovery was completed, and silence returned, without a shot being fired.

Life here was if not enjoyable at least quite pleasant. The shelling was annoying, but not frequent enough to cause more than a little discomfort. It even gave us a subject for conversation.

'We stopped quite a packet this morning – the 88s had us taped to a yard.'

'88s! Oh, that's nothing – you wait until the Nebelwerfers catch you, then you'll know all about shelling!'

'That's nothing, is it? Well, that burning house over there was hit by an 88 – and look at the shape of it! No Nebel could do that!'

Dick Bethell used to visit us regularly. He strongly approved of our little Command Post in the cellar because we had all the maps and air photos displayed on the walls instead of stuffed into my haversack, as they usually were. He liked our intelligence system, too. A careful log was kept at each OP, noting the time and place of every movement seen, and the logs of both OPs were carefully compared, the results marked on my map. In this way, by comparing each day's results with the rest, we were able to build up a pretty good picture of what was where on the other side.

The German Platoon HQ gave themselves away by frequent and regular comings and goings. The relief of lookout posts was deduced from movement at regular times, and so on. All this provided food for our harassing fire to feed on. Ian came in unannounced one day and was so impressed that he got his Intelligence Officer to pool the Battalion's logs with ours. Between us we built up a good picture of the front, which must have helped our successors when the time came for them to cross the river and take Venlo itself.

What pleased me more than anything was the interest that all my party took in what was going on. One day I came back from a round of the OPs to find them studying the logs and air photos and comparing them with the map. Their comments and suggestions were so apposite that I had another map mounted and gave them the task of keeping it up to date. They did this so well that I made theirs the master map, checking their work thoroughly, of course. That was a great boost to their morale and drew the team even closer together.

Soon it became the normal thing for an informal conference to assemble each evening after supper to discuss the day's events – and anything else that came to mind, from the way to run an Army to jobs after the war. Often there would be as many as twelve people in that small cellar, each taking his turn at settling the affairs of the world, and all of us enjoying it.

After two weeks of this static warfare, the Regiment was pulled out of the line and sent to Asten for a rest of exactly four days. It had been in action for fifty-four days, two short of two months, a long time to be at instant readiness to fire, day and night, with all wirelesses manned, Officers on duty at every Command Post, and Patrols and local Defence Posts on continuous alert. It is a long time, too, for the gun detachments to be always on call to rush to their guns at a moment's notice. Most of the time and in all weathers, from pouring rain to freezing cold, their only cover at night was a makeshift tarpaulin shelter. They had thirteen or fourteen moves in the period, most of them at night, and lasting for most of the night, to be followed by from six to twelve hours' hard work digging gun-pits and the rest. As often as not, just as they had got things ship shape in would come the order for another move, and they would have it all to do again. The marvel is that all the equipment was kept in excellent condition, in spite of all the weather could do and the difficulties of maintaining it.

Monotony was the chief enemy. Almost the only things to look forward to were letters from home and the weekly NAFFI issue – cigarettes and chocolate, soap and toothpaste and such like. Each man was able to buy about two shillings [ten pence] worth, and its arrival was eagerly awaited. It says a lot for the efficiency and understanding of the Officers that there were never any complaints, and such grousing as there was was of the normal humorous and friendly kind. The Battery Captain, Ray Bristowe, can take a lot of the credit for this. He lived mostly in the Waggon-Lines, seeing to the supply of rations and petrol and ammunition, and performing 101 domestic chores that were essential to the efficiency and happiness of the Battery.

A well-organised Battery in war is a wonderful thing. It is split into so many widely separated parts – OPs, Tac HQ, Gun positions, Wagon lines, for example – and all are dependent on each other. If one fails the whole unit suffers. Control and supervision is not easy and it is now that the value of peacetime discipline and training is apparent. The Officers and NCOs who made the best job of it were those who had absorbed the methods and ideas passed on to them by the pre-war Regular Army: those were the people who could maintain proper discipline without losing the personal and friendly touch; who could be democratic in spirit without introducing crackpot democratic ideas. 179 Field Battery was bequeathed to me in excellent condition, and I look back on it with wonder and admiration.

Chapter 35

Christmas on the Maas

From ghoulies and ghosties,
And long-leggedy beasties,
And things that go 'Bump' in the night,
Good Lord, deliver us.

181 Field Regiment RA, December 1944

After a short rest we came back to our old position near Maasbree. Our friends the Scots Fusiliers were out of the line, so for most of the time we had no OPs out. Life in the Battery was quiet too, because the policy was to appoint a 'duty Battery' to fire all the harassing fire tasks from a place well clear of the main positions. So, with no OPs to man and little shooting, we were able to start thinking about Christmas.

The enemy gave us one jolt before the great day. I was peacefully asleep in a little room next to the Command Post when a tremendous explosion woke me. The door came down on my bed, the window and shutters blew out with a crash of broken glass, and a flame appeared to shoot across the ceiling – all of this in the waking instant. I felt the heat of the explosion and waited, with my arms covering my head, for the ceiling to come down. Finding I was unhurt, I slipped on my greatcoat and dashed out to see what sort of a shambles there was.

In the Command Post I found bewildered confusion. Bricks and mortar were everywhere: the room was full of dust and there was a large hole in the wall by the door. The dog (who was still with us at this point) was cowering under a table. Moss Waters was swearing like a Trooper because a telephone had fallen on his head, but apart from that no one was hurt.

I hurried to the kitchen: the door had been blown against the far wall. Bombardier Dodd was wandering round in a daze saying 'Good job I moved over from by that door.' The Dutch family peered out of the cellar and murmured '*Nix goot!*'

Upstairs in the officers' dormitory I found most of the roof off and Philip Mulholland sleeping peacefully in the debris.

It was a miracle no one was hurt. Returning to the Command Post, everything was still in chaos. I stung the men into action, telling them to be back to normal and ready to accept fire-calls in ten minutes. The old 'Grappler' and I collected some men and searched the woods and orchards round the house.

To our great relief we found nothing there. Before that, I thought an enemy patrol had 'bazooka-ed' us, and it had been a nasty feeling sitting in the bull, as it were, waiting for the next shot to strike.

The puzzle was, what had hit us? It couldn't have been a shell because someone would have heard it coming; a rocket would have done much more damage, so we ruled that out; and it wasn't a bazooka. The only remaining possibility was a time-bomb, but how could a time-bomb have got there?

The problem remained unsolved for several days. Then we were given warning to keep a lookout for two German soldiers who were said to be going about disguised as nuns, carrying the time-bombs under their skirts for use as occasion offered. Then all was clear. I remembered seeing a pair of them plodding through the mud near our house. If they were in fact soldiers, what could have been easier than placing an innocent-looking tin against the wall as they passed? I had been thinking what wonderful women they were to go on with their duties so close to the enemy.

The morning after the explosion we moved to the harassing fire position, feeling very disgruntled that our nice house had been so knocked about and that we should have to celebrate Christmas in the ruins. But when we came back, on Christmas Eve, we found everything back to normal. Our rear party had repaired the hole in the wall and the farmer's sons had mended the roof. The lofts were set with tables and benches, decorated with streamers and tinsel and boughs of evergreen. Here was a real feeling of Christmas in the air, heightened and completed by the arrival of a bumper mail from home. You have to go to war to really understand what the arrival of the home mail means.

Then came a shocking blow. The Bosch had been seen by the Dutch having his Christmas Dinner two days early, so it was opined that he might be intending to try and catch us on the hop with an attack while we were eating ours. So the order came to us: 'Hundred-per-cent alert!'

All the turkeys and pork were ready for cooking; extra rations of all kinds were up. It would not keep, so it looked as if we should have to spoil it all by snatching at the food piecemeal. That, I decided, just would not do. After turning it over in my mind I reckoned that we could get round the letter of the order without breaking its spirit by relieving half the guns at a time and by making the others fire double rates if an attack should come in until the banqueters got back to their places. I was sure that the Colonel would agree to this (or I would not have done it), but it seemed unfair to unload responsibility on to him by asking permission to 'interpret' the order, so we just did it and said nothing about it until afterwards.

The day dawned bright and sunny after a hard frost and the nip in the air was exhilarating. Festivities started in the traditional way, with the Officers taking early morning tea – laced with rum – to the troops in bed. This was hugely enjoyed and gave rise to plenty of soldiers' wit. 'Don't forget the bread and butter next year!' said one humourist.

After going round and seeing everyone in the 'Firing Battery' (i.e. the part that does the firing), I went down to the Wagon Lines. There the drivers had billeted themselves on the families of a small hamlet, to the liking of both parties to the contract. As I was leaving I saw a pair of legs sticking out from a lorry. Investigation revealed the owner as the Chief Fitter. I wished him the usual wishes and asked why on earth he was working on this, of all days. 'Can't afford to have a truck out of action – Christmas or not,' he replied, which was typical of the spirit in the Battery. If there was a job to do they did it, even on Christmas Day, with no apparent urgency to spur them on.

As the time for 'dinners' drew near we trooped up to the loft, now even more decorated than before. 'Easy' Troop and half Battery HQ were seated at two long tables, cracking nuts – typical of the soldier, anything on the table is eaten at once, regardless of its place on the menu.

The air was thick with smoke and full of the roar of conversation. In a little alcove great dishes of turkey were being marshalled into position. Crates of beer were clinking as people seized bottles from them and passed them round. Everyone was merry and everyone was chattering.

The cooks slaved away at the dishes, dumping great slices of turkey, pork, beef, stuffing, potatoes and greens until the plates could hold no more, whereupon they were whisked away by the Officers and Sergeants – mess waiters for the day. There was hardly room to move, but soon everybody was helping and the roar subsided a little as each gave rein to his appetite.

I went from group to group and soon exhausted my store of repartee as each took time off from eating to make some wisecrack or other. When the plum pudding was on the way, I went to give the cooks a pat on the back. Here I found Howarth with his sleeves rolled up, lending a hand – that chap could not resist cooking. He at once sat me down to a plate of turkey, and it was done to a turn. The Ritz could not have done it better! In a very short time that mass of food had disappeared and the horde of joyful and distended soldiery wandered off to their dug-outs to sleep it off. Their place was taken by 'Fox' Troop and the rest of Battery HQ. It was a splendid blowout and a break in the monotony that did everyone good.

The Officers' dinner was also a great affair. That was held in the evening. We had several guests. We picked up the Adjutant, Walter Matthews, when we went to RHQ in the morning to pay our respects to the Colonel. They were taking the war very seriously and had postponed their dinner, so we said Walter must come and help eat ours. James Robertson, who was to take over the Battery from me, was there, and Neil Brodie of the RSF who had some men guarding our exposed flank, and we also had the Adjutant of the RSF, Hugh Cowan. I think he just dropped in (most welcomely) because the Scots were keeping their celebrations for Hogmanay, so he thought he had better make sure the Sassenach Battery behaved themselves.

Bombardier Dodd did us well. It was a lovely dinner! Imagine a typical Dutch parlour with the usual religious statuary, the ancient family groups on the walls, the lace curtains over the blackout blinds. There is a roaring stove in a corner, and a dim oil lamp glimmers through the tobacco smoke. Stir in a dozen or so British Officers, of all types, close the door, pass the whisky round and the picture is complete.

Afterwards we started to play Vingt-et-un, but it was soon clear that it was an evening for song, not cards, so we closed the game and sang. Song after song was sung and the evening became comfortably rowdy. I think I brewed some rum Punch: if so that was probably the cause of Neil being dumped into his truck like a sack of wheat after he had demonstrated the strength of his stomach by making two hefty batmen stand on it in ammunition boots. Hugh Cowan was draped tenderly over him and the truck vanished into the icy night. The Scots Fusiliers were out of the line, so Hugh and Neil could let their hair down. We had to hold back very considerably, in case the attack should come in, but it did not seem to affect our enjoyment at all.

Said Ian a day or two later, 'What did you do to my Adjutant, Dick? I haven't been able to get any work out of him for two whole days!'

Now I had to tear myself away from 179 Battery. The Colonel was doing some reorganising and Dick Moorshead had been sent home for a rest. As I was by far the senior Major, Dick Bethell said I must take my place as Second-in-Command. So James Robertson spent Boxing Day going round with me, learning the ramifications of the outfit, and I departed for RHQ the next day. I hated going. Only four months had passed since I took command, but it had seemed an age. So much had happened, events had followed each other so quickly. Each event, short in itself, had been drawn out by tension and a faster rate of living until a battle or a period in the line became marked in my mind as an epoch.

Officers and men were individually, almost without exception, first class, and together they were a friendly but ruthlessly efficient team. They were always high spirited and always ready to smash the Bosch.

Shortly after I left, Howarth was awarded a 'Commander in Chief's Certificate' instead of the Military Medal for which he had been recommended. It came as a complete surprise to him, and he was amazed and delighted. The bewilderment on his face gradually relaxed into a beaming smile, then he broke the ice with: 'What's this for? Cooking in the face of the ruddy enemy?'

Chapter 36

The Second Fall of Tilburg

At last he rose, and twitched his mantle blue:
Tomorrow to fresh woods, and pastures new.

John Milton

181 Field Regiment RA, December 1944/January 1945

I found that RHQ had no idea about keeping warm! In the Mess there was a stove crammed full of wet peat. Two sparks were alight and a thin trickle of steamy smoke could be seen when the lid was opened. I made a mental note that if I was to stay alive I must do something about this. I gave this job first priority, and it took me exactly two days. After that we had good fires for the rest of the war.

We stayed at Maasbree until the first week of the New Year, which gave me a chance to get on good terms with the Officers and men. There was Walter Matthews, the Adjutant, who had Christmas dinner with us in 179, his assistant Deryck Martin, Bob Livie the Survey Officer, Tomlinson the Intelligence Officer and John Shaw, the Quartermaster. A very efficient Signals Officer was attached, and there was the doctor, and a dry little Scottish parson. The last member of the Mess was a Dutch boy, Dicky Brown. We picked him up in Eindhoven, where he had lost all his family and acquired an intense hatred of Germans. He wanted to enlist with us, but we couldn't do that, so we enrolled him as our interpreter – and a very good one he was.

The cold was now intense. My normal dress was a leather jerkin over my Tilburg fleece, and under that battle dress, three cardigans, shirt and vest, pyjamas, ankle-length woollen pants and two pairs of socks: quite a bundle, but I was never cold, and my movements were never impeded as they would have been by a greatcoat. I used that as an extra blanket at night. The enemy hardly stirred – I expect he was feeling the cold more than we were.

The last event at Maasbree was a party on New Year's Eve to which all the HQ RA Officers came. The CRA (Lyndon Bolton) and I had a good laugh about our first meeting, which now seemed so long ago. He was kind enough to say that he was glad he did not send me back to base then.

We then had a short rest at Deurne before going to Maesyck, where we did practically nothing, and then we got the grand order: 'Go to Tilburg, and have a real holiday!' Off we went, like a lot of schoolboys. We found that it had changed. Every street we wanted to turn into was newly marked 'No Entry'. Wherever we tried to park, MPs pointed to 'No Parking' signs. The maple leaf of the Canadians appeared everywhere, but the red lion of the 'liberators' was not recognised. The people were apathetic and unfriendly. Evidently the Canadians had rubbed them up the wrong way. To cap it all, we were given an inferior part of the town for our billets. It was a complete anti-climax. We managed to get everyone in, but billeting was most difficult, with every obstacle put in our way. Our Mess was in an uncomfortable little café-cum-pub with two marble-topped tables and a few wooden chairs for furniture. We explained to the owner that his café was now hired by the British Army, and that he would be paid rent for it, and put '*Café geslotten*' on the door. But still the customers came in for their drinks, staring dully at us as we went about our business.

I could stand it no longer. There was a big house across the way where our Billeting Officer had been defeated when he tried to get us in there in the first place. I decided that we would go over. The owner, Herr Siegers, was quite peremptory to Dicky Brown, saying that we would spoil his carpets. I told him we had been civilised once, and had even had carpets in our houses, but he ranted that his house was far too good for soldiers. That riled me. I told him that nothing was too good for British Soldiers and that we were going to have our Officers' Mess there. At that he changed and was all over us, saying he would be delighted and so on. With that, we moved in.

Next day no fewer than three women came and wanted to know why they had been left out of the billeting scheme. 'Why can't we have a nice Tommy like the others?'

'I'm sorry' we answered, 'You should have spoken earlier – they're all settled in now!'

Settled in they were. Many had started drawing their rations and living with the families. The women did their washing and mending for them, and that very day a young girl was seen wearing a hat modelled on the Tam o' Shanter She was the forerunner of a fashion in Tilburg! Yes, the troops were in clover, and the townsfolk were delighted to have them.

It says a lot for those Shropshire lads that they won the people's hearts so quickly, and kept them. It confirms my belief that the men of 181 were an exceptionally nice lot. Indeed, I cannot remember there ever being an unpleasant incident, and I don't think the Colonel ever had to hold a 'petty sessions'.

Moss Walters and Jonah paid us a visit when we were settled in to tell us that 179's billets could be improved on. I told him that they were no worse than the rest. 'Yes, I know,' said Moss, 'but we thought we would come and see if you had a vestige of Battery feeling left.'

We quickly became friendly with our family. Herr Siegers was an anxious, dyspeptic-looking little businessman and his wife was a quiet, elderly matron. Then there were three daughters. Annie, the eldest, was broad, and heavy. The second, Reit (or Titte), was a beauty: she was about sixteen, slim and golden-haired, with a charming expression. Lastly, there was Corrie, a long-legged schoolgirl of twelve or so.

The trouble was that Dicky was the only one who could talk to them. Siegers spoke a little French and German, but our conversation with the others was limited to smiles and *Goede morgen* and *Goede nacht*. However, Dicky made great headway with Reit. As a rule they stayed in the kitchen in the evening, whither the batmen also congregated. Sometimes we would invite them to coffee and drinks and pass a pleasant hour talking French to Siegers, or forcing Dicky to take his eyes off Reit and interpret for us. Sometimes Reit would play the piano with Dicky dutifully turning the pages for her, of course. Next morning Bain would tell me that we had spoilt their evening by taking the family away.

So for a time life passed pleasantly and without incident. But soon the rumble of war reached us again, in the form of 'top secret' orders to reconnoitre gun positions for the breaching of the Siegfried Line and the clearance of the Reichswald (Imperial Forest). The affair really was top secret. I was to go to the town of Graves – and vanish! I was to step into a truck belonging to a Canadian regiment that was already in the line near Nijmegen and not a soul was to know where I went after that. The Siegfried Line was a tough nut to crack, so it was essential that the Bosch should not suspect that it was to be stormed until it was too late for him to reinforce it.

On a cold afternoon we arrived in a wooded country, flat and dreary under a covering of snow, and the CRA showed me some old gun positions. We were to 'double-gun' them – put two guns where only one had been before – thus the Germans would not be able to estimate our strength, even when they discovered that the old position was again occupied.

'Will these do?' asked the CRA.

My stomach went cold at the thought of the damage just one shell or bomb could do to guns packed so tightly. But I knew there was no alternative: all I had to decide was whether the guns could do their job without hitting the trees in front. I measured the angle with my eye.

'They'll do', I said.

Then the Canadians undertook to prepare the site and dump the ammunition for us. They were very pleasant, friendly people.

Tilburg was as we left it. Every so often a V1 or Flying Bomb would pass over us, on its way to Antwerp, which was our supply port. It was odd to watch them streaking across the sky. They were the first attempt at a pilotless aircraft, and as such seemed a little uncanny. They looked ugly and square and unfinished and they made a noise like an ancient farm tractor, but they were very effective at first. One or two got off course and fell near Tilburg with very loud explosions. The Dutch were very alarmed at this: they had not been bombed before and found it rather a shattering introduction.

All this time the Colonel was on leave, so much of the preliminary planning for the battle fell to me. I had a most interesting time attending various secret conferences and in due course, as the time came for more people to be let into the secret, I took the Battery parties forward to the positions, still under pledge of secrecy.

The gunner plan hinged on getting our Regiment forward the moment the first objective fell. The attack was a deep one, and we could not otherwise make the range. Unfortunately, the place allocated to us was thought to be one large minefield. 'The main track will be swept and cleared,' said the CRA, 'then you must clear lanes on either side to put your guns into. It's difficult, but it's the only place, and you must be damn quick about it – everything depends on your fire being available at once!'

I didn't like the sound of that at all: we had infinite faith in the ability of the Sappers to detect and clear a minefield, but not much in our own efforts. However, there were still a few days left, so the motto to adopt seemed to be 'Eat, drink and be merry!' Here old Siegers came to our aid, suggesting that we should have a party, and promising to supply the girls and food if we did the rest. It seemed a good idea, so we went ahead with it, though I could not help wondering why he should suddenly become so interested in our entertainment. I was even more surprised when he came to me one morning and asked if he could have some photographs taken as souvenirs. One had to be on the watch for treachery and ulterior motives in war and I racked my brains to try to see what he was up to. The only thing that I could think of was that he would have some photos of a handful of unimportant officers, which couldn't possibly be of any use to the Germans, so I made no objection.

Later on, it struck me that he probably wanted them as proof that he had actively collaborated with the British as an offset to rumours that he had been unduly friendly with the Germans. I saw no reason to withdraw the permission as I had no use at all for the cold-blooded mob vengeance that was handed out to collaborators.

The party was a great success [see plate]. The old man certainly knew where to find pretty girls. The belle was a lively brunette called Villi, but some of the others ran her close. One called Anna made a dead set at Deryck. It was really very funny to see how quickly she captivated him. She looked at him and suddenly turned on all she had. You could almost see blue electric sparks cross the gap between them. From then on, he was her slave. Such is 'animal magnetism'.

So successful was the evening that it seemed impossible to end it. At last we played 'Auld Lang Syne'. That went down awfully well and there was a pause while they said what a delightful game that was. Then the party broke up into small groups and looked like finishing. But it wasn't! Villi was busy organising, and just as we expected to say goodbye we found ourselves in a ring for 'Put your right foot in ...' etc. She thought a repartee was expected to our parlour trick. The party went on at a great rate until it flagged from sheer exhaustion.

We moved from Tilburg in perfect secrecy. No preparations were made to give away that we were going. We poked our heads into the kitchen to say goodbye and thank you and off we went, at twenty minutes' notice. The drivers were not even told where they were bound for until they were well on the road.

Our destination was some miles beyond Nijmegen and we were adjured to be hidden in our new positions by dawn. The attack was to be some days later. We were gradually closing on the River Rhine

Chapter 37

Clearing the Reichswald

With banners furled, the clarions mute,
An army passes in the night;
And beaming spears and helms salute
The dark with bright.

Herman Melville

181 Field Regiment RA, January/February 1945

The night move from Tilburg to Nijmegen was, I think, the most chaotic I have ever experienced. It would have been perfectly simple, but someone decided to close the main road for repairs and routed us by a by-road. It was some by-road, too: track through a marsh would have been a truer description.

All three Divisional Artillery Field Regiments were travelling that night, and we were the last of the three, so there was quite a chance that our tail would be caught in the early morning light even if things went well. Progress was a crawl from the start. The road itself was bad enough to account for some delay and a huge bulldozer ignoring the one-way traffic orders did not help much. It caused block after block. Then we came to a prolonged halt, and it was obvious that something more than the road was holding us back, so I went forward to see. We had then been on the road for six hours and had covered precisely nine miles.

I wormed my way up the column on foot, my car squeezing its way through as best it could. Four of 190 Regiment's guns were well ditched. There were drivers asleep with their trucks blocking the road: they had a rude awakening. There were Officers asleep too, who got a very rough side of my tongue. Some of them looked aggrieved at being cursed by someone from another Regiment, but it was their job to go ahead and find the blockage, not to take the opportunity to make up lost sleep.

At last we reached the cause of the trouble, where the road had crossed a marsh. I say 'had' because there was now no road left – just a quagmire. Two guns and their tractors were well and truly bogged down, and on

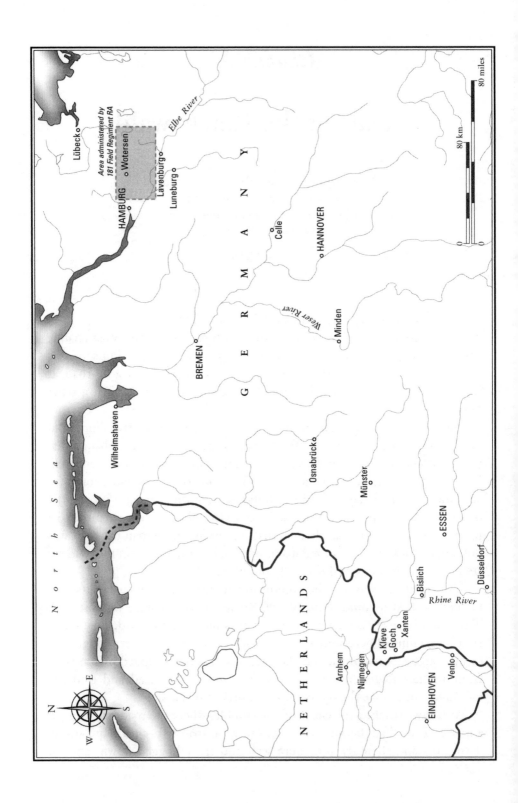

either side of the track too, so that there was only a narrow gap between them full of soft, clinging clay.

A Sapper Officer was in charge and he was giving each approaching driver the best possible orders to ditch his vehicle irretrievably. 'Its soft here, driver – get up all the speed you can, and rush it!' The driver did so, the gun and tractor skidded and plunged. The wheels threw up sheets of liquid clay as they dug in up to the axles, and there was another truck ditched. It looked hopeless. A quick glance showed that there was no way round. Overhead, a flying bomb clacked its way, its tail of fire streaming behind like a meteor. The time was 4.00 am – and we had to be under cover by dawn.

The Sapper was junior to me, so I took charge. I remembered that a pair of mules will shift a gun through mud that will halt a six-horse team because mules will pull slowly and doggedly, while the horses thrash and plunge like mad when they feel the extra drag, and then give up. I determined to see if this applied to mechanical traction.

People were shouting and milling about the place, getting in each other's way, and there was so much confusion that it took a minute or two to get silence and attention – to get the hounds looking towards the huntsman, as it were. Then, between us, we did a very neat recovery job, rescuing a gun and a tractor that seemed to be permanent fixtures. Then I got hold of a driver and held his attention until he really understood that he was to engage his lowest gear, and just *crawl*. To my delight, the plan worked like magic, the reason being that the full power of the engine was applied without the wheels spinning and cutting through the surface.

When the column was moving again I went back to Tilburg to get a recovery vehicle. I could not find one. Two more bombs streaked past, but this time their trails were the colour of the morning star against the pale blue sky of approaching dawn. So the night was over. If we were not under cover by dawn, it was not for the want of trying. Anyhow, there was no more that I could do, so I set a course for Nijmegen and, I hoped, breakfast. It had been a hard, hunger-making night.

To my delight, the road was completely empty. The horse–mule idea really had worked! Better still, I found RHQ at breakfast. Reports were coming in still and one Battery was what the Navy call 'adrift'. It was not on the road, as I had just come that way, so I saw no point in scouring the country and sat down to a meal.

Just as I was getting my teeth into it the Colonel arrived like a hurricane, wanting to know what the devil we had been doing all night. Regarding the missing Battery, he did not at all approve of my theory of 'Leave them, and they'll come home,' so I was soon batting down that blessed road again. It was a journey wasted, because they had come by the road that was supposed to be closed. It was not closed at all – all our troubles of the chaotic night had been quite needless. Unfortunately, the lost Battery had thrown its advantage away by taking a wrong turning, and arrived much later than any of us ... making me miss my breakfast.

The Division broke through the out-posts of the Siegfried Line as planned and our reconnaissance parties went forward with some misgivings. It looked as if the minefield did not stretch as far as our new position after all, but we took no chances, prodding and 'sweeping' the area with great care. I think I found the only mine, and it was well clear of where we wanted to go, so the Regiment was able to move in according to plan.

After that the battle was complicated by floods and soft ground, which the enemy made worse by breaking the banks of the river above us, very nearly cutting us off. We managed to get out in time and advanced on Cleeve from another direction.

Five days later the town of Goch fell: we were through the Reichswald and the smaller Hochwald. Those were days of strenuous moves and long bouts of firing while the Infantry worked through the woods. Plans changed so quickly that I often had to round up my party just as I had scattered them to get the position ready. At those times, I used to wish for a hunting horn to sound the recall. That or a trumpet would have saved a lot of careering over the country.

When the division reached the line Xanten-Geldern it was relieved and we were sent back to Tilburg again. That was quite a triumphant homecoming. The advance parties travelled through the night and I knocked at the Siegers' door at 7.00 am. After a moment or two Reit's pretty face appeared, two eyebrows lifted, and the head drew back. Then a hand came round the door and hung our 'Officers' Mess' sign on the nail again. The door swung open and we were almost pulled inside. Quite a greeting for so early in the morning! Our return was very popular because we brought the family some excellent beef from Germany. They had been short of meat for a long time.

While we were there I heard that I had been awarded the Military Cross, which was a pleasant surprise. I knew that one was coming to Nigel but did not expect to be on the list myself.

The next event for me was a sudden grant of seven days' home leave. The Colonel was away at the time, but was expected back that day. Not until I was on the way to the airport did the message arrive that he had been promoted to command an Infantry Brigade and would not be coming back to us. The Adjutant sent a jeep after me to bring me back, but the story has it that he timed it so that my plane would have taken off before it arrived. At any rate, I got home all right.

While waiting at Waterloo for the 1.25 am train to Devon, a soldier took a dislike to my face and punched me on the jaw, nearly knocking me out. A friend commented, 'Through the war without a scratch – he meets his Waterloo on the Southern Railway!'

Chapter 38

Crossing the Rhine

And on the river pours – it never tires;
Blind, hungry, screaming, day and night the same
Purposeless hurry of a million ires,
Mad as the wind, as merciless as flame

John Masefield

181th Field Regiment RA, March 1945

Back to Germany, and after a bit of hitchhiking I caught up with the Regiment again. Dick Bethell's place had been taken by Pat Keene, who had been Second-in-Command of 190 Regiment, and preparations for crossing the River Rhine were in full swing. We were on the last lap. We had hung our washing on the Siegfried Line, as the wartime song had prophesied – though it had taken four years to get there.

As the Allies had already tampered with nature by introducing artificial moonlight, it was no surprise to find that the reconnaissance of the flat, low-lying country of the Rhine Valley was to be done under cover of artificial fog. It was effective, but not at all pleasant. It was produced by smoke from portable oil burners, which hung over the land in a dismal evil-smelling haze – nearly as bad as a London 'pea-souper'. We had to prepare gun positions round a farm called Vinen, about 2,000 yards from the river bank, and jolly glad we were to escape from the murk and get back to the fresh air and sunlight when this was done.

The River Rhine is, according to Montgomery, the biggest water obstacle in Europe. It is no mere Thames: it is far, far wider, and takes quite a time to cross in a motor boat. All the bridges had of course been blown, and the enemy was defending the opposite bank, so the troops were faced with an assault crossing to be made at night.

The Infantry were carried in a Funny known as a 'Buffalo' [see plate]. This was simply an unarmoured steel box with enormously wide tank tracks, which made it possible for the vehicle to cross soft mud and boggy ground and also served as paddles to propel it when afloat. Each took about ten men. Boats and motor rafts were also used. Tanks were floated across by attaching huge air bags to give them buoyancy.

Three or more crossings were made at widely separated places during the night, each of which we supported by fire. Our old friends the Highland Division crossed first some miles to our left, and then 44 Lowland Brigade started. We had a running commentary on their progress from Jimmy Robertson, with the Scots Fusiliers. 'Starting now,' he said. 'Shelling very heavy on both banks ... We are about halfway over and going well ... Shelling still heavy ... Now under the far bank, foothold established.'

A little later, he told us they were safely ashore – the Rhine had been crossed. As far as Monty was concerned, the war was over. The rest was only a matter of time and the relentless elimination of the German Army. Barring some colossal error on our part, there was no possibility of the Germans staging a comeback.

*

But it did not seem like that to us yet. The river crossing was to be followed by a parachute and glider landing by an Airborne Corps of two Divisions – the British 6th Airborne and the US 17th. Our next job was to try to smooth their path by laying a carpet of shells on all known enemy AA guns.

A bright and sunny morning found us hard at work at this task. It was an unsatisfactory one because we were forbidden to fire after the planes appeared, so we knew that many of the guns whose crews had been cowering under our fire would come to life again as soon as we let up. But it would have been too risky to let our shells cruise alongside the incoming aircraft.

At 10.20 am – long before we expected it – we heard a steady roar overhead: we were directly under the path of the British Division. Frantic orders to stop firing made all the wires red hot, and there were we, in the front row, with nothing to do but watch. From then until 1.30 pm flight after flight zoomed over us in a steady, unhurried stream ... Dakotas carrying parachutists, four-engined Halifaxes towing gliders, two behind every plane, and Dakotas and others loaded with guns and stores for parachuting to the troops: it was magnificent. There were 1,700 aircraft and 1,300 gliders in all, of which half were in our stream.

Ahead we heard the AA that we were powerless to deal with thicken into a continuous roar. The gliders were an especially easy target. Soon after passing us they cast off the two ropes and then had to swoop slowly through the punishing 'flak' and land. Many were hit. The official figure of those destroyed is four per cent, but the wreckage we saw later seemed more than that. Certainly the two anti-tank Batteries had fifty per cent casualties before landing. The CRA of the 6th Airborne landed – as he described it – 'with the glider round my neck, all my staff killed or wounded, and my wireless out of action'.

We could not see the actual landing because the planes vanished into a haze of smoke and dust that rose like a fog over the dropping zone, but it was most successful, and soon we were answering their calls for fire. They had been purposely dropped within range of our Artillery. Their role was the quick expansion of the bridgehead, not the more usual one of dropping right behind the enemy lines, as at Arnhem, there to hang on by their teeth until the main force can catch up. It was a strategy that suited the event admirably, but there will probably never be agreement as to which is the best way to use airborne troops.

181 Field Regiment was the first of the gunners to cross the river and, to our intense annoyance, the papers reported us as the 81st [see plate]!

I was told to find positions near Bislich. The Regiment was to follow almost on my tail and I was to force a way for us, regardless of who else might be crossing. We had been given absolute priority officially, but at such times one is apt to be shouldered out if one is not aggressive.

So I arrived at the crossing, ready to do battle with the rest of the Army, but a pleasant surprise was in store. I was met by a young Officer of the Rifle Brigade who was in charge of the crossing and someone had so impressed him with the urgency of our mission that he was in a complete flap. All he could say was '181 has priority – ABSOLUTE PRIORITY! Priority over everything – make way for the Gunners!' Surprisingly enough he was efficient as well as in a flap, so we crossed like a royal procession.

The advance parties crossed on a motor raft with a Sapper at the wheel. The morning was lovely and sunny and we were enjoying the trip when suddenly, out of the blue, one single shell burst on the river with a crack. The enjoyment left us and we were back to reality in an instant: the middle of the Rhine is no place to be shelled. No other shell came near us, but I took the hint and hurried the Regiment away from the landing point as quickly as ever I could.

We sited the guns and took over a house, telling the German family to go. There was no question of sharing it with them: our orders were strict; there was to be absolutely no fraternising, or 'fratting', as it was soon called. That brought out the best in a young girl of fifteen or so. Her family were aghast at being turned out of their home and lost the power of thought or movement. This young heroine sized up the situation and took complete charge. She found a house and organised granny and the kids, and her father and mother, shifted the bedding and essentials and had the place clear in no time. We could not help admiring her common sense and practical ability. Her efforts were wasted, as it happened, because we swept on without dropping the trails of the guns and spent the day advancing through a small forest, much of which had been set ablaze by our earlier shelling and was still smouldering in places.

In the afternoon we dropped into action near Hamminkeln, on the glider landing zone. What we saw of the damage done to them did not encourage us to go to war by glider. That night we were suddenly called upon to fire at very short range to a flank when our previous ranges to the front had been to the order of 10,000 yards or more. Apart from causing trouble because the guns were not all sited to fire in that direction and had to do a quick move, it meant that we were in a pretty sharp salient with the enemy close enough to call for active defensive measures.

This salient lost us our good friend Dicky the Dutchman. For some reason the German family in our farm – which we had not evacuated – induced him to go to another farm to fetch one of their relatives. Why he went was a mystery because Dicky hated Germans and was most unlikely to do one a good turn. If only he had reported to the Command Post before going, as everyone was supposed to, so that the Adjutant or myself knew where they had gone; if only he had obeyed this simple, common-sense order, we would have told him that the farm was in the enemy salient. As it was, he took a motorbike and rode straight into a withering blast from a Spandau.

We suspected the family of treachery and sent all the men to a prison cage for questioning. There the sixteen-year-old son was shot trying to escape. Perhaps it was Old Testament justice, but it didn't give us Dicky back ... and I think we were all struck with horror at the unnecessary loss off two such young lives, even if one was an enemy.

Dicky's body was recovered and buried on the farm with the nearest to full military honours that we could manage. It was a sad moment when the little form, sewn up in a blanket, was lowered into the grave.

So ended the Battle of the Rhine. After that, the enemy had no option but to pull out as fast as he could, fighting tough delaying actions as we penetrated deeper and deeper into his country. With the Russians attacking in the east there was no hope for him. Prolonging the war merely increased the casualties on both sides, but Hitler would not hear of surrender. The German soldier fought gallantly to the last, holding us at every river, and only giving in when he was forced to his very knees.

Thus we enter the last phase of the War in Europe.

Chapter 39

Victory in Europe

Like as the waves make towards the pebbled shore
So do our minutes hasten to their end;
Each changing place with that which goes before,
In sequent toil all forwards do contend.

William Shakespeare

181 Field Regiment RA, April/May 1945

No time was wasted in starting the pursuit. In our sector 6th Airborne Division took the lead with 15th Scottish following them up and ready to attack through them whenever they were seriously held up. In particular, we seemed to be specially marked for river crossings.

We passed through Bocholt, Munster, Osnabruck, Minden and Hannover and then had to force a river crossing at Celle. It was at Celle that we first came in contact with German atrocities, for Bergen Belsen – the extermination camp of evil memory – was only a mile or two away. The CRA advised us to go and see it as an education in the vileness that man can descend to, but I felt too busy to go. We heard all about it from the drivers of our water carts who were sent to help the RAMC and others who took charge there. Our men were shaken to the core that human beings could be so maltreated. Thousands had died or been murdered and those who survived were skeleton-thin, scarcely able to move and degraded below the level of animals.

From Celle we went to Ulzen, and there we had quite a sharp engagement. A Battery of 190 Regiment commanded by John Stephenson – who came to my Regiment after the war – caught the limelight here. They were part of a detached Battalion Group that was surprised one night when they were bivouacking in a village. A German patrol in half-tracks penetrated the perimeter and set some of the houses on fire. In the midst of the confusion and near panic that arose, Stephenson collected some men and got one of his twenty-five pounders into action, knocking out several of the German trucks and putting the rest to flight. His quick action undoubtedly saved the Battalion from quite a nasty situation.

Our next obstacle was the River Elbe, which we crossed in front of Lauenburg [see plate]. This was a 'set-piece' operation, which took some time to prepare. To start with, we had to evacuate all Germans living within five miles of the river, so as to ensure the secrecy of our plans. That was a very unpleasant job. People pleaded pitifully, but we could not let them stay. One case was particularly difficult. We were asked to let an old woman, who was said to be bed-ridden, stay. That sounds an obvious case for mercy, but a woman would have to stay to look after here, and the husband of that woman would have to stay too ... and then there would be a son who could not leave alone. In no time at all the whole spy organisation could be in residence. In this case, we sent the doctor to see the old woman and find out how ill she actually was. He reported that she was quite able to stand the move and shortly afterwards we saw her departing happily on the top of a loaded farm cart.

We settled into a nice country house. There I was met on the stairs by the daughter of the house, dressed in riding breeches with her hand on the butt of a pistol. '*Was vollen sie hier?*' she demanded haughtily. '*Schliepen camra*', I replied, giving her, I think, quite the wrong idea. However, she did not use her pistol on me, so the reconnaissance proceeded as planned.

In the course of time we crossed the river. I went in a Buffalo and felt most unsafe as there was only a few inches of free board and the river was wide. A few sprays of machine-gun bullets ruffled the surface, and there was a little shelling, so when we landed I got the hell out as quickly as I could. Then I remembered that my motorcyclist orderly was in the next Buffalo, and feeling rather ashamed of myself for not waiting for him went to look for him. The relief on his face when he saw me repaid my trouble a hundredfold. He would not have known where to go if I had gone on without him.

For several days we pushed on, more or less in the direction of Hamburg. There were a few skirmishes, but no real fighting. I had the last shot of my war fired at my jeep at the crossroads of a village called Dassendorf. The shell burst just behind us, and we shot down the road like a scalded cat. General MacMillan saw us as we slowed down again and remarked, 'That made you shift!' He was dead right – it did.

Then one day Pat Keene remarked that the war might end any day, but I just didn't believe him. It had gone on so long and the Bosch was so stubborn that an end did not seem possible. I said I would believe it when it came.

I wrote a letter home to my son, aged seven, who was just going away to school. He kept it and it is reproduced in the plates section. It shows the confidence, the acceptance of death and the weariness of the time.

But events began to convince me on 4 May when we got a warning not to start anything new. About that time we had a most extraordinary order – one which tickled our sense of humour. It was worded something like this:

> By kind permission of the GOC-in-C XXX Corps the –th Wehrmacht Division will fight a battle to round up a SS Battalion that refuses to surrender. The area of the battle is out of bounds to British troops.

So the great German Army had come to that. The end could not be so far away, after all.

Shortly after I went for a swan about on the Autobahn to see what it was like. I had not gone far when I came upon a long column of vehicles halted by the side of the road. As I passed them I had a funny feeling that there was something different about them. Suddenly, the penny dropped. They were German trucks; German uniforms. It was an Airforce Unit coming to surrender en masse. We tactfully took little notice of each other and I continued my drive, but I must confess that my scalp prickled a little. I felt like a sheepdog when a pack of hounds visits his farm.

The final message came at last – just two words, HOSTILITIES ENDED. There was no cheering or elation, just a kind of stunned feeling and an intense thankfulness that one had lived to hear those words.

The reality of the war's end was brought home to me by the closing down of the RHQ Wireless Control Set. It had never stopped as long as any Battery of ours was in action and its whirring noise was so continuous that no one noticed it. Night and day it was ready to answer the hard-pressed OP Officer's call and give him the firepower he needed. It was the key link in the wireless chain that bound the many scattered parts of the Regiment into one united fighting machine. Now its work was finished – the splendid Regiment was no longer required.

'Close down,' said the Signaller, and the out-stations prepared to comply. When all were ready, he pressed his switch for the last time ... 'Close down now. Out!'

And so the war ended for me as it had begun – with the click of a switch.

Postlude

Joyful are the thoughts of home,
Now I'm ready for my chair,
So, until morrow-morning's come
Bill and mittens, lie you there.

John Clare

181 Field Regiment RA, May/June 1945

Shortly before the war ended Pat Keene said to me, 'Be sure to choose good billets next time we move, as it may be the last move before we leave Germany.' With this in mind, I selected a very nice small *Schloss* called Wotersen [see plate]. To look at, it reminded one of a large English Baroque or Georgian house, set in beautiful grounds. Some of the rooms were magnificent and the furniture was in excellent taste, pleasing to look at and comfortable to use.

The owner was a Count von Bernstorff, who was, I believe, hanged by the Russians while a prisoner of war.[1] His wife, who was living at Wotersen, was an English woman and she had another English woman – also married to a German count – staying with her.

When I first looked over the place before moving in, I found a Gunner Captain waiting for me as I went out. Diffidently he asked if I knew that there were two English ladies living there. I said that I had found that out and was not going to turn them out as they were not German by birth.

'Thank heaven for that!' was his reply. 'One of them is a cousin of mine!'

So we let them stay and became quite friendly with them, holding that it was not 'fratting' to talk to British-born people.

In these pleasant surroundings we became petty governors, responsible for law and order and for seeing that the people did not starve until the normal local government could be set to work again, under the control of the Allied Commission. Each Battery Commander was given a large area to look after and I had seven villages as my share. It was all very interesting. I called my *Burgomeisters* in to a conference one day at which we discussed their problems, making it quite clear that they would be held responsible for any disturbances in their districts. They were just like a group of

English well-to-do farmers and country businessmen, all in their Sunday best, some with heavy gold watch-chains across their waistcoats. It was impossible to feel any animosity against them. They were completely sincere, making the best of a bad job, and the meeting was more like one between landlord and tenants than one held in the aftermath of war.

During this time we saw the start of the lowering of the Russian 'Iron Curtain'. It was soon clear that the Germans were terrified of the Russians by the streams of refugees that came across the Elbe, pouring into Western Germany. The leaders were lucky, but soon we were told to close the crossings of the river and of the Elbe–Travers canal. That dammed the stream of people and huge bivouacs began to form at every bridge, increasing in size each day. People pleaded to be allowed across, but we had to harden our hearts and say 'No'.

An eighteen-year-old girl aroused my admiration. She was a young lady of good family and rode up to Wotersen like a warrior Amazon, mounted on a fine horse, with feed and pack on the saddle as self-sufficing as a cavalry trooper. She had somehow managed to slip across the river and had come to ask the English Countess to intercede for her family.

We could hardly bear to deny anything to one so brave – and such a fine-looking, open-air beauty. But she went away disappointed, vowing that she would get her family out of the Eastern Zone if she had to swim the Elbe to do it. And I for one hope she succeeded.

The Germans did not seem to bear any ill-will towards us: they seemed glad that the war was over and were only too ready to turn to the occupying army for anything they wanted. Our locals would have been as friendly as those of an English village, if we had allowed it. The children refused not to frat. It was quite useless to chase them away. They liked soldiers, and they liked to see what was going on, so when told to go they just ran off and popped up a few yards further on. The British soldier is not very good at frightening children!

Being wise after the event, I think the question 'To frat, or not to frat' should have been left to the Commander on the spot. Of course, there must have been many with hatred in their hearts, and many who would have turned against us given the chance, but the man on the spot should be quite capable of judging the temper of the crowd. The British Private soldier is no fool at this, either. If he doesn't like the atmosphere, he either keeps to himself or beats the place up. Certainly he is not fooled for long.

To my mind, a little more friendliness would have paid dividends in the future. The theory was that the Germans had, by the atrocities of the SS, put themselves beyond the pale and must be made to feel ostracised. But you cannot tar a whole nation with one brush – there is good and bad in every community.

In spite of our aloofness, there was, I think, quite a father–son relationship. The Germans accepted the fact that it was a stern father, but knew that they were being treated fairly. Montgomery did a lot to improve the relationship when he broadcast to the British sector. He spoke in German. He did not gloss over the past, nor did he condone or forgive. He told them what they must do for their own salvation, and how it was to be done, and he gave them hope. I was told that his use of the friendly 'Du' instead of the formal 'Sie' made a tremendous impression. It made them feel that he was leading them, not merely governing impersonally. Cooperation in the sector improved noticeably after the speech.

There was quite a lot of fun at Wotersen as we wallowed in relaxation after the tension of the war. There were my German lessons from six-year-old Julia, daughter of the other Countess. She would take me round the garden, chattering about the birds and flowers, telling me what the name of each was. Her mother had divorced her husband and later she returned to England, renounced her very musical name (which I forget) and became plain Mrs Grub!

One evening we went to see *Peer Gynt* at the Hamburg Opera House. The drive to the theatre showed what bombing can do to a town. If anybody thinks our towns were the last word in ruin he should have seen Hamburg in 1945. We drove through four or five miles of desolation. The rubble had been cleared from the road to the verges, where it formed a broken wall. Heaps of charred stone and bricks showed where there had been houses. In many of these heaps, a dim light glowed – the family were living in the cellar. They had to. There was nowhere else to go.

There was just one little T-shaped block left standing and the centre of this was the almost undamaged Opera House. There, in the centre of devastation, we enjoyed an excellent performance.

Into the middle of this calm existence came a sudden bomb shell – for me. A War Office telegram arrived asking if I wished to command the Anti-Tank Regiment of the 6th Airborne Division, which was then in England, preparing for the Japanese War. I knew they were glider-borne, and I remembered the impression of 'glider riding' formed at the Rhine crossing, but the call to independent command was a strong one. I had hoped to get a Regiment after the North African campaign and had been recommended, but I had not made a big enough mark to offset my youthfulness and soon became resigned to having missed the boat. Now, here was my chance. Anyone can sit in a glider if he has to, I told myself, and accepted the offer.

Nothing happened for a week or two. Then, when I had almost forgotten about it, a telegram arrived. 'Fly soonest' it said. So I flew soonest.

Not until I had officially accepted the Regiment and had signed a paper volunteering for Airborne service did the War Office Staff Officer remark casually, 'Of course, gliders are dead, you know – your Regiment is to convert to parachuting shortly.'

That gave me a shock. I had never had the slightest intention of becoming a parachutist, but I had not the face to back out at the last moment. So I became one.

And 181? Our grand Regiment? In course of time it slowly died. First the guns were taken away, then the trucks. Officers and men were demobilised or posted to regular units until only a rear party was left, and one day the Quartermaster handed over the final key and nothing remained. Through some error it isn't even listed in the Royal Artillery War Commemoration Book.

But something did survive. Years later I wrote to the King's Shropshire Light Infantry and sent them one of the worsted bugles that we used to wear on our sleeves. They put it in their Regimental Museum and I like to think that, by that token, the spirit of 181 returned to the Regiment from which it came.

Notes

1 Albrecht von Bernstorff (1890–1945) was a member of the Solf Circle, a gathering of German intellectuals opposed to the Nazi regime. He was possibly shot by order of Joachim von Ribbentrop, Nazi Foreign Minister.

Appendix

Military Structure and Terms in the Second World War

Level	Rank Commanding	Location and Role
Brigade Headquarters	Gunner Brigadier (CRA)	The CRA worked alongside the General commanding the Division
Three Royal Artillery Regiments with Regimental Headquarters (RHQ) per Brigade	Colonel for each Regiment, plus: The Survey Section Royal Signals Troop The Light Aid Detachment REME to repair guns and trucks. The doctor and his Regimental Aid Post The padre	The Colonel lived at Brigade HQ and worked alongside the infantry Brigadier, co-ordinating targets and fire plans
Three Gunner Batteries per Regiment, each with eight twenty-five pounder field guns	Three Majors, Battery Commanders and three senior Captains as second in command (the Battery Captain)	The Battery Commander lived with the Infantry Battalion Commander, constantly in touch to provide gunfire support
Two Troops of four guns each in each Battery	Six junior Captains, Troop Commanders	Troop Commanders' key role was to man the Observation Posts (OPs) with the forward Infantry Company. Here they could see what to shoot, report on activity and discuss likely targets with the infantry

Index of Abbreviations

AA	Anti-Aircraft
ACV	Armoured Control Vehicle
BC	Battery Commander
BEF	British Expeditionary Force, which was evacuated from France at Dunkirk
BTE	British Troops Egypt: controlled the base (i.e. not the units fighting) troops
CO	Commanding Officer
CPO	Command Post Officer, senior subaltern who supervises fire control. The Subaltern was either a Lieutenant or a Second Lieutenant
CRA	Commander Royal Artillery
DSO	Distinguished Service Order, awarded for highly successful command and leadership during active operations
GHQ	General Headquarters
GOC	General Officer Commanding
HD	Highland Division
HQ	Headquarters
KOSB	King's Own Scottish Borderers
LAA	Light Anti-Aircraft units and their guns
LAD	Light Aid Detachment (vehicle repair), REME
LST	Tank landing ships
M&V	Meat and vegetable stew
MC	Military Cross, issued for gallantry in presence of the enemy to warrant and junior officers (below the substantive rank of Major) of the Army
MM	Military Medal: award for the other ranks for gallantry on land in presence of the enemy
MO	Medical Officer
MP	Military Police, 'Red Caps' because of the red covers on their hats
NAAFI	Navy Army Air Force Institute, responsible for retail and leisure services

OP	Observation Post
PT	Physical Training
RA	Royal Artillery
RAF	Royal Air Force
RAMC	Royal Army Medical Corps
RAP	Regimental Aid Post (medical)
RASC	Royal Army Service Corps responsible for transport and supplies
RE	Royal Engineers, 'Sappers', responsible for building roads, bridges, civil engineering activities, clearing mines and demolition to hold up the enemy
REME	Royal Electrical and Mechanical Engineers, responsible for vehicle (and gun) repair and maintenance
RHA	Royal Horse Artillery
RHQ	Regimental Headquarters
RQMS	Regimental Quartermaster Sergeant
RSF	Royal Scottish Fusiliers
VC	Victoria Cross, Britain's highest award for conspicuous courage and bravery by members of the armed forces in the face of the enemy

Index of Names

Index of Places

Index of Military Units